Victims of Terrorism

Also of Interest

International Terrorism: An Annotated Bibliography and Research Guide, Augustus R. Norton and Martin H. Greenberg

† *Terrorism and Hostage Negotiations*, Abraham H. Miller

† *Terrorism: Theory and Practice*, edited by Yonah Alexander, David Carlton, and Paul Wilkinson

Terrorism and Global Security: The Nuclear Threat, Louis René Beres

Self-Determination: National, Regional, and Global Dimensions, edited by Yonah Alexander and Robert A. Friedlander

Insurgency in the Modern World, Bard O'Neill, William R. Heaton, and Donald J. Alberts

† *U.S. Policy in International Institutions: Defining Reasonable Options in an Unreasonable World*, Special Student Edition, Updated and Revised, edited by Seymour Maxwell Finger and Joseph R. Harbert

Global Human Rights: Public Policies, Comparative Measures, and NGO Strategies, edited by Ved P. Nanda, James R. Scarritt, and George W. Shepherd, Jr.

† *Contemporary International Law: A Concise Introduction*, Werner Levi

Arms Transfers to the Third World: The Military Buildup in Less Industrial Countries, edited by Uri Ra'anan, Robert L. Pfaltzgraff, Jr., and Geoffrey Kemp

War of Ideas: The U.S. Propaganda Campaign in Vietnam, Robert W. Chandler

† *Violence and the Family*, edited by Maurice R. Green

† *Stress and Its Relationship to Health and Illness*, Linas A. Bieliauskas

† Available in hardcover and paperback.

Westview Special Studies in National and International Terrorism

Victims of Terrorism
edited by Frank M. Ochberg and David A. Soskis

Few events can place as great a stress on a person as being taken hostage during a terrorist attack. The hostage, who often has led a quiet existence up to that time, is suddenly subjected to stress that would seem almost unbearable. Yet, hostages cope with their situations, at times with unusual defenses—sometimes even to the point of developing affection for their captors.

This book relates scientific and clinical understanding of stress, captivity, and coping to the ordeal of the hostage-victim, focusing on the perspective of the victims themselves and examining what can be done to reduce their suffering. Evaluating actual events, the authors look at the behavior, reactions, and residual problems of those who have been hostages in terrorist attacks and similar events. Discussion centers on the hostage-victim's psychological and physiological reactions, as well as on the phenomenon of victim/terrorist alliances—the so-called Stockholm Syndrome.

Frank M. Ochberg, M.D., practices psychiatry in Michigan, where he recently served as director of the Michigan Department of Mental Health. He functions as psychiatric advisor to the U.S. Secret Service and is a consultant to the Federal Bureau of Investigation. As associate director for crisis management at the National Institute of Mental Health, he participated in the National Security Council Special Coordinating Committee on Terrorism. Dr. Ochberg is clinical professor of psychiatry at Michigan State University and medical director of the St. Lawrence Hospital Mental Health Services. **David A. Soskis**, M.D., is clinical associate professor of psychiatry at Temple University School of Medicine and attending psychiatrist at the Institute of Pennsylvania Hospital in Philadelphia. He is chairperson of the Task Force on Psychiatric Aspects of Terrorism and Its Victims of the American Psychiatric Association and serves as a consultant to the Federal Bureau of Investigation.

Victims of Terrorism

edited by Frank M. Ochberg
and David A. Soskis

Westview Press / Boulder, Colorado

Westview Special Studies in National and International Terrorism

Copyright © 1982 by Westview Press, Inc.

Published in 1982 in the United States of America by
Westview Press, Inc.
5500 Central Avenue
Boulder, Colorado 80301
Frederick A. Praeger, President and Publisher

Library of Congress Cataloging in Publication Data
Main entry under title:
Victims of terrorism.
  (Westview special studies in national and international terrorism)
  Includes index.
  1. Terrorism—Addresses, essays, lectures. 2. Hostages—Psychology—Addresses, essays, lectures. 3. Victims of crimes—Psychology—Addresses, essays, lectures. 4. Stress (Psychology)—Addresses, essays, lectures. I. Ochberg, Frank M. II. Soskis, David A. III. Series.
HV6431.V5   362.8'8   82-2572
ISBN 0-89158-463-3   AACR2

Printed and bound in the United States of America

Contents

Foreword

This book deals perceptively and compassionately with a very old problem in a very new context: human responses to human cruelty.

There are now more working scientists than there have been in all of history combined. Multiply this example many times over and we begin to realize how suddenly we have been thrust into a world of enormous complexity since the Industrial Revolution and especially in this unique century. Our power—both for better and for worse—suddenly dwarfs all of history. This power is, above all, significant in relation to our conflict-laden history as a species.

Throughout our historical record, over thousands of years, conflict between groups has been common, often destructive, varied in content yet similar in basic themes. Human societies have a pervasive tendency to make distinctions between good and bad people, between in-groups and out-groups. This sorting tendency is very widespread, readily learned, and susceptible to harsh dichotomizing between positively valued "we" and negatively valued "they."

Hostility between human groups is likely to arise when the groups perceive a conflict of vital interests, an unacceptable difference in status, or a difference in beliefs that jeopardizes self-esteem. Such situations tend to evoke sharp in-group/out-group solidarity, with drastic depreciation of the out-group by the in-group. Perceived threat from an out-group tends to enhance in-group solidarity and tightness of group boundaries and to encourage punishment of those who deviate from group norms. Human groups seem readily able to find a threatening group. Tyrants have understood this for centuries.

Justification for harming out-group members rests on sharp distinctions between "we" and "they," between putative good people and bad people. Such justification is readily provided by assumptions regarding (1) the damage they (members of the out-group) would do to the in-group; (2) the damage they would inadvertently do to themselves; and (3) classification of the out-group as essentially non-human.

Many different political, social, economic, and pseudo-scientific ideologies have been mobilized to support these hostile positions. Although such intergroup hostility varies widely in content, from time to time and from place to place, the form is remarkably similar.

It is easy to put ourselves at the center of the universe, attaching a strong positive value to ourselves and our own group, while attaching a negative value to many other people and their groups. Groups have been specified not only by ethnicity but by religion, race, language, region, tribe, nation, and various political entities. The same principles seem to apply across different kinds of groups. Can human groups achieve internal cohesion, self-respect, and adaptive effectiveness without promoting hatred and violence? A deeper understanding of factors that influence ethnocentrism could have much practical value in resolving intergroup conflicts. In my judgment, this is a critical area for scientific effort in the future.

To threaten, injure, or kill innocent bystanders in a circumstance of political, religious, or other ideological conflict is an ancient form of human behavior. But in the twentieth century such behavior is abetted by an array of available technologies that dwarf all previous reality. From gas chambers to instant world-wide televised threats to atomic bombs to diverse miniaturized weapons of devastating power—the old terrorism is rapidly becoming transformed into a number of variations on the theme of holocaust.

There has been so much hatred, cruelty, and killing in the history of our species that we would be foolhardy to dismiss the Nazi holocaust as a unique event that cannot reoccur. That holocaust vividly demonstrated the human capacity to justify harm with glib, vacuous explanations that appeal to the most destructive emotions. Once again, as so often in history, out-groups were blamed for virtually all social ills and personal frustrations. Once again, the destruction of the powerless was made palatable to the powerful. There is so much of that tragic delusion in human history that we must be alert to possibilities of recurrence. But now there is more. The Nazis brought to this gruesome task a level of sophistication in modern organization and technology that exceeded prior similar events. And the world has moved since the 1940s to even more formidable organizational capability and destructive technology.

Small-scale terrorist episodes may not seem to present such a formidable capability. But they do. If they continue to spread in widening circles, with greater publicity, more powerful weapons, and a more pervasive multiplicity of threats, they are capable not only of injuring many innocent victims but also of arousing repressive responses by powerful governments in democratic societies as well as totalitarian ones. The quest for ways to improve communication and understanding between groups, to foster social justice, and to fairly resolve conflicts is of great importance in any event—and of authentic urgency in the face of pro-liferating terrorism.

In a world replete with hatred, rising crime, spreading terrorism, an abundance of small wars, and growing talk of an immense war, this is a subject that must be pursued with utmost vigor. Science must do whatever it can; indeed, its boundaries must be opened to encompass these critical issues. High standards of careful, objective scholarship must be applied. A deeper understanding of conflict and its resolution is no longer just an optional fascination, but a vital necessity for the human future.

The authors' concern in this volume is mainly with a small but impor-tant, poignant, and neglected sector—the victims of terrorism, and how we can help them. They thoughtfully seek ways to understand the ex-periences, to ameliorate the suffering, and when possible, to prevent it.

In the aftermath of World War II, the world gradually rebuilt itself, often with remarkably hopeful results. Economic recovery was widespread, colonialism ended in much of the world, aims of political freedom flourished, health improved along with technical advancement and rising standards of living.

But by the late 1960s and early 1970s, much disillusionment had oc-curred. Most regimes in the world were still, to say the least, highly authoritarian. The dreams of political freedom and economic well-being were anxiety-laden for many and nightmarish for some. Prejudice, cru-elty, international conflict, poverty, and disease were all still rampant. Indeed, the paradoxes of suffering and impotence in the midst of abun-dance and capability were never more vivid. And the contrasts of the world were highlighted as never before by mass media of unprecedented reach and immediacy, as well as by governmental propaganda ma-chines.

In this setting, a resurgence of terrorism occurred, not only in tradi-tional hotbeds of conflict and international intrigue, but even in tradi-tionally peaceful settings of university life. In one such university, I began to reflect on these matters and to engage some of my students and colleagues in these reflections. It was my privilege to be associated with a remarkable group of gifted, dedicated, and idealistic people—at once scholarly and oriented to socially useful actions. They went on to make a variety of contributions to our present understanding of stress and coping as well as aggression and conflict resolution. Several of them are substantial contributors to this volume; one of them is its coeditor. Frank Ochberg is a wise, ingenious, compassionate physician who has gone deeply into problems of terrorism—from origins to negotiations to victimization. His leadership is apparent in this book and in the field. David Soskis, as coeditor, has worked closely with him in fostering creative collaboration between professionals in law enforcement and the behavioral sciences.

In biological research, behavior is viewed in the framework of adaptation. How does behavior meet adaptive tasks—i.e., requirements for survival and reproduction? Sometimes this is easy, routine, habitual, unremarkable. Sometimes it is difficult, risky, troublesome, alarming. These latter occasions are the ones we call stressful. But what makes them so difficult? Essentially, they are appraised by the individual or those important to the person as jeopardizing opportunities for survival and/or reproduction—however these may be defined in a particular group. Coping with life-threatening experiences is a distinctive and difficult feature of medical and nursing care. It has not, however, been the object of much systematic research in medicine. To the extent that life-threatening occasions have been studied, the emphasis has been on impact, distress, and incapacity. Much less attention has been given to effective ways of responding, meeting stern challenges, even learning from difficult experiences. In other words, the clinical literature on life-threatening situations is long on stress and short on coping. Over the past three decades, I have had the privilege of being involved in many studies with many remarkable associates in efforts to probe the biology and psychology of stress and coping—adaptation under difficult circumstances.

Among its other uses, the present volume constitutes a significant contribution to our understanding of stress and coping in an area so far little explored—and indeed very difficult to explore. Such understanding of human adaptation, even in its darkest recesses, can contribute to the prevention of disease and disability. The authors explicitly take their analysis in this direction. More generally, the articulation of biomedical and behavioral sciences in research on stress and coping, as exemplified in this volume, is an approach of considerable significance for health problems in the future.

The present volume illustrates the needs and opportunities for research on terrorism and its victims. It also highlights the need for the relevant sciences to transcend their traditional boundaries and achieve a level of cooperation among disciplines rarely achieved in the past. The important real-world problems do not come in neat packages that fit the traditional disciplines. The stakes are too high to permit a complacent avoidance of the challenge.

David A. Hamburg
Director, Division of Health Policy
Research and Education
Harvard University

Acknowledgments

Many individuals and groups have provided encouragement and assistance without which this book would have been impossible. The editors wish to thank the U.S. Public Health Service, the Forensic Psychiatry Department of the Institute of Psychiatry in London, New Scotland Yard, the Training Division of the Federal Bureau of Investigation, the National Institute of Mental Health, and the Michigan Department of Mental Health for sharing their resources and providing help. Many of the chapter authors in this book had the opportunity to meet and to begin the interdisciplinary work that characterizes our efforts at the Fourth Seminar on Terrorism sponsored by the International Center for Comparative Criminology and the Law Enforcement Assistance Administration, which was held in Evian, France, in 1977.

A research sabbatical granted by Temple University allowed David Soskis to devote considerable uninterrupted time to the preparation of this book while working at the FBI Academy in Quantico, Virginia, and with Professor Abraham Kaplan at the University of Haifa in Israel. Our families have provided us both with needed encouragement in this task and with substantive editorial help. Most of all, however, we acknowledge the victims of terrorism and their families who have given us, and all clinicians, lessons in coping.

Frank M. Ochberg, M.D.
David A. Soskis, M.D.

Introduction

Frank M. Ochberg
David A. Soskis

This is a book about the victims of political terrorism. In it, we have tried to bring together the perspectives of theorists, practitioners, and persons who have themselves been victimized. This is not the first book to grapple with the problem of terrorism, a problem that has returned again and again in the final decades of the twentieth century to disturb and haunt us just as we thought it was on the wane. Previous works have considered the history of terrorism as a political device, its use by government and by dissident groups, theories of etiology, police and military responses, and the impact of modern terrorism on the operations of the criminal justice system. During the last several years there have also been a profusion of legislative hearings on terrorism, conferences sponsored by the U.S. State Department and the FBI, and a growing number of seminars organized by and for major corporations that perceive their overseas employees as potential victims.

The scope of this book, while broad enough to fill volumes, is still quite narrow when compared with the material encompassed in most definitions of "terrorism." The reasons for this narrowed focus have grown out of the broader-based activities we have just mentioned. General, but necessarily superficial, considerations of terrorism have occurred with sufficient regularity over the past five years to provide us with a common partial set of concepts and reference points. Each successive restatement of these common concepts has been followed by a recommendation to focus future attention on one or more specific areas that had been relatively underexplored. This is our aim; focusing permits deeper exploration and such digging may unearth new nuggets of value to all of us.

Before we begin a detailed exploration of our chosen field, two perspectives may be useful. First, especially for those of you who do not routinely work on the problems of terrorism, we would like to provide an overview of what we mean by this term and a description of some of the issues it raises. Second, especially for those of you who *do* work on the problems of terrorism, we will set forth our own views on the role of psychiatric issues and perspectives in this field. These views and their implications will be developed more fully in Chapters 6 and 10 of this book.

By now it has become commonplace for one man's terrorist to be another man's freedom fighter or revolutionary hero. The very word "terrorist" carries a significant negative moral valence; terrorists never refer to themselves as such. The historical and psychological truths of these statements should influence both our choice of definitions and the amount of time we spend debating them. They should not, however, prevent us from making definitions, and in fact may help us by pointing to characteristic terrorist conceptual modes. We have found the approaches to definition given below useful in our work, although many will disagree with them, one hopes for constructive reasons.

Our first approach to definition is a formal one, but one that we believe is well-suited to the context of terrorism in the twentieth century. It is a variation of the definition formulated by Justice Meir Shamgar of the Israeli Supreme Court, a specialist in international law: Terrorism is the use of murderous violence to achieve political ends that does not obey the rules of war. These rules, as expressed, for example, in the various Geneva Conventions, deal with what are considered relatively "inhumane" weapons, what classes of persons (such as young children or the infirm elderly) are considered "noncombatants," and what are acceptable standards for treatment of prisoners who are unable to offer further physical resistance.[1] The rules of war, though often disobeyed, are real; they have emerged in the course of history out of the tension between what is best and worst in human nature and experience. Although the meanings of the terms used in this definition can be and have been debated, it is the dictionary definitions rather than the philosophical meanings of "murderous" and "political" that are useful here. In any productive endeavor we need some presuppositions; not everything can be problematical at the same time.

Another useful approach to definition begins with one or several paradigmatic cases that serve to anchor and help evaluate defining and explanatory concepts. We define what terrorism means by pointing and saying "this." We present such a specific example as the first chapter of this book—the experiences of Gerard Vaders during the takeover of a Dutch train by a group of South Moluccans in 1975. We point to this incident, which will be described in detail, and say, "For us, this is terrorism." Another incident that comes close to exemplifying "pure" terrorism was the taking hostage of Israeli athletes by a Palestinian group during the 1972 Olympic games in Munich.

The Moluccan incident is explored in some depth later on, but a few comments now concerning the Munich Olympics may help delineate the core "terrorist" concepts. First, terrorism breaks the old rules without necessarily establishing new ones. Many Americans rely on the conventions of sport to insulate them from the psychological issues sport expresses and explores. For them, it was a particular shock to see the Olympic Games violated so openly and brazenly. For the terrorists and their supporters, this was precisely the point; they wanted to recontextualize the event and felt morally justified in doing so. Why should anyone be allowed to sit comfortably in his living room while others remain stateless and oppressed?

The perspective behind this approach was probably best articulated, in imperfect but highly accurate English, by a Palestinian terrorist who was discussing another incident of this period (the September 1970 "Triple Skyjacking"). He commented that "it is a severe entry into their minds; nevertheless it is an entry. They had to ask the question: Who are these? Why are they doing that?"[2] This statement, especially the term "severe entry" (with its associations to rape) helps explain the compelling intensity of the Munich drama and the primary emotional reactions and secondary defensive postures it aroused in people all over the world. This formulation also reminds us that fear may be the central emotion for the victim, but not for the spectator, and that the occurrence and control of terrorist incidents is closely related to issues of publicity.

Other recurring themes in modern terrorism that were seen in the Munich incident have been discussed extensively elsewhere: a passionate cause, usually in reaction and revenge to a perceived past injustice; a dedicated, sane, and competent leadership; operatives who are prepared to die for their cause; financial support from interested outsiders or from "appropriations"; understanding of and access to the technologies of international air travel and of portable weapons; and a democratic government that values human life and will not turn the incident into an instant massacre.

It is generally acknowledged that although terrorism is not the major source of mortality or of political change in the twentieth century, what it is and what it means merit our careful attention and study. Certainly, events in Munich and Tehran have shown that no country, whatever its economic or military strength, is immune either from terrorist incidents themselves or from the significant social and political disruption they cause. But the reasons for concentrating on the victim's experience may be less clear, and we want to articulate them.

Since the victim of terrorism is often a symbol of the government under siege, and because the media provide an immense audience for released hostages once the dramatic incident is over, these victims have a profound impact on public opinion and public sentiment. Only a government or a public that understands these victims is prepared to cope rationally with what they say and do. A public that overreacts in outrage to the victims' helplessness may precipitate harsh, simplistic counterterrorist measures that play into the terrorists' desire to discredit the government. In other words, if a public joins some victims in identifying with the terrorist-aggressors and their cause, it may undermine the morale and confidence of those in government, from policymakers to police, who must respond officially when an incident occurs. If the public is perplexed and alienated by the entire process, the bond of trust between government and governed that is necessary for the survival of democratic institutions may be weakened. On the other hand, a public and government that are reasonably aware of the repertoire of human responses that may be utilized by men and women under severe stress—including the stress of terrorist threat and captivity—will be able to make rational decisions about national policy on terrorism and the appropriate means for managing incidents that occur.

There is another, even more important, reason to consider the victims of terrorism. They suffer. Unfortunately, their suffering may be neglected or misunderstood when the tumult and drama surrounding the notorious event have subsided. There are medically sound approaches to the diagnosis and treatment of such suffering that can and should be brought to bear on these cases. Psychiatry can make a real contribution because it is uniquely equipped to care for the victim of terrorism in those areas where he or she suffers the most: the wounds to the mind and spirit, as well as to the body, and the physical and psychological consequences of these wounds in terms of human experience and behavior. Although psychiatry's traditionally broad focus, encompassing social, cultural, and political factors, has hindered its attempts to deal with certain types of problems, this focus is clearly necessary for any realistic appraisal of the contexts and consequences of terrorist victimization. For instance, since the terrorist's victims are often the unwitting and unwilling proxies for an assault on the state itself, it might be argued that this group uniquely merits direct governmental reparation and aid for care and rehabilitation. Israel has assumed this position with respect to its citizens and their families. The U.S. government has not yet committed itself formally on this issue, but has given it serious and humane consideration in the programs developed to help the captives returned from Iran. We hope that this volume will help to advance the search for an appropriate government role with respect to U.S. victims of terrorism.

Although the current wave of transnational political terrorism has certain unique characteristics, victimization itself is certainly not new. Coping, and the stress of captivity, have been studied in considerable detail, especially in the period during and after World War II. To our knowledge, however, there has never been any attempt to integrate expertise on stress, on coping, and on captivity in order to understand the impact of victimization by political terrorists or to relate this expertise to the work of those charged with combating terrorism. This is the aim of the present volume.

We should acknowledge at the outset that we have based the organization of this book on several presuppositions. We accept as both a fact and a challenge that no single current professional discipline or theoretical perspective can either say all that is useful about the victim of terrorism or translate what others have said into its own language without distortion. We are content to leave the tunnel vision and the simplistic explanations to the terrorists. We feel that different, sometimes conflicting, perspectives will mutually illuminate each other and that the only source of "objectivity" in a field like this is a spectrum of reports by different observers of the same "facts." We acknowledge the imperfection of current theoretical formulations, including our own, and see successive approximation as the most fruitful process for theoretical development.

In practical terms, this means that we have selected the authors of this volume to reflect one possible spectrum of perspectives that we consider illuminating. We have begun with the account of an actual victim, both to anchor our theorizing in human facts and to remind us who the ultimate consumer and judge of our services must be. We have presented Gerard Vaders's account in considerable detail, although this mode of presentation may appear strange to those unfamiliar with the "raw material" of fields like psychodynamic psychiatry. Such a detailed account tries not to prejudge relevance; what we are trying to avoid is a story that merely illustrates the author's or editor's favorite explanatory concepts. Readers may use this account as a benchmark for evaluating the conceptual frameworks expressed here or elsewhere, and as a laboratory to test their own preferred theories. (We refer to Gerard Vaders's account at several points in this book to illustrate this checking process.)

Subsequent chapters focus in turn on the concepts of stress, coping, and the effects of captivity. Dr. Walton Roth reviews various theories that have been proposed to explain how people react to major stressors on a short-term basis. His perspective is medical and the concepts he introduces bridge the mind-body gap. Dr. Jared Tinklenberg goes on to explore the more psychological responses of "coping." Both he and Dr. Roth discuss specific unconscious defense mechanisms utilized by victims of terrorism. Dr. Leo Eitinger, who speaks from the personal experience of Nazi terrorist captivity, extends these perspectives to long-term effects on psychological and physical functioning, including second-generation effects. In the next chapter, Dr. Martin Symonds describes the approaches he has found most useful in treating the victims of personal crimes. Dr. Symonds has had professional experience both as a police officer and as a psychiatrist, and his clinical approach is based on extensive experience with the people and institutions with whom and with which a victim of terrorism is likely to interact.

We then consider several less conventional, but potentially enlightening, concepts about terrorist victimization. This theoretical chapter is followed by Dr. Rona Fields's description of some actual techniques and problems involved in clinical research with victims of terrorism. Dr. Fields extends our focus geographically to the conflict in Northern Ireland and introduces the special problems of the child victim, in whom the terrorist event or milieu interacts with extensive developmental change.

Authors of the next two chapters introduce the perspectives of a relatively new group of professionals who have had, and will continue to have, a major impact on the planning and implementation of programs for victims of terrorism: law enforcement officers who also possess an academic-research orientation and background in the social or behavioral sciences. Both authors are faculty members at the FBI Academy in Quantico, Virginia. Thomas Strentz, with a background in clinical social work, extends our understanding of the Stockholm Syndrome by discussing his own observations and interviews with participants in a wide range of terrorist incidents. Conrad Hassel, with a background in law and criminology, considers the problems and possibilities associated with collaborative work among professionals in law enforcement and behavioral science. Finally, we conclude this volume with some guidelines for future planning of both ends and means that have emerged from our own work on this book and in the field it explores. This final chapter includes specific guidelines for clinicians who may be called upon to work with former hostages or victims.

As dramatic and gripping events, acts of international terrorism have made a big splash on the world scene. But such acts are inherently transient, and hostages in places like Entebbe or Tehran have often been displaced to the small print even before the incident has ended. What many do not see or feel are the waves that international terrorism has repeatedly made over the surface and through the substance of our lives. Although it is the direct victim of terrorist violence who is actually tossed, and sometimes lost in the crest, the waves move and change us all.

Notes

1. *The Law of Land Warfare*, Field Manual FM 27-10, Department of the Army, Washington, D.C., July 1956. An illuminating discussion of some of the ethical and social implications of these laws can be found in Axinn, S.: "The Law of Land Warfare as Minimal Government." *The Personalist*, October 1978, pp. 374–385.

2. Interview on "Hostage," ABC Television Network, January 30, 1978.

1
A Case Study:
Gerard Vaders

Frank M. Ochberg

The clinical method of inquiry often begins with a close look at a single illustrative case, which we shall do here. By beginning with the experience of a person who has been a victim in a terrorist incident we remind ourselves of the standard by which our analysis, explanation, and plans must be judged. Unfortunately, there are many victims of terrorism to choose from. No experience could be more helpful, though, than that of Gerard Vaders, a mature and sensitive Dutch newspaper editor who was held hostage for twelve days in December of 1975. Vaders's story illustrates the major issues that arise from the hostage situation: the roles open to the victim, stress, coping, and psychological effects. The detail and richness of his account will allow the reader to test out several of the perspectives presented in this book and any that he or she brings from outside. I do not intend to diagnose or psychoanalyze Vaders's behavior. I am grateful to him for the time he took to tell me his story, and for the courage he showed in taking notes while he was a hostage.

The Incident

At 10:00 A.M. on December 2, 1975, a train bound from Groningen to Amsterdam was boarded and stopped by seven masked gunmen on a flat, dreary piece of land near Beilen. During the takeover, the engineer was shot and killed, and during the ensuing period of negotiation under duress two hostages were executed. One terrorist and a hostage were injured when an automatic rifle discharged accidentally. The assaulting group were of the Free South Moluccan Youth Movement; their cause was the separation and independence of their homeland from Indonesian rule. Their demands included release of political prisoners from Dutch and Indonesian jails, publicity for their cause, policy changes in Holland regarding Moluccan independence, and safe passage out of the country. They held 52 hostages at the outset, but allowed the number to dwindle to 23. Their weapons included pistols, automatic rifles, and sham explosives taped menacingly to all exit doors.

One year after the incident the Moluccan terrorists were in prison beginning 17-year sentences, and Vaders was in his bustling news room, telling me the story he would never forget:

"How do I feel now? It is complicated. I know I need to get back to this life, and to leave that other. But there are many who are still sitting on that train, waiting. Waiting for Godot.

"From the beginning it was different for me. I recognized the situation. The moment the Moluccans came in I felt back in the war. I was thinking, 'Keep your head cool. Face the crisis.' I knew there would soon be choices. Times to take risks. For instance, it was risky to sit there taking notes. That destroys your anonymity. I made the choice and took notes."

After the train seizure, as Vaders and the other passengers were herded from one compartment to another, his coat and briefcase were left behind. He thought, "I don't have anything to write on—I've left my note pad in my briefcase. Ah, but I could take notes on this. . . ." (Some papers in his pocket that had to do with his daughter's school.) It was clear to him at that moment, some 30 minutes after the train had been halted, that he could keep a running diary of events and impressions, and that doing so involved greater risk than blending in with the crowd. In a matter of seconds, he had decided to take his notes openly.

I asked whether his feelings at the beginning of the siege were like any others he had experienced.

"There was an early experience. I must have been 17. I was sleeping in the room with my brother and all of a sudden the SS were standing there with machine pistols. They were on a reprisal raid because the resistance had murdered a Dutch collaborator. We were sent to a concentration camp in Holland. Every morning we had hours of 'apell'—lining up in freezing weather. But I was young looking and had fair hair. I came to the attention of the SS officer in charge. He asked my age and I lied, 'Sixteen.' I remember him saying, 'My God, are we fighting children?' I was released the next day.

"There was also a time of similar feeling during the Ardennes offensive, when I came under fire. And in 1948 in Indonesia two hand grenades were thrown at me and I saw them at my feet. Neither one exploded."

We returned to the train: "They threw the door open. There were two or three of them wearing black woolen balaclavas. I knew they were South Moluccans. The others thought PLO, but on their rifle butts you could see the colors. I recognized it from Indonesia."

Vaders produced the worn piece of paper (a Dutch school announcement) with his handwriting on the reverse side. It translated roughly, "10:07. Just past Beilen. Door slammed open. The barrels of a rifle and a sten gun are pointed inside. Shots are heard, hard and dry. In a reflex movement someone reaches for a gun barrel—an act of recklessness that goes unpunished. Another shot; it misses. The colors of the South Moluccans republic are stuck onto the gun butts: red, green, white, and blue. The hijackers are extremely nervous. Black woolen balaclavas over their faces so that only the eyes and nose can be seen. A lot of shouting and some more shots."

Vaders put away his notes and went on.

"Although the memories are vivid, it wasn't so much a memory as a realization that I would have to mobilize reflexes like in the war.

"I still have guilt over the war. I did nothing bad, but not enough good. Not enough for the Jews. My sister did more and was in Dachau. Then I chose not to take too many risks.

"But on the train I did risk. I decided to write and to do it openly.

"For the first 10 minutes I felt cool. Cooler than usual. I was even looking for humor in the situation. December 5th is our Sinterklaas holiday when we give poems as presents. I was thinking how I wouldn't have to write poems this year.

"The others on the train were either sitting still or following orders. The Moluccans had us tape paper over the windows and many were doing that. One man seemed a little too aggressive. That was Mr. de Groot.

"I was taping windows, too. I asked them if anyone was hurt. They said the driver wanted to be a hero and was shot. I asked if an ambulance should be called. They said, 'No. He's dead.' But he wasn't dead yet, we later found out. I sat down and took notes.

"They saw me writing and didn't say anything at first. But then they returned. One of the Moluccans said, 'Come with me.' I was led at gunpoint to the front of the compartment, beyond the passenger section. One held a rifle to my head and another pointed a revolver. They said they would shoot if I tried to run and of course there was no way to escape. Then I could see two of the Moluccans fixing chains and what I thought were explosives to the handles of the doors. I said to myself—and I suppose eventually all of the others reached the same conclusion—if we tried to escape or if anyone tried to rescue us through those doors, many, many would die.

"I wasn't left there for long. Someone tied me up with my hands behind my back and then tied me by the arms to the doorway so that I was like a curtain. I faced away from the passengers and towards the pool of blood from the driver. People could walk past me, under my arms. I knew they were planning to execute hostages."

Vaders's memory was particularly vivid for this part of his ordeal. He was in considerable pain, strung up across the passageway for over three hours. Afterwards he wrote, "My feet felt like slabs of raw meat. The rope chafed my wrists. Straight in front of me I could see part of the baggage area and the legs of the dead driver. From the way he was lying I got the impression that he had indeed resisted. I grieved to think of how his bravery had proved fatal.

"Through the window I could see the Drenthe countryside, gloomy and vague in the mist. Several times I tried to look behind me through the glass of the connecting door. Each time they raised a pistol and I stopped trying. After about half an hour I saw the yellow nose of a train drawing slowly alongside on my left. It stopped opposite the baggage area. The door opened and I caught a glimpse of someone in a blue railway uniform. Then I heard shots. The door slammed shut and the train moved out of sight.

"You quickly lose all sense of time in such a situation. I don't know exactly what time it was when a girl in a brown-orange dress and several Moluccans crept past me. Eleven or twelve o'clock perhaps. The Moluccans came back alone. I heard later that she had been freed because she was pregnant. She took Hans Prins's blood specimens. (Prins was a captive who had convinced the captors he was a doctor. 'Can you prove you're a doctor?' the Moluccans had asked him. He answered truthfully, 'No.' But since then he was known as 'the doctor.') At the other end a woman and her child have been released. And an Indonesian girl. Why the Indonesian girl? A case of blood being thicker than water after all?

"It must have been about two when the door behind me opened again. A tall young man opened the door facing me and squeezed past. Then I felt a second man go by. To my surprise he was Dutch. He looked like Pronk (the Minister of Overseas Development) and for one mad moment I thought: 'Has he come to negotiate?' He was wearing a blue jacket and blue or grey trousers. He went through to the next compartment and stopped. He looked puzzled, but outwardly quite calm. Two Moluccans came up to him and stood on either side, their guns pointed at him. For perhaps a minute nothing happened. Then they continued into the baggage area, carefully stepping over the feet of the dead driver. I could no longer see them, but I felt what was about to happen and my heartbeat quickened. After a few seconds two or three shots were fired. Several days later I learned that it had been Robert de Groot, 33-year-old father of three children. (Although those in the train believed him to be dead, de Groot had managed to escape.)

"When they came back I saw that at least two of the three had tears in their eyes. One of them, whom I later got to know as Paul, had a sensitive and intelligent face. He asked, 'Can you understand us, sir?' 'I can understand your case' was my diplomatic reply. Paul had earlier told Mrs. Kruyswijk: 'Anyone who thinks that this is a game is making a mistake.' There was no longer any question of making that mistake. He continued: 'We don't hate you, but we have no choice. The Bible says there is a time to kill. The time has come. We don't hate you as people.' Another young man who was called Djerrit said: 'How could I hate you? My wife is Dutch.' We found out later that this was a lie. They must have wanted us to like them."

Vaders told me how, while he was hanging in the doorway, the Moluccans killed a soldier. The first terrorist demand had said that hostages would be shot every 30 minutes until their request for a bus, a plane, and political recognition was granted. "I could see one of them shooting and hear a howl like a dog.

"They let me down in the afternoon. Prins, the fellow hostage who had convinced everyone he was a doctor, massaged my arms for an hour. This was my first contact with another hostage during the ordeal. I tried to keep up the contact."

Evidently, Prins played a crucial role for many of the hostages, and possibly for the Moluccans as well. He was, according to Vaders, robust, energetic, courageous, and good humored. When he worked the circulation back into Vaders's aching arms, "he was so energetic that the sweat flew off his forehead." Vaders felt comforted, and remained reasonably calm, unaware then of the singular terror that awaited him.

The passengers shared what scraps of food they had brought with them and talked of trivial things. There was some discussion of Moluccan history. At least one hostage remarked how badly the Moluccans were treated by the Dutch government. Darkness came, and with it the cold of the Dutch winter.

Vaders began shivering. He asked the terrorist known as Paul, perhaps the most sympathetic of the lot, if his coat could be brought from where it was left up front. Paul looked apologetic. "They had used my coat to mop up the blood of the driver. Then one of the passengers gave me another coat. Afterward I learned it was the coat of the dead solider."

Vaders managed to sleep that night, although he awoke at one point with abdominal cramps. Paul gave him some ointment to "rub on where it hurts" and Vaders was able to return to sleep.

"The next morning I was full of fear. Sweating. Cramps in the stomach. Fighting away panic.

"Now I took notes by stealth."

Whatever calm and poise Vaders had experienced the first day had vanished by the second. This was evident to him the moment he awoke. The second day was to be even grimmer than the first.

It became clear that a resolution was not near. Several hostages had been shot, although there was some confusion about who was killed and why. The specter of more executions was a reality. And when one of the terrorists announced that in case of an attack everyone was to lie on the floor to avoid being shot in the crossfire, the possibility of military liberation suddenly loomed as another threat.

Vaders had difficulty remembering the events of this second day and he asked if I wouldn't rather read a translation of his notes, which I did while he left the room for a short break. I read them slowly:

"On Wednesday, the second day, reality slowly dawned on people, but not to the same extent on everybody and in some cases not at all. At one point one of the hijackers (I think it was the one with dark glasses, Eli) told us that he was expecting an attack by the anti-terrorism police unit and that, since he did not want us to get hurt, we should lie on the floor if there was a shoot-out. A 74-year-old woman, who had turned out to be very self-centered, replied 'I'm not going to do that—my dress will get dirty.' Others were speculating about whether they would be entitled to claim compensation. But most of us were counting the hours in fear.

"From time to time the Moluccans would group together and excited commands in Malay would be issued over the loudspeaker. They grasped their weapons determinedly and rushed down the gangway. That was frightening. A tap on the shoulder even more so. What did it mean? Throughout Wednesday it indicated that the 'sentry' (the person tied in the door) had to be relieved. The record was still six hours, but I was to break it. The normal tour of duty was two or three hours, although it was not always equally divided. In the meantime the news of the execution of two hostages had filtered through, and that destroyed any remaining sense of security.

"Now that the unthinkable has become a real possibility, we cannot think about anything else. Every movement the hijackers make is studied for its meaning. When they laugh, everyone is relieved. When they pull down their black balaclavas hearts beat quicker and palms begin to sweat.

"The women may be in less danger, but no one feels safe. Although Eli gave one of the women his scarf when she was cold, he said: 'We're so emancipated that we also shoot women.'

"Life goes on. Hans Prins compiles a list of the medicines we take. About twelve o'clock we share the last sandwiches. I get one but my stomach has shrunk so much that I can barely swallow it, despite my hunger.

"There's a rumour that a bus is waiting at the crossing further up the line to take us all to Amsterdam airport. A plane is standing by. The hijackers ask the conductor if he can drive the train. He hesitates: 'I've seen it done and I know more or less how it works, but the brakes were locked when the communication cord was pulled and I don't know how to free them.' The hijackers are angry. We say: 'Let him try. You must trust him,' but they walk away and nothing happens.

"It never gets completely light in the train. The newspapers over the windows create a permanent dusk which deepens into total darkness. Everyone is making plans. Hans Prins puts one forward: an appeal to the Government, public opinion, and the trade unions (at the suggestion of Laurier, who is chairman of the metal workers branch of a union). It is read out and approved, although there are comments like: 'It's nowhere near strong enough.'

"We put the plan to the Moluccans. It fits in with their own plans in that they have decided to send a young Chinese who only speaks English (and has a British passport) to the nearby farm where the police have their headquarters. He is allowed to take our appeal as well as their demands. At first they threaten him: 'If you don't come back, we'll shoot one of the hostages.' Hans Prins and I offer to go in his place. We can explain the situation. But Paul says quietly: 'He has nothing to do with all this. He can stay there.'

"There's also a plan for Prins to meet the police halfway with a rope tied round his waist, to explain how things are in the train, but it doesn't come off. The idea of having to talk with a long-range rifle aimed at you is not very pleasant.

"One of the demands was for megaphones. They are provided together with a field telephone so that there is a direct line to the police. We also get food and blankets from the Red Cross: sandwiches, milk, apples, and oranges. For most of us this was the first food for twenty-eight hours. It doesn't all go quietly. I hear swearing over the loudspeaker and then an order: 'Move those people away from the bushes.'

"Is there a bus coming or not? Apparently one was promised, but dusk becomes night and the chance is gone. The disappointment inside the train is very great. People sit apathetically staring straight ahead.

Seventeen-year-old Irma Martens, who was on her way to school in Hoogeveen and was worried yesterday about missing a test, cries softly to herself: 'Why doesn't Den Uyl (the Prime Minister) send a bus? Why doesn't he?'

"Tonight things begin to go wrong with Grandpa and Grandma, a clergyman and his wife who are 84 and 83 respectively. They call each other 'Dad' and 'Be.' They had been to Haren for the christening of their grandchild and were put on the train by their daughter Mia. Grandma says, with an air of relief: 'It's a good thing Mia brought us to the train, otherwise she'd be thinking that the car had broken down and we were stranded.'

"It started that evening. There were rules for going to the lavatory. You asked a Moluccan, 'Can I?' He asked the man by the lavatory if someone could come. Only if his answer was 'Yes' could you go. The hijackers didn't want any surprises and the gangway had to be kept clear. But that evening Grandpa broke all the rules. He stood up. 'Sit down, Grandpa,' said Djerrit, not unfriendly. 'No, no,' came the reply. 'We've got to get out. We've got to visit someone, you see.' 'Doctor' Prins calmed him down with sleeping pills and Valium provided by the Red Cross.

"The nights are endless. By four in the afternoon it's practically dark and in the morning it only gets light about nine. The red light stopped working after just three nights, but after that some light from the army or police searchlights came through the cracks and holes in the newspapers. We called them the 'goons' eyes'. But if it was foggy it got pitch black. Then time stood still and we slept a little, or rather dozed. Occasionally there was a moan or the sound of someone quietly crying. Using suitcases we made an improvised bed for Grandpa and Grandma. There was a hole in the middle that couldn't be completely filled with coats and Grandma commented: 'You've bought a funny sort of bed—the middle bit's missing.' But the first nights made us feel safe. Everyone shifted about in their seats, trying to keep warm and not to think too much. The worst that could happen to you was two to three hours 'sentry duty.'"

Vaders returned to his office as I finished reading his notes. He picked up where the notes left off.

"On the second night they tied me again to be a living shield and left me in that position for seven hours. Eli, the one who was most psychopathic, kept telling me, 'Your time has come. Say your prayers.' They had selected *me* for the third execution. They didn't exactly say so, but they didn't have to. Eli would stare at me without saying anything. The others spoke nervously in their native language. During that long night I thought of many things and I had different impulses. One was to reason with them. But I suppressed that. I thought it would only strengthen their resolve. The second impulse was to flee. I would have had to untie both hands, both feet, and the door. I had one hand slightly free, but I would not have had time to do the rest.

"I was preparing for execution. Making up a balance. My life philosophy is that there is some plus and some minus and everyone ends up close to zero. Some say that is pessimistic. I think it is realistic. I was 50 years old. It had not been a bad life. I'm not happy with my life, but satisfied. I had everything that makes life human."

"But you weren't executed," I said. "How did you feel?"

"You won't believe this. Disappointed.

"I had the impulse to say, 'Let that man go and let me go in his place,' but the words stuck . . .

"I felt . . . I feel guilty." He looked sad.

"In the morning, when I knew I was going to be executed, I asked to talk to Prins, to give him a message for my family. I wanted to explain my family situation. My foster child—her parents had been killed—she did not get along too well with my wife, and I myself had at that time a crisis in my marriage behind me. I hoped my wife would get a new purpose in her life by concentrating on the child. There were other things too. Somewhere I had the feeling that I had failed as a human being. I explained all this to Prins and the terrorists insisted on listening. But when I expected them to lead me away, they instead told me to sit and wait. They had an emotional discussion in Malay and then let me sit with the other passengers."

Vaders interrupted his story to say that two Dutch psychiatrists, Dr. Mulder and Dr. Bastiaans, said later that they felt the Moluccans had planned to execute him but changed their minds after hearing his long message to Mrs. Vaders. I agreed. He was no longer a faceless symbol, and had not come across as a hero. His human flaws, and his humanness, were exposed and the Moluccans could not conspire to kill him.

"After that they didn't isolate me anymore. They said, 'We have others to kill.' I was sitting next to this woman and across from a young man named Bierling, a 33-year-old father of two. They came and pointed to Bierling and led him away and shot him.

"The days went by and we somehow knew there would be no more executions. Only Eli, the psychopathic one, wanted a fourth killing, but the others talked him out of it. People calmed down and even told jokes. The Red Cross sent in cigarettes and a broom, which we used to keep the place tidy. We settled into a new world 30 feet long, 8 feet wide, and 7 feet high.

"We still had bad moments. There was a line connecting the terrorists to the police that we could have used to speak with our relatives, but the bureaucrats wouldn't allow it. I could see the line out of a tear in the newspaper covering the window and I thought, 'That should be a life line but it isn't.'

"Then we had our first hot meal in three days sent into us. It was a stew. But the authorities on the outside didn't think to provide spoons or paper plates. We had to lick the food off some pieces of plastic cups and our fingers.

"There was a growing sense that the authorities were mishandling the situation, that the wrong people were in charge, that we should have heard from the Prime Minister or the Minister of Justice, and not just the mayor of the little town of Beilen.

"That same day there was a major incident when Djerrit, one of the terrorists who was always fiddling with his weapons, dropped his sten gun. It went off with a bang, sending a bullet through Paul and smashing splinters into three hostages. I thought there would be panic. We didn't know what had happened and all the Moluccans were looking about wildly, loading their weapons and shouting above the moans of those who were injured. Paul was bleeding from the face and eventually left in an ambulance. I was worried when Paul left. He was sensitive and intelligent and he seemed to balance out Eli.

"Before long the tension eased again and we went back to small talk and boredom. Even the Moluccans relaxed. They could go around unarmed. Djerrit once left his sten gun in the lavatory."

The final week was difficult for Vaders to recall in detail, but the Moluccans had allowed Vaders more notepaper, and his diary recorded the events:

"Saturday, December 6. The first game has started. . . . Each has to guess how many coins the others are holding in their hands.

"16:05. Oasting, who up to now has been quiet and said little, suddenly explodes: 'When we're free we're going straight to the Hague to hold Den Uyl and the rest of his gang hostage.'

"21:00. We hear a rumour that the first man executed, Robert de Groot, is not dead but only wounded in the back.

"Evening. Grandma Barger is helped into bed. Her handbag is lying on a seat. She says to her husband, 'Nobody will steal it, will they? I can leave it there.' They chatter on for quite a while, in dialogue that is straight out of a turn-of-the-century novel. She asks, 'Would you like breakfast in bed? I'll clean an orange for you.'

"Sunday, December 7, 8:45. Crackers with cheese and ham. Prins brings the food round on a board belonging to Verver, the estate agent. There's a model of a property development on it. We also get food in jars. It may be good stuff, but it has to be warmed up with hot water and there is none. Eventually we warm the jars by putting them between Grandad Smit's legs. He is 82 and has stomach trouble.

"Sunday, 10:20. Walter Timmer holds a makeshift service. Matthew, 14.22. Peter walked on water, until he lost his faith and sank. By way of justification, the Moluccans ask him to read Ecclesiastes, 3, 1-15: 'To every thing there is a season.' The passage includes these significant lines: 'A time to be born, and a time to die: a time to plant, and a time to pluck up that which is planted. A time to kill, and a time to heal. . . . A time to love and a time to hate.'

"On the first day Paul had said: 'It is now the time to hate.' Then we said the Lord's Prayer with the minor textual differences between the Roman Catholic and Protestant versions.

"Sunday morning. Four people behind us are playing dominoes. They have made paper dominoes. Grandad Smit is an authority on the game and explains how it can be played in different ways.

"The hijackers come and ask us to change their guilders into smaller coins. They're going to play cards.

"Laurier comes round to tell us that during the night the Moluccans were doing something outside under the train. The worst fears come at night and he thought that they planned to blow up the whole train at twelve. He had a plan ready. The hijackers didn't know, but one window on his side had been cracked by a fragment of a bullet. If things went wrong, he intended to throw his case through the window and dive after it. (In fact the hijackers were trying in vain to repair the heating.)

"Sunday, 16:05. Eli says that the clergyman and his wife, Grandpa and Grandma Barger, will be released. Prins has to help them. They're happy again. What style they have! They say: 'Is it fair to the other passengers to leave?'

"Verver, Rob de Groot's father-in-law, asks us what we think of the rumour that Rob survived the execution. He says hopefully: 'He was in the army. He does know about that sort of thing.' I tell him that after the shooting I heard them say 'Tidah mati' (not dead). He goes back to his seat slightly reassured.

"Sunday, 16:30. It seems almost certain that four people representing the South Moluccan Republic in Exile have come to the train to negotiate. All but two of the hijackers were in the front (empty) carriage.

"Later Eli says to Prins: 'They're trying to make us nervous.' Prins: 'Yes, that's why you must stay calm. I'm trying to keep the passengers calm.' Eli: 'Yes, I know, but if the passengers do anything stupid, we can play the same game.'

"Sunday evening. We are playing games—places in Holland beginning with an 'A' and so on. Prins says, 'If anyone has suggestions for Christmas dinner, now's the time to speak out.'

"The police cheer us up by bringing up three more searchlights, but no food is brought (it's the Lord's day) and there is no more food or drink (not even water).

"Monday, December 8. Cold, some of us entwine our hands and do exercises to get warm. One night Timmer couldn't sleep. He made an ABC. A is for Ada, his wife. H is for Hate. But he couldn't find anything for Q. He says: 'We should have parted after Paul and Ter Veer were wounded and we held that service. Now we're back in the old situation of two opposing sides.' He goes on: 'The rights of man include the right to food: it's a scandal that no food was brought on Sunday.'

"Monday, 15:00. We get Hot Pot. The ladies get sanitary towels but there is no tobacco.

"Tuesday, December 9. Frits Santing has got his radio working. We hear again about the seizure of the Indonesian consulate in Amsterdam. Then they take the radio away again, possibly to the driver's cabin. They try to prevent us from hearing the news, but we regularly catch snatches of it. On the radio they refer specifically to 'the terrorists.'

"Tuesday, 10:00. Mr. Albracht is massaging Mrs. Van der Giessen's legs. Last night she sat behind us playing games again. I spy, etc. Brave old Grandad Smit, who had kept quiet about his stomach complaint, gets baby food and milk that we warm up between our legs.

"Tuesday, 11:00. A plane flies low over the train. Somebody says: 'They've started running sight-seeing trips.' I suck at my empty pipe for the taste.

"Tuesday, 12:35. Eli says to Timmer: 'They're leaving us to stew in our own juice.' Djerrit gives me a hand-rolled cigarette. Timmer says that he's been thinking about the Moluccans all night: 'Their problem is that they don't dare to trust us: they've said so themselves. We must help them get over that. They're prepared to let us go if the Government will do something in return.'

"Tuesday, 14:00. They've agreed to send Laurier's letter and the first part of my story outside. It'll be a pity if it gets lost on the way. Later I see Eli busily reading my story. Then he tells me: 'It can't be done. There are too many details in it.' I ask: 'Give it back. It's worth a lot to me.' He promises he will.

"Christian patience notwithstanding, Timmer is getting fed up with a woman who is forever complaining. When she's constipated she talks about it incessantly, and when she's got diarrhoea she makes us all suffer. At night she drinks other people's water. Timmer would dearly like to give her a slap in the face.

"Tuesday, 14:30. It's surprising how many mutual acquaintances we have.

"Late on Tuesday afternoon. Warm soup, marvellous! But we only get small portions. Is this meant to weaken the hijackers? They're getting all they want. We're becoming less and less choosy. We drink buttermilk, coffee, and soup one after the other out of the same cup. Grandad Smit dozes off more and more often. A few days ago he said to me, 'I don't care about dying, as long as I don't suffer.'

"Tuesday evening. Last night was comedy night. A sample: a man buys a new car but a week later he brings it back to the dealer. The gear box is ruined. A new gear box is put in but a week later he's back again, same story. 'What on earth are you doing to it?' asks the dealer. 'Well, you know, the normal thing: first, second, third, fourth, and then into R for race.' Tonight it's proverbs: 'Where there's life, there's hope.' That's a good one. Hans sings softly: 'While Moluccans watched their flock by night, all seated on the ground . . .' Hans and I discuss the plan to get the train moving again. They'll have to remove the explosives: we might push the wrong button, open the doors, and blow up the lot of us.

"Wednesday, December 10, 9:45. We've got a new game—Mastermind with figures instead of colours. Playing this game it becomes apparent how poorly we are able to concentrate. One of the Moluccans does something stupid with his pistol and it goes off. No one is hurt.

"Wednesday, 10:05. Djerrit and another Moluccan go up front. Shots are fired. They are shooting at sea gulls.

"Wednesday, 11:30. Someone has made a draughts board. We hear a siren in front of the train. A long conversation through the megaphone follows. The only thing I catch is, 'We want to negotiate.' It's the Moluccans. For one reason or another it makes no impression on the passengers; at least, there is no trace of excitement.

"Wednesday, 13:30. Frits suddenly says: 'This is the 196th hour.'

"Wednesday, 15:50. Prins makes Grandad Smit lie down on a makeshift bed. All this time (even at night) he has been sitting straight up, virtually motionless, with his shoulders hunched under his coat and his hat pulled down low over his eyes. We wrap him up in blankets. He has never asked for anything and didn't tell us that he takes pills for his stomach. He tries to join in the games. To give him something to do, we ask him to make paper chessmen, which he does very handily. He even joined in the 'bicycling' exercises.

"Wednesday, 16:40. I note: 'There's probably a good reason why no one has yet come to negotiate. It's now too late for anyone to come today. Did the Moluccans' request come as a complete surprise?'

"Grandad Smit is lying on his bed like a corpse. You can certainly put hijackers under pressure by delaying, but it's a double-edged sword.

"Wednesday, 17:00. The constant presence of armed Moluccans by the doors and both ends of the carriage has made Mrs. Van der Giessen so nervous that she doesn't dare go to the lavatory anymore. The people nearby help her get over it.

"Thursday, December 11. Hans Prins and Riet Overtoom are making a sleeping bag out of two blankets. They use Private Stevens's (not the solider who was executed) army sewing kit.

"Thursday, 12:00. The Moluccans have let it be known that if no one has come to negotiate by 12 o'clock they will start executing people again. They're bluffing, but still. . . .

"Thursday, 12:30. No negotiators. Water and milk have run out.

"15:00. The hijackers have spent most of the afternoon up front. Negotiators must have arrived. They come back laughing but talk in Malay and I can understand nothing.

"15:05. Wonderful news: Grandad Smit is released. Tears run down his cheeks. Confused, he shakes hands and shuffles forward. Mrs. T. Bakker de Bruin (74) can also go. Her voice trembling, she asks, 'Can I take my friend with me?' Jack answers, 'Get a move on. Don't ask questions. Be glad you're getting out—Timmer will be!' Later it emerged that they had intended to release Mrs. Hansen, who had had an asthma attack.

"Thursday, 15:30. Riet Overtoom makes a sleeping bag for Djerrit.

"Evening. For a change we hear the news. Manusama and Mrs. Soumokil have been here with two others. In the evening Manusama flies to The Hague. The radio describes the release of Smit and Mrs. Bakker. The atmosphere in the train is supposed to be 'good.' What do you call 'good'? It was good to hear the comment of a Mr. Van Andel on the radio about how to deal with the hijackers. He said that the desire for revenge should be resisted. The Moluccans muttered in agreement.

"Friday, December 12. The morning rush hour at the privy is over. The stench is less now that we have disinfectant. Prins had asked for antiseptic fluid. First they sent us one block to hang in the lavatory bowl. As if there was water for flushing. Actually, the whole organization is poor. In twenty-four hours we received 18 lunch packets for 24 people. In each packet there were 4 sandwiches, a slice of currant bread and an apple. That works out at 3.75 sandwiches per day per person. This may be meant to starve them out, but we're the ones who are going hungry, not the hijackers. Today especially we talk about food. We plan the meals we'll eat when we're free, and the things we'll buy.

"Friday, 12:00. 'We've been here 242 hours,' complains Frits. We supplement the few sandwiches with the porridge and rusks we got for Grandad Smit.

"Friday, 13:15. An excellent meal: hot soup, boiled fish in butter sauce, carrots, and mashed potatoes. Our spirits improve remarkably, although people do get irritated now and again, even by little things like cigarette smoke. Private Thijs Stevens says, 'I'll start with the ice cream.' In a few days he may be able to have all the ice he wants, but not quite the kind he has in mind.

"Friday, 15:00. The radio says that Mrs. Faber has stated: 'The mood in the train and the condition of the passengers are good. Their lives do not seem to be in immediate danger.' Obviously this is meant for our families, but the effect on the Moluccans is quite different. Somebody says that Eli has asked for someone to come and repair the heating system, but nobody comes.

"16:30. Eli must have torn a strip or two off the others. Probably they went outside without taking enough precautions. There's a meeting going on. The train is quiet and tense.

"It's getting colder. The trick is to keep your feet warm. It's difficult once they get ice-cold. Some wrap themselves in blankets from the waist down. One or two handymen make beds incorporating spare seats. We have more leg room now that quite a few hostages have been released.

"Saturday, December 13. Beautiful blue sky, with only a few clouds on the horizon. These days we are hardly guarded at all. By day the Moluccans go virtually unarmed. At night two of them stay awake: the rest sleep. We might be able to overpower them, but in such a small space one shot could be catastrophic.

"Saturday, 10:30. Laurier hears that his letter got through and has been released to the press. He is hoping for a telephone call.

"11:30. They are hanging up blankets against the windows. They keep out the cold but they also make it even darker. Wientje Kruyswijk thinks they're doing it to tease us, but that's rubbish.

"12:15. The press seems to be incapable of giving an accurate, comprehensive report of what is going on. It seems that for days it's been impossible to register births and deaths in Beilen (the town hall had been turned into an Emergency Centre). We are supposed to be under great psychological strain. That's true enough and it also applies to the hijackers. We can count ourselves lucky in that there's a 'doctor' among the passengers.

"13:00. The women get half a cup of milk.

"13:45. The hijackers stick plastic rubbish bags over the windows in their part of the carriage—not exactly an indication that they're thinking of surrendering.

"14:45. Food: meat, potatoes, and peas. 'Next time we'll ask them for nasi goreng' (an Indonesian specialty), I say to Kobus. 'I don't think there'll be any left over for the passengers,' he answers. Prins says: 'I'll come and eat nasi goreng at your place.' Jack replies: 'Sure, in cell 580.'

"16:15. We haven't noticed any more negotiations going on. Djerrit must have had bad news. He strikes his forehead and walks up and down the gangway. He sits on the arm of a seat with his head in his hands, crying. It's dead quiet. Two Moluccans begin to sing a duet, an Amboinese song intended to comfort him perhaps. Eventually he lies down. Crying, he takes the pocket Bible which he took from his wife without waking her up (otherwise she would have stopped him). By the light of a torch he crosses out something on the flyleaf and then reads. Later on he is unusually gay. Strangely enough we feel sorry for him, even though he is an accomplice in the murder of three hostages. There is an excellent programme about the South Moluccans on the radio.

"Sunday, December 14. There is ice inside and outside the double-glazed windows. We are wrapped in blankets, but I slept reasonably well.

"In the morning Hans Prins telephones through the following information to Dr. Kox and the Emergency Centre in Beilen: 'One patient, male, eczema, inflammation of the scrotum and groin, spreading. One patient, male, purulent infection of foreskin. One patient, male, stabbing pains in the back, left below the ribs, urine dark-brown. Age 47. Physical and psychological condition rapidly deteriorating. One patient, female, age 72, asthmatic bronchitis, general physical and psychological condition quickly deteriorating. Acutely short of breath at times. One patient, female, age 61, serious oedema of both feet, barely able to walk. Feet and ankles twice the normal size. One patient, male, age 63, operated at the base of the spine in January 1975. Sitting painful. Most passengers are in danger of becoming infected as a result of continued sitting and no change of underwear for 13 days.' For the fourth time Prins asks for clean underwear, especially pants. Women's sizes 42, 48, and 50; gents 6, 7, medium, and large. And not paper ones! We ask for paper tissues instead of kitchen rolls.

"Sunday, 9:10. The news agrees that we've had a cold night. Some comfort. The train must be white with frost. The Thought for the Day on the radio is given by Vicar Glasveld. He says that Rob de Groot asked permission to pray before his execution. The Moluccans prayed with him. That's perfectly possible. He also recalls Timmer's prayer in which God was asked to find a solution for both Moluccans and hostages.

"9:45. Water is streaming down the walls. According to the news, the police are warning people not to drive out to see the train.

"10:00. The Moluccans bring us a glass of milk. I say to them: 'It's an old custom of war to cease hostilities in the winter. Why don't we strike camp and meet again in the spring?' Kobus replies in English: 'Who knows?'

"10:15. They are getting their things together. Is something happening?

"As happens frequently in such dramatic affairs, the end came unexpectedly. All morning they were pushing and shoving stuff around. They seemed relaxed, but they were also continually busy with their guns. Bullets clattered to the floor. Time passed. Something was in the air, but what?

"11:45. Timmer calls for attention but the Moluccans ask him to wait. They put cigarettes and matches in their pockets. Djerrit asks Prins: 'Where's the ointment for sore hands? Can I keep it?' I ask: 'Are you going?' He shakes his head. The telephone rings. This is the 290th hour. Djerrit has unloaded his rifle. He opens a small window and pretends to fire. The firing pin clicks. He carelessly tears the newspaper from the windows. He rips down more with his sten and another rifle.

"The sound of a helicopter comes nearer. Djerrit again pretends to fire. 'Dead,' he says. We don't yet dare really to hope. They are cracking jokes in Malay.

"12:00. It is over. Prins asks Djerrit: 'Hadn't you better take away the explosives?' He starts to laugh: 'We've made fools of you for 13 days —it's fake.' He goes and gets a stick: 'Now you can have them as a present.' Kobus says: 'Stay in your seats for now.' They leave. Prins passes out Hacks throat sweets. Then they return with Manusama and Mrs. Soumokil leading. Manusama says: 'It's all over.'

"Some of the Moluccans cry. Timmer leads us in prayer. 'On Your day, the day of the Lord, we stand before You.' He calls it the day of reconciliation. He says that both sides here had their difficulties: 'We are all made in Your image. We all bear responsibility and hope to make that clear.'

"He wishes the Moluccans strength in the days ahead. Then we say the Lord's Prayer. The Moluccans shake a few hands. The police are coming."

The presence of positive feelings toward the Moluccans, both on the train and at the time of this interview, more than one whole year later, is clear in Vaders's account. He put it this way:

"You had to fight a certain feeling of compassion for the Moluccans. I know this is not natural, but in some way they come over human. They gave us cigarettes. They gave us blankets. But we also realised that they

were killers. You try to suppress that in your consciousness. And I knew
I was suppressing that. I also knew that they were victims, too. In the
long run they would be as much victims as we. Even more. You saw their
morale crumbling. You experienced the disintegration of their personalities. The growing of despair. Things dripping through their fingers.
You couldn't help but feel a certain pity. For people at the beginning with
egos like gods—impregnable, invincible—they end up small, desperate,
feeling that all was in vain."

The Aftermath

Following the incident, Vaders lost a great deal of weight and had a
long illness, which went undiagnosed from the summer of 1976 until a
gallstone operation in November brought relief. His relationship with his
wife improved dramatically. There was much discussion, reconciliation,
and a decision to spend far more time together.

He wrote some stories that were critical of the government and they
brought a great many threatening calls and letters. The government
claimed he was sick, several colleagues spread rumors that he had made a
deal with the Moluccans to spare his life in return for a favorable press,
and a police dossier emerged claiming that he had Communist connec-
tions. He drank more and smoked more, then cut it all out precipitously.

His eldest (natural) daughter had a great deal of difficulty watching all
the aggression leveled at him, dropped out of school, and needed some
psychological support.

He had no dreams and no fantasies that he can remember during the
siege, but beginning one week after release he had nightmares for one
week in which he was threatened by guns. These have not recurred.

His negative feelings about the way the government handled the case
have abated. He is willing to help develop future policy and sits on a national committee for this purpose. But he notes that the Ministry of
Justice is very sensitive to criticism. "They think they do their best and
that we should just express gratitude."

There is another part to Vaders's story. In 1977 the Moluccans struck
again. On Monday, May 23, in the first of two coordinated attacks, 4
Moluccan youths seized the primary school at Bovensmilde, released
Moluccan students, and held 5 teachers and 105 children hostage. At the
same time, 9 other Moluccans commandeered the train from Assen to
Groningen, holding 56 passengers hostage. Both areas were cordoned off
by Dutch national police, field telephone links were established from the
terrorists to an improvised crisis center in the basement of the police
headquarters at Assen, and a national command post was established at

The Hague. The government's initial posture was to demand release of all schoolchildren prior to any negotiation, and to publicly announce that no hostages would leave Holland. The terrorists demanded safe passage to an unspecified foreign country for themselves and 21 convicted Moluccan terrorists in Dutch prisons (several of whom were relatives of these latest hostage takers). They gave a deadline of 2 p.m. on May 25, threatening to blow up themselves and their hostages if their demands were not met.

Two hours before this deadline the government agreed to talks without release of the children and conceded a landline connection between the train and school for the use of the Moluccans. The deadline passed without incident, and on the next day the first hostage was released for medical reasons: a 7-year-old schoolgirl with abdominal complaints. Throughout the following night and into the morning of Friday, May 27, all of the children were released, many of them suffering gastrointestinal disturbance and dehydration. One teacher was also released. There followed two weeks of relative calm, during which time attempts at negotiation and mediation failed to break the impasse. Toward the end of this period, 2 pregnant women and 1 ailing man were released from the train. On dawn of the 20th day, Saturday, June 11, the Dutch marines attacked both sites, killing 6 Moluccan terrorists. Two hostages were killed in crossfire at the train and several more were injured. There were no casualties at the school.

I spent the first week of the siege with the negotiators in the crisis center and had a day to renew my acquaintance with Vaders. (An account of my experiences with the crisis management team may provide some useful insights into the issues that arise around actual efforts to help former hostages, both adults and children. This account is presented in the Appendix to this chapter.) We met at the psychiatric wing of the vast Academic Hospital in Groningen. Now each of our roles was very different. Having come from the forward command post, where the landlines from the terrorists at the train and school were ringing on the desks of the psychiatrist-negotiators, I had become a step-cousin of the crisis management group. And, in a way, so had Vaders, for he was making regular visits to the train station in Groningen, another "front line" where the relatives of hostages had gathered to share their fears and hopes for welcome news. Several ex-hostages, in close cooperation with the mental health and medical professionals at Groningen, generously gave their time and personal experience in an attempt to comfort the vulnerable relatives, who had become victims themselves.

Vaders met me on Friday afternoon when the siege was in its 5th day. We greeted one another warmly. He looked well, and began telling me about the "old train group." The 23 ex-hostages from the episode of December 1975 had held regular meetings. The last one was on April 19. "We are all feeling some more stress now, but rallying. Aftercare, in a way, failed for us. The professionals were not interested enough and they began too late. We are hoping to help out so that this won't occur this time."

Three members of the old group—Timmer, Prins, and Vaders—have leadership roles today. They are concentrating on compensation issues, and on listing the symptoms previous victims experienced, including careful attention to the time course of these symptoms.

Relatives of those involved in the current siege ask Vaders many questions: "How hard are the terrorists? Did they allow hostages to go to the toilet when they want? Will the hostages have their thoughts altered? How long do the changes last?" Vaders has told family members that in his experience the hostages do not think very often about their family members. This is probably a defense against fear of death. (Grinker and Speigel made the same observation about Air Force pilots in World War II. Successful flyers cleared their minds of thoughts of home and functioned effectively. Near the end of their tour of duty, when they could not help but think of home, their fear of death and anxiety increased, and their flight performance diminished.)

Vaders noted another amazing fact. The positive feelings that the old train group had about the Moluccans have vanished completely. Vaders explains that he and his fellow ex-hostages have mobilized their aggression against the Moluccans. He hedges and says, "I am not sure I recognize this in myself, but my wife says it is true, so it must be so."

After some more talking about the current situation, particularly the concern of the doctors about one middle-aged hostage on the train who has a history of depression, authority problems, tension headache, and hospitalization in this psychiatric facility, we leave for Vaders's home.

On the way home Vaders expressed some interesting ideas: "It was a great help to myself to be of any assistance to the families of victims. In a way you have to relive your experience. It may be arrogant but I think I deepened my insight and my thinking about the whole affair. I hope these victims learn. I hope the terrorists did too. I certainly hope they learn. We can't relax, can't say we have a solution, a strategy. The losers learn more than the victors. The victors fight the last war. The losers change and improve. For example, the Moluccans were quiet at the beginning this time. They gave a longer deadline. They had time for relaxation and for equilibrium. They took 54 hostages so they had more time to avoid personal relations. They were more rational and less emotional. Their demands were less demanding. But they crossed the boundary by taking children."

Later he remembered, ironically, "I told them near the end of the siege that it was a good idea not to fight in the winter. I said let's stop and come back in the spring!"

At home Mrs. Vaders was engaging, friendly, and open. But she reported feeling extremely guilty about her own hostility toward the Moluccans. This came over her rather suddenly and caused a clinical depression. "I was raised with very liberal values. We were the outcasts of our 'red-neck relatives.' It hurts me particularly to have these feelings."

The 23-year-old daughter and 17-year-old stepdaughter were there also. Both were concerned, but emotionally unaffected, by the current siege. The elder, a tall, attractive, well-spoken young lady, described how she gave up psychiatric social work after finding her colleagues harsh, bitter, authoritarian, and even cruel in relating to her after her father's victimization. Now she is moving on to a different academic career and doing quite well. His stepdaughter was calm and composed.

Finally, Vaders led me upstairs to show me memorabilia from the old train: the original notes he took; one of the mock explosives, a heavy cylinder wrapped in tape with an exposed fuse; pictures and newspaper articles. We both knew that the story of which these relics formed a part was far from over for him, for his family, and for the current and future victims.

Impressions

Gerard Vaders is a human being who is alive today because he overcame the natural inhibitions that cause us to shroud the intimate life details and displayed his true self to committed executioners. Ironically, this display of humanness could only occur after Vaders reconciled himself to death. Of course there can be no certainty in conjecture about the precise reasons for the Moluccans' change of mind, nor can we know for certain why they chose him for execution in the first instance. As a note-taker and newsman (he told the Moluccans that much but never admitted editing the largest paper in north Holland) he stood out from the crowd. As a living curtain, suspended between compartments of the train, he was the nearest thing to an inanimate object. Disposing of curtains is easier than disposing of persons.

Vaders told me that he insisited on telling Prins all the details that should be conveyed to his wife and family, and he gave a great deal of background so that Prins could understand the message. The Moluccans tried to hurry this process at first, but Vaders was quite resolute and managed to overcome their objections. This is reminiscent of Judge DiGennaro, who was kidnapped by Italian terrorists, and who told me, "I gave up all hope of life and I was free to be brave." Bravery did not mean attempting escape (he was bound and blindfolded throughout) but rather telling the captors exactly what was on his mind. Vaders showed a certain blend of courage and resignation that may have reminded the Moluccans of themselves.

His initial response to danger was classical. There was a period of arousal in which he felt cool, assessed the threat, and made physical and mental preparations. He was not particularly aware of bodily needs, visceral changes, or the falling temperature in the train during this beginning phase. However, he did suffer a collapse of sorts after the first night ended. There are phases in the stress response. Vaders may have entered what Hans Selye calls the "stage of exhaustion." Several other hostages in different settings have reported striking changes in their ability to function smoothly after dawn of the second day, or after the first period of sleep. The phenomenon is recognized; the mechanisms are not fully understood.

Vaders's reponse to danger was also idiosyncratic to a degree. Stress researchers have emphasized that both physiological and psychological patterns show striking individual differences, related to life history rather than the form or intensity of the threatening stressor. The other victims on the train were showing varied patterns of activity, emotion, and interaction throughout the siege. (Dr. Roth's chapter on stress will review and develop these concepts.)

To cope with captivity and the threat of death, Vaders employed several familiar devices. Researchers in this field, such as Dr. David Hamburg and Dr. Richard Lazarus, call these "coping mechanisms." First, Vaders assumed a familiar role. He became a journalist. In this role he could concentrate his attention, conserve his energy, and feel a certain amount of professional self-esteem. Preserving self-esteem is often more important to the individual than preserving life—a striking finding in the examination of these hostage incidents. Furthermore, Vaders gathered information throughout his ordeal. Good copers do this. The ability to scan the environment, to perceive quickly and accurately, to gain further knowledge from a peer group in a similar plight, are all critical mechanisms for coping and survival. In addition to employing these mechanisms, Vaders affiliated with his fellow captives. The ability to form and preserve affective bonds is necessary for normal human development, is adaptive in negotiating the usual life crises, and is critical in extreme situations such as captivity. Dr. Leo Eitinger and others who have studied concentration camp survivors have documented and developed this point. (Dr. Tinklenberg's chapter on coping will expand on these perspectives.)

Vaders had a mild case of the "Stockholm Syndrome," which consists of a positive bond between hostage and captor and negative feelings on the part of the victim toward the authorities. In the case of Vaders, the negative display toward government was more intense than the affection for the Moluccans. Both feelings began in the early days of the siege, crested in the immediate aftermath, and diminished over time. Some positive feeling toward the kindlier of the captors remains; negative feelings toward government officials have abated. This is by now a recognized feature of hostage situations. It does not occur in every instance, but is frequent enough to be considered by police in the management of protracted negotiations.

The Stockholm Syndrome is the most clearly identified and acknowledged "unique" psychological reaction associated with terrorist victimization. As such, it will occupy our attention repeatedly in the course of this volume. It is far from being completely understood or explained. This incompleteness invites useful contributions from a variety of perspectives provided by differing backgrounds in theory and experience. It is a challenge for us to find or to fashion new concepts to fit new facts.

Finally, Vaders suffered a series of physical and emotional aftereffects that are characteristic of hostage situations. His weight fell markedly, not only during the period of captivity and restricted intake, but also afterward. His protracted abdominal distress may or may not have been due to gall bladder disease. Gastrointestinal dysfunction after prolonged stress is not uncommon: a variety of mechanisms and target organs may be involved. Changes in eating, drinking, and smoking habits bridge the processes of physical and emotional re-equilibration. For instance, emotion affects appetite, appetite affects nutrition, nutrition affects physical health, which in turn affects appetite and emotion. Dr. Eitinger's chapter on the effects of captivity will focus on this psychosomatic interaction and on its short- and long-term consequences in a broad range of captives.

Vaders did rather well psychologically, and, as noted, his marriage emerged stronger than before. In several other cases victims have described feelings of "rebirth" and returned to family and friends with a new resolve to place relationships on firmer ground. The fact that Vaders's daughter had difficult days is, sadly, a common occurrence. Loved ones suffer by extension of the trauma into their lives, and they may not be protected by the mobilization of support that occurs within and around the identified victim.

Eighteen months later, as an expert on victimization, Vaders was quick to recognize familiar patterns of behavior in the relatives of hostages. He could engage in "peer counseling," and he found that the opportunity to serve others improved his own morale. But he already had something to offer—a sense of reality and a spirit of community.

APPENDIX:
PSYCHIATRIC PERSPECTIVES ON AFTERCARE
FOR RELEASED HOSTAGES AND THEIR FAMILIES:
A DIARY ACCOUNT.
(SECOND MOLUCCAN INCIDENT, MAY 1977)

What follows are notes from a diary I kept during the first week of the siege, when I was a participant-observer in the crisis center. These notes will provide an idea of the surroundings and concerns of the psychiatric staff, and of the actual victim-related part of the crisis-management process.

1 P.M.: We are joined by Professor Van Dijk, who is tall, imposing, warm, and, of course, has a Van Dyke beard. Also present are Dr. W.G. Mulder (no relation to Dick Mulder, the negotiator), and Dr. Plaggemans. This is the best-equipped psychiatric facility in Holland, a large teaching center with a good budget, staff, and reputation. We are in a spacious room with a constant flow of sandwiches and beer. (Incidentally, the same was true at the crisis center and medical command post.) At one end on a huge blackboard are listings of names and telephone numbers: police, fire department, doctors in Assen, Groningen, and The Hague, the crisis center, the medical center, the ex-hostage consultants, and others. By now, I recognize most of the names and the numbers. Our conversation is animated. First they tell me about the families who are massed at the station in Groningen and are surprisingly mutually supportive. Here is where the ex-hostages are making their major contributions, answering all sorts of questions that husbands and wives have about conditions inside the train, changes of mood that go on, problems that occur upon reunion.

We talk about care of the children in Bovensmilde. A female pediatric psychiatrist, Dr. M.C. Kho-so, is advising. She took care of the children who were terrorized last year at the Indonesian embassy. Then the first psychiatric symptoms appeared one week after the incident. But those children were not as physically ill as these. We hear reports of more and more sickness in Bovensmilde. Now we fear an Echo virus epidemic. Many children are reportedly apathetic. Some fear standing up and playing near the windows. Some have been reported home with their parents, lying down in the living room. Most children do not say much about the events (remember it is less than forty-eight hours of freedom). Some parents have employed the advised "play therapy" and it seems to be working. Most of the children would be described as normal and experiencing an expected amount of relief and joy. We discussed the issue of returning to school. Is there any sense in using "flooding"? The doctors here agree to take at least a week to ten days before returning the children to any school. Also, most of the parents adamantly do not want to send their children back to *that* school in Bovensmilde. It had been fire-bombed recently and it is on the border of the white and Moluccan sectors. The parents want their own white school!

It is explained to me that there are two white groups in Bovensmilde. The middle class work in Groningen—they will undoubtedly move out of the community. The others have lived there for generations. They will stay, but they are the hard core anti-Moluccans. Thus, the migration will further increase the polarization of that community.

Children from the school are reporting that the first day the terrorists explained to them their reasons for fighting, talked about their far-away country, and about their parents' service to the Dutch. The children were allowed to get books, papers, pencils, and then were made to sit on the ground. There was undoubtedly positive feeling toward the Moluccans. It is not clear now if there are four or five terrorists in the school. One of them was disliked by the children, but the others were friendly and popular. On the first day the Moluccans were very irritated by the younger children. Also, on that day there was some shooting out of the windows, which scared the children. Later, however, the Moluccans were cuddling the youngsters.

Dr. Van Dijk observes that it is very good to have the children in a group at this point. For instance, one was asked, "Were you afraid?" And he replied, "No, no!" But some other children said, "Yes you were, you were crying . . ." and the child admitted his fears and began to talk about them. Reports of anxiety and apathy are higher for the children at home than those who are in the hospital. This reflects a good deal of the literature on the positive value of affiliation during moments of shared stress.

One parent decided to have none of this psychiatric intervention, locked his child in a bedroom, disconnected the phone, and even unwired the door bell, then left the house so that his boy could get some rest. This account plunged us into a discussion of the role of the public health official and the school when parents disagreed with treatment plans. It is a sticky issue. Hopefully, the rapport among parents, doctors, social workers, students, and teachers will be good enough to allow collective planning and full appreciation of what each is trying to do. It seems to me that the school is the proper vehicle for restoring trust, calm, and confidence, and that the best role for the public health and mental health officials is that of consultants to the authorities in the school system. Fortunately, the relationship between the medical and educational community is excellent.

The psychiatrists at the hospital have noticed some bizarre actions among their regular patients, probably triggered by the current siege. One patient ran amok, ripping a sink off the wall, spewing water everywhere, then blurting out, "Deliver me of my solitude machine." Afterwards it became clear that he was feeling the isolation of the victims in the train. Another man called up from South Holland asking to be executed instead of the four teachers at the school. In another instance, a properly credentialed physician felt he had been summoned to the crisis center, and actually made it past the guards before it was discovered that he was completely deluded. These dramatic, highly publicized events do stir the imaginations of those on the brink or over the brink of psychosis.

Now we review the plans for receiving hostages once they are liberated from the train. First, they will pass through a very brief administrative screen. Just their names will be taken. Actually, 56 of the 57 hostages are already identified by name and family members are in contact with the psychiatric center. Secondly, there will be a short interview with one of the very experienced psychiatrists. Third, they will go with the nurses for a shower and change of clothing. After this the police will be allowed two or three minutes for an interview if necessary. Fourth, in the presence of psychiatric staff, they will be encouraged to take coffee, drinks, to stay or sit and otherwise relax as they please in the room in which we are now sitting. Fifth, they will have one to two hours for ventilation with members of the psychiatric staff. The idea here is that they talk and talk and talk and talk. Sixth, they will reunite with family members, in groups of five to ten persons. Social workers who already know the families will be present. Seventh, after watching from a discreet distance, psychiatric staff will attempt to resume contacts. Finally, the released hostages will be advised to stay in the gymnasium of the hospital for 24 hours. This will be a strong suggestion, but obviously there is no compulsion involved. I inquired about the need the police might have for interrogation and was told that the agreed-upon plan delayed intensive interrogation until two or three weeks later.

2:30 P.M.: We are receiving further news reports from the Assen hospital. A few of the 27 children have been sent home, but several are too ill to return. We still don't know the cause of the illness but we have heard that lumbar punctures have been performed on all of the children. One of the mothers of a released child has become ill. Is there a possibility of meningitis? Could this be a ploy to frighten the Moluccans? We are not sure of the facts, and since I am out of contact with the crisis center I don't really know. It seems highly unlikely that a doctor would make a public announcement about performing lumbar punctures if he had not done so.

3 P.M.: Now 12 parents in Bovensmilde have been diagnosed as having the same illness as the children. We debate whether it is an epidemic or a ruse. The discussion turns to talk about who has the medical responsibility for the teachers and hostages in Bovensmilde: should it be here in Groningen or there? The Groningen psychiatric staff agree that it is better to have treatment close to home, to locate the responsibility and psychiatric follow-up care itself within the affected community. Financial specialists have been summoned to analyse the costs of aftercare in Bovensmilde and Groningen, and to send estimates to the Director of the Ministry of Health, Dr. Van Londen, at The Hague.

Next we discuss the aftercare program for children and their family members. Although this is being run at another site, the psychiatrists sitting here with me have been consulted. The program is first aimed at the children, their parents, and their siblings. The entire affected population is divided into three groups. This grouping is based on the way parents grouped themselves at the library in

Bovensmilde while they were awaiting the release of their children. The emphasis is on short sessions to allow family life to continue around the social and psychiatric interventions. First, there was a medical screening process, then social work screening. Thirty social workers are involved. Later, child psychiatrists are brought in. What is under intensive discussion now is the development of a school program away from the school. There is a newly opened child psychiatry facility in Bovensmilde. It currently has 30 patients and can hold 80. That is the facility that is planned for use.

The plans call for a day program from 10 A.M. to 3 P.M. six days of the week. Children will attend in two shifts, on alternate days. There will be group talks, creative drama, with the whole group together for lunch. In the afternoon there will be free play and parents and other children (family members) will be invited in. There will be an opportunity for parent-child groups. Then they will go home together. We talk about relating this program to the other members of the community in Bovensmilde. It might be risky to form an "enclave of victims" and sacrifice some of the natural bonds that exist with community members who were not directly affected by the incident.

2
The Meaning of Stress

Walton T. Roth

After a terrorist siege has ended, the authorities and survivors survey the damage that has been done. Physicians may describe the bodily damage in terms of physical injuries, but in addition to any direct injuries each participant in a terrorist incident has been exposed to a situation in which many subtle physical changes may have taken place in response to a stressor. These changes may be only temporary or they may have varying degrees of permanence. This chapter will focus on our current understandings of the human stress response. A diverse group of concepts have been developed to explain this response and its relationships to health and disease. Each of these concepts and approaches focuses on an aspect of this universal human phenomenon, which may be useful for understanding and intervening in the experience of victims of terrorism. The discussion is based on a medical perspective that encompasses both physical and psychological reactions.

The Physiology of Stress

The response of the human body to threatening situations occurs in three basic systems: the skeletal muscular system, the autonomic nervous system, and the endocrine or hormonal system. To the outside observer the most obvious component of the stress response is the "fight or flight" behavior allowed by the postural and motor functions of the skeletal muscular system. Somewhat less obvious are the numerous adjustments of the autonomic nervous system that support the "fight or flight" response. The autonomic nervous system regulates other physiological systems that are usually beyond voluntary control, such as the constriction and dilation of blood vessels or the rate of digestion. Although recent research has shown that some voluntary control of these functions can be learned through biofeedback, this control is far less than we usually associate with voluntary activities such as the movement of limbs.

TABLE 1
Autonomic Nervous System Responses to Stressors

Organ	Response
Eye	Dilation of pupil
Heart	Increase in pacemaker rate
	Increase in conduction velocity of excitation
	Increase in strength of contraction
Arterioles (small blood vessels)	Dilation of coronary arterioles
	Constriction of peripheral arterioles
Lungs	Relaxation of bronchiolar muscles
Stomach and intestines	Decrease in motility
	Decrease in tone
Skin	Sweat secretion
	Piloerection (hair stands on end)
Adrenal Medulla	Secretion of epinephrine (adrenaline)
	Secretion of norepinephrine (noradrenaline)
Genitalia, male	Inhibition of erection
	Facilitation of ejaculation

Autonomic regulation is accomplished by adjustments in the balance of two principal divisions of the autonomic nervous system: the sympathetic and the parasympathetic. These two branches are distinct in terms of their autonomical location and pathways, and when they are stimulated they usually have opposite effects on the organs that they control. For example, sympathetic stimulation usually increases heart rate, whereas parasympathetic stimulation decreases it. This sympathetic nervous system is, at least initially, the one that is activated during stress. Some of the effects of this activation are listed in Table 1. The heart beats faster and more strongly, blood is diverted from the skin to the muscles in preparation for "fight or flight," the airways to the lungs open more widely, and digestive activities are suspended. The evolutionary significance of such changes is clear: they prepare the organism for immediate physical effort to meet the challenge of the stressor.

The parasympathetic nervous system, on the other hand, may be either inhibited or activated during stress. It is sometimes difficult to know if an observed change is produced principally by sympathetic or parasympathetic effects. For example, the pupil of the eye dilates under stress, a change that could be obtained by stimulating the sympathetic system or by inhibiting the parasympathetic system. Both of these systems have a baseline rate of activation, and it is essentially a change in the balance between these rates that produces effects on many of the end-organs in response to stressors. Although this balance usually shifts to the sympathetic side under stress, there are some exceptions. The syndrome of vaso-vagal fainting represents an increase in parasympathetic activation in which heart rate slows and blood pressure drops, producing the loss of consciousness. Parasympathetic activation under stress is observed when subjects react with an increase in activity of the gastrointestinal tract resulting in diarrhea.

Many autonomic nervous system changes can be perceived directly by the person undergoing stress and may increase his feeling of fear. An interesting example of this is Gerard Vaders's reactions to watching Robert de Groot being led past him in the Moluccan train incident. At first Vaders misperceived this man as the Dutch minister of overseas development and wondered if negotiations had begun. In fact, de Groot was being led away to be executed, and Vaders's realization of this as they went by was accompanied by his own perception of the resultant autonomic change: "I could no longer see them, but I felt what was about to happen and my heart beat quickened. After a few seconds two or three shots were fired." Here, the signal value of the autonomic change told the hostage what was really going on, even though part of him did not want to acknowledge the terrible reality of the situation. Later in the same incident, Vaders's perception of the breakdown in his initial adjustment also was accompanied by clear autonomic signals: "The next morning I was full of fear. Sweating. Cramps in the stomach. Fighting away panic." He used this signal of depleted resources to modulate his initial stance of taking notes openly: "Now I took notes by stealth."

Endocrine or hormonal responses to stress are even more widespread in their consequences than autonomic responses, but are usually not perceived directly by the subject in the same way. Table 2 lists some of the hormones and other chemical substances that have been measured by stress researchers and found to change during or after stress. These chemical changes are interrelated in very complex ways that may have major consequences for health. The anterior section of the pituitary gland secretes stimulating hormones that act as the regulators of other endocrine organs such as the adrenal gland and the thyroid. The hormones released by the adrenal cortex have effects on most body systems that result in widespread changes in body chemistry. Feedback systems exist to counteract the swings in hormone levels produced by stress. As in the case of the autonomic nervous system, stress affects an endocrine system that is already operating at some baseline level that may vary from person to person.

The overall integration of the muscular, autonomic, and endocrine

TABLE 2
Endocrine and Other Chemical Responses to Stressors

Substance	Source	Change of Serum Level Immediate	Change of Serum Level Post-Stress
ACTH (stimulates adrenal cortex)	Anterior pituitary	Up	--
TSH (stimulates thyroid)	Anterior pituitary	Up	--
GH (growth hormone)	Anterior pituitary	Up	Up
ADH (regulates water retention by kidneys)	Posterior pituitary	Up	--
Glucocorticoids (steroid hormone)	Adrenal cortex	Up	--
Mineralocorticoids (steroid hormone)	Adrenal cortex	Up	--
Epinephrine (adrenaline)	Adrenal medulla	Up	--
Norepinephrine (noradrenaline)	Adrenal medulla	Up	Up
Thyroid hormones	Thyroid	Up	Up
Insulin	Pancreas	--	Up
Androgens	Testicles	Down	--
Estrogens	Ovaries	Down	--
Pepsinogen	Stomach	Down	Up
Free fatty acids	Adipose (fatty) tissue	Up	--
Lipoproteins	Liver	Up	--
Coagulation factors V and VIII	Liver	Down	Up
Fibrinogen	Liver	Down	Up
Uric acid		Up	--
Iron		Down	--

response systems is accomplished in the brain. The hypothalamus and the limbic system of the human brain control specific patterns of autonomic and endocrine response. These more "primitive" portions of the brain are connected through several pathways to the cerebral cortex or "thinking" portion. Although the cortex is more remote from the pathways in the nervous system that directly control the stress response, it often initiates the entire sequence by perceiving a situation as being threatening. In the case of Gerard Vaders, the entire stress response was initiated by a process of perception and interpretation: "They threw the door open. There were two or three of them wearing black woolen balaclavas. I knew they were South Moluccans. The others thought PLO. But on the rifle butts you could see the colors. I recognized it from Indonesia." The cerebral cortex is an unnecessary signal system if the stressor is pain or some other physical stimulus such as heat or cold.

However, immediate physical discomfort does not always constitute the prime source of stress for people involved in terrorist situations. After all, the value of hostages as a means for threat depends on their remaining alive and relatively uninjured.

One of the most careful and thorough descriptions of this response process has been given by Hans Selye in his work on the General Adaptation Syndrome.[1] Selye emphasized that there is a sequence of events that occurs in prolonged and severe stress. His particular description of stress stages is based on the response of the adrenal cortex of rats exposed to severe stressors. Stage one is divided into two phases. In the shock phase, the adrenal cortex is normal in size but is being stimulated by the hormone ACTH from the anterior pituitary gland. In the counter-shock phase, the adrenal cortex has enlarged. In stage two, the stage of resistance, the adrenal cortex has returned to normal size but is still secreting more steroid hormones than before. (In a sense, this is an adjustment to chronic stress.) Stage three, or the stage of exhaustion, only comes about when the stressor is intense and prolonged. During this stage the adrenal cortex enlarges again, but this time it is unable to provide sufficient steroid hormones and becomes depleted. At this point, the organism becomes vulnerable to infection and other diseases.

It is unlikely that corticosteroids would become exhausted during human captivity lasting a few days or even a few weeks. But hostage situations such as the one in Tehran have, unfortunately, made it necessary for us to consider longer-term consequences. Selye's scheme serves to emphasize that the immediate stress reaction may be quite different from the prolonged stress reaction. Furthermore, substances that are repressed during stress may rebound to higher than normal values when the stressor is removed. As noted in Table 2, this is what happens with the digestive hormone, serum pepsinogen. These findings imply that the termination of stress may itself affect health.

Activation and Performance

A person's ability to think and act is modified during stress. Psychophysiologists studying the effects of stressful situations on performance have used the concept of psychological activation or arousal to unite the complex of physiological changes that we have outlined and to explore their effect on performance. Psychological activation is low when a subject is relaxed and drowsy and high when the subject is emotionally excited. One generalization that has emerged from the many experiments relating activation level and performance is that the relationship between these variables forms an inverted "U." Performance on a wide variety of tasks is optimal at intermediate levels of activation. Too much or too little activation decreases performance. Furthermore, the optimum arousal level for simple tasks is higher than that for complex tasks. One might say that the performance of simple, and possibly boring, tasks requires a degree of alertness that would interfere with the performance of difficult tasks, which require a more relaxed mental state. Some tasks that show this effect include motor coordination, perceptual discrimination, and vigilance. Activation level has been manipulated experimentally by the administration or threat of electric shocks, by the presentation of continuous loud noise, and by forced sleep deprivation. The analogical relationship of these methods to conditions existing for victims in many terrorist incidents is clear.

One of the abilities that activation affects is a person's state of attention. At high levels of activation, attention may be so sharply focused on a few relevant parts of the stimulus field that it misses other relevant stimuli. For example, stimuli presented near the center of the visual field might be detected whereas other signal stimuli in the periphery may be missed. For some tasks this narrow selectivity of attention is advantageous. In the Stroop test,[2] subjects must report the color of words printed on cards as quickly as possible after they see each card. The task is hard because the words are color names, and when a subject sees the word "red" printed in blue ink he may say "red" instead of "blue" or may take longer to give the correct answer. There is evidence that under conditions of high activation, subjects do better at this task because their attention is riveted to the color of the word and there is less tendency to read the word. In general, however, such abnormal focusing of attention is detrimental to overall performance.

Within a given situation, such as a terrorist incident, individual levels of activation vary. Some people are more prone to high activation in emotional situations or take longer to return to a relaxed state after becoming excited. These people perform complex tasks poorly under stress. According to the findings of Eysenck and his coworkers, people with introverted personalities are chronically more highly activated than people with extroverted personalities.[3] As a result, introverts may perform simple or boring tasks better than extroverts because the activation level of the extroverts is suboptimal. Under severe stress, however, the extrovert may do better than the introvert, because the activation of the introvert would be too high, while the activation of the extrovert would move into the optimal range. Gerard Vaders refers again and again to the helpfulness and high level of functioning of one of the hostages, Prins. A great part of Prins's activity involved "extroverted" interactions with others and concerns about the outside world.

One interpretation of this narrowing of attention at high levels of activation is that the subject attempts to resist the distraction of arousing stimuli. Noise shocks and other emotionally arousing events not only increase physiological activation, but also distract attention, and this may explain some of the performance deficit at high arousal levels. To a certain extent, however, the allotment of attention (a concept very closely related to the allotment of effort) is dependent on the plans and needs of the organism. For instance, the sleep-deprived subject can restore normal performance and adequate activation by exerting compensatory effort, but motivation to perform well and feedback about performance are crucial to sustaining and modulating the effort required. The importance of motivation and feedback in this context is echoed by the reports of many former hostages concerning the vital role played by information from the outside (for example, the importance of the radio news broadcast to the Moluccan train hostages) and the way that feedback and encouragement from fellow hostages helped them successfully adapt to the hostage experience.

Stress as a Cause of Disease and Death

Evidence of varying quality suggests that stressors and the emotions they produce can result in disease and death. The effects of the stressor may be immediate or delayed. At one extreme are reports of death occurring within minutes or hours of an individual's experiencing an emotion-arousing situation. In these cases the victim usually had a history of cardiovascular disease or was of an age where cardiovascular disease was likely. However, Herbert and Mead have collected accounts of deaths following closely after stress situations in young, and presumably healthy, people.[4] Some of these accounts have come from anthropologists and missionaries who tell how members of primitive tribes may die of unexplained causes within a few days of eating a taboo food by mistake or after learning that witchcraft had been practiced against them. For example, in Australia a man's enemy would point a bone at him, and if the effects of this pointing were not counteracted by appropriate magic the victim would fall sick and die within a few days. In these situations the beliefs of the society reinforce the beliefs of the individual that he will die, or, in the case of breaking taboos, that he should die. The behavior of dying persons in these societies is not fear and agitation, but more hopelessness and acceptance of death.

There are also anecdotal reports about people in Western societies who have died simply because they were firmly convinced that they were about to. For example: "An assistant was hated by the students of a col-

lege. They condemned him in a joking manner to death, carrying out the
ceremony in a serious manner. The assistant was held with his head on
the chopping block, eyes bandaged, while one student made the noise of
a swinging ax, another dropped a warm, wet cloth on his neck. The assistant died instantly."[5] The same authors cite other examples of the lethal
effects of panic.

Research on the effects of stressors over a few months' time indicates
that fear and anxiety are not the only stressors that affect health. Rahe,
in a series of studies, employed a questionnaire designed to measure life
change. Subjects are questioned about both unpleasant changes, such as
the death of a family member or having been fired from work, and pleasant changes, such as a vacation or a job promotion, that have recently
affected them. It appears that either type of change results in more
sickness in the near future. In one study, American seamen filled out the
questionnaire before going on a cruise. They were divided into high- and
low-risk groups on the basis of total life changes they had registered on
the questionnaire. In the first month at sea the high-risk group had
almost 90 percent more sickness than the low-risk group. Although this
difference declined over the ensuing six months, the high-risk group still
had more illness than the low-risk group at the end of the cruise.[6]

Life events, especially when mediated by their meaning to the subject,
do not always have negative effects on health. Anticipating a significant
event in one's life may actually decrease the probability of death. Phillips
and Feldman discovered that death rates decreased in the six months
before birthdays and increased afterward, reaching a peak in the first
three months following the birthday. The greatest variation was noted
among distinguished people, for whom the ceremonial occasion of the
birthday would have elicited the greatest social response.[7]

Long-term followups of people exposed to stressful conditions such as
prison camp incarceration often suggest that such situations have far-
reaching consequences for the survivor's health. Even many years after
their liberation, prison camp survivors have had higher mortality and
morbidity rates than age and sex-matched comparison groups. Eitinger
and Strøm found that mortality rates were greatest among those
prisoners who had been exposed to the worst conditions and that this
higher death rate persisted at least fifteen years after release. More than
the expected number died of tuberculosis and other infectious diseases
and from accidents, lung cancer, and coronary artery disease. Eitinger
and Strøm also examined registered diagnoses of survivors who had
come into contact with the National Health System, and learned that ex-
prisoners had much higher incidences of tuberculosis, neurosis and ner-
vousness, alcohol and drug abuse, gastric and duodenal ulcers, and com-

plaints of back pain. The incidence of cardiovascular disease in this group was not significantly higher. Dr. Eitinger's discussion of the long-term effects of captivity on health follows in Chapter 4.

Among survivors of prison camps it is difficult to separate the effects of stress from other, more specific disease factors such as starvation, infection, and physical trauma resulting from hard labor or torture. Of course, these effects are hard to separate even in theory, since stress probably decreases resistance to infectious disease. In any case, prison camp survivors differ considerably from most hostages, who are seldom held as long or under as severe conditions. (However, recent terrorist incidents, such as the one in Tehran, may foreshadow a change in this pattern.) It is possible that starvation in prison camps actually reduced the subsequent incidence of coronary artery disease in some prisoners whose normal diets had been associated with this health problem. It also might be misleading to apply mortality and morbidity statistics for prison camp survivors to terrorist hostages, since captives who were soldiers may have been healthier than average when captured, and those who survived extremely harsh conditions may have been the healthiest members of their group.

Certain diseases are apparently related to stress in various ways. In so-called psychosomatic diseases, the quantitative relationship between psychological and physical factors is much less clear cut than the relationship between infecting agent and infectious disease, for example. Stress can have either an etiological or a modulating effect on psychosomatic diseases, depending on the individual and the intensity of the stress response. Alexander and others have singled out the following diseases as being stress related, to varying degrees: bronchial asthma, essential hypertension, ulcerative colitis, certain types of dermatitis, rheumatoid arthritis, thyrotoxicosis, and peptic ulcer disease. Certain general symptoms such as headaches, menstrual disturbances, eating disorders, and sleeping disorders are also often stress related. It is not surprising, then, that these diseases commonly flare up in predisposed persons during prolonged hostage situations.

Stress Responses and Disease Mechanisms

Although the above examples show that stress influences health, they fail to specifically tie physiological stress response and disease together. Now we will try to do this theoretically by matching several different formulations with the facts. Physiological stress reactions may exemplify what Cannon has called "the wisdom of the body," because they prepare the organism for increased muscular effort in emergencies. The process of evolution favored those physiological changes that enhanced an animal's ability to fight or to flee. Changes that occur in the stress response are similar to those that take place during strenuous physical activity. This complicates the use of physiological indicators to measure emotion in "real life" situations.

That this parallelism of stress response and response to physical activity creates research constraints can be clarified through an example from one of our own experiments. We were interested in verifying the relationship between increased heart rate and emotional stress during everyday activities. Subjects in our experiment wore light tape recorders that recorded their electrocardiograms during a twenty-four hour period.[8] During this same time the subjects kept diaries of their activities and rated the emotional arousals they experienced with each activity. Physical activity was also measured. Depending on surrounding circumstances, heart rates associated with different physical activity levels varied tremendously. For instance, when one subject, a psychiatrist-in-training, was sitting, his heart rate was between 80 and 90 beats per minute. While he was hurrying from place to place, it was from 100 to 120 beats per minute; during sleep his heart rate reached a low of 50 beats per minute. Such variations are typical. At one point on this subject's recording, in the late afternoon, his heart rate increased to 105 beats per minute without an accompanying increase in activity. This occurred when the subject was conducting a group therapy session in which he began to get angry at what one of the patients was doing. This anger, which from an evolutionary standpoint began to prepare the psychiatrist to punch the patient in the nose, illustrates two points. First, the amount of increase in a physiological variable due to the emotion may be very small compared with variations that take place during mild physical effort. Second, it illustrates how, in modern civilization, an originally physiologically adaptive response is no longer useful. Nowadays emotional arousal rarely precipitates immediate fighting or fleeing. For terrorist hostages, motor activity either to fight or to escape would seem to make much more sense. Unfortunately, this response is often impossible for hostages, and has occasionally led to tragic consequences when attempted. Thus, the victim of terrorism often finds him- or herself unable, for prolonged periods, to pursue vigorous physical activity, even though action would seem to be the best response.

A central paradox in psychosomatic theory is that the psychological stress response is an adaptive mechanism that helps the body keep functioning, although at the same time the stress response itself can theoretically lead to breakdowns and to disease. How can mechanisms that have evolved to protect the body become mechanisms of destruction? One possibility is that extreme emotions can elicit extreme physiological responses that are no longer adaptive and may even be incompatible with life. This might apply to cases in which death occurs within minutes or hours of stressful events.

Cannon thought that in cases of voodoo death, extreme activation of the sympathetic nervous system could have caused death. Some symptoms of such activation might be elevated heart rate, sweating, enlarged pupils, and fever. On the other hand, Richter's research indicated that such activation might be parasympathetic. In his experiments, wild Norway rats forced to swim in a tank died quickly, especially if their whiskers were clipped before the rats were put in the water. (Rats use their whiskers to orient themselves.) The rats did not die from drowning but from heart rate slowing and cardiac arrest, which points to massive vagal stimulation, i.e., overactivity in the parasympathetic nervous system.[9] In a milder form, this phenomenon has been observed in vasovagal fainting attacks in humans exposed to a stressor such as the drawing of blood: heart rate and blood pressure drop. The relationship of the autonomic nervous system to different kinds of emotion is complex in that emotional arousal usually stimulates both the sympathetic and parasympathetic pathways. However, anxiety is usually associated more with sympathetic discharge, and depression or giving up with parasympathetic discharge. Thus, in autonomic terms, extremes of either emotion might have lethal cardiovascular effects.[10] This is not usually the case because of the numerous regulatory mechanisms the body has to prevent excessive swings in physiological functions; people with preexisting heart disease, however, might be unable to regulate these excesses.[11] Sometimes neither the patient nor his physician is aware that heart disease is present. Certainly the presence of pathological changes in cardiac and vascular function in older men in Western societies is the rule rather than the exception.

The importance of considering emotional responses other than anxiety, as well as the interaction of these responses with preexisting cardiovascular disease, has been illustrated by Engel and Greene. Engel found that people often die in situations characterized by intense emotion, fear of losing control over the precipitating situation, and feelings of hopelessness. They have often "given up" psychologically shortly before death.[12] Greene and his coworkers studied sudden death in patients, most of whom had a history of preexisting coronary heart disease. Typically the patients had been depressed from one to three months, had become involved in an arousing situation at home or at work, and had been returning to their baseline state of depression when death occurred.[13]

Another possible model for the relationship of stress response to disease is that continued activation of a physiological mechanism that is useful in acute stress situations leads to pathological changes that would not take place if the activation were only brief and intermittent. For example, the increase in blood pressure that occurs in acute stress is too minor to be harmful and has the evolutionary purpose of preparing the person for physical action. If the stress continues at a low level for a longer time, however, the mechanism that regulates blood pressure can be altered so that blood pressure is maintained at a higher level even when the stressor is removed. It is as if the thermostat had been turned up. The net result is a decreased life expectancy due to hypertensive complications. Early man, who relied on hunting for his existence, was better served by these mechanisms. In the first place, he was more likely to benefit directly from reacting to stress with physical activities of fight or flight. In the second place, he seldom lived to an age where the complications of elevated blood pressure would be noticed.

Variations in Stress Responses

What is stressful to one person may not be stressful to another. Moreover, the stress response itself does not create an identical physiological reaction in everyone. These variables may explain why some people develop stress-related diseases and others do not, even in the extremely stressful situation of terrorist captivity. This is clear in the accounts of Gerard Vaders and others who describe the reactions of a fairly large group to the stresses associated with a terrorist incident. It will be useful, then, to consider some sources of variability in more detail.

First, some kinds of stressors produce specific kinds of physiological response. Some of this differentiation is simply due to the fact that the human autonomic nervous system has specific regulatory tasks that are not related to stress itself. For example, extreme cold and extreme heat may both be stressful, but the autonomic changes that conserve heat (such as peripheral constriction of blood vessels, shivering, and suppression of sweating) are the opposite of those that dissipate heat. For instance, Gerard Vaders and the other captives on the Moluccan train found cold to be a major stressor. Often, as in this case, the hostage-takers share the same stress, and reactions of both groups must be considered by those attempting to resolve the incident.

Another type of differentiation lies more on a psychological plane. This type of *stimulus-response specificity* is based on experiments pioneered by Lacey that indicate if the stressor requires attention to the external environment, the heart rate decreases, whereas if it requires attention to internal processes, the heart rate increases. An example of the former situation is a vigilance task; an example of the latter is doing mental arithmetic in the presence of outside distraction. It is interesting that although heart rate differs between the two situations, skin conductance (which has often been used as a physiological correlate of psychological arousal) rises in both. In other words, increased heart rate does not always accompany increased skin conductance and psychological stress.

People also differ greatly in their patterns of response to stress. An individual, however, will often react consistently to different stressors, a phenomenon called *response specificity* or *stereotypy*. Some people are heart rate reactors; others are blood pressure or muscle tension reactors. This labeling refers to the variable that shows the most change, and does not mean that most people react exclusively in one way no matter what the situation. Instead, quantitative differences in reactivity occur in various systems. It is generally assumed that these idiosyncratic differences in reactivity patterns are based on genetically determined anatomical differences, but it is possible that some types of physiological patterning can be learned.

Another source of variation is *emotional specificity*, a term used to describe reactions to stressors that may differ depending on whether the subject experiences fear, anger, or other emotions. Under some circumstances, anger may cause diastolic blood pressure to rise, whereas anxiety or fear may produce a fall. In general, the cardiovascular response to anger-provoking stimuli is similar to the effects of norepinephrine, and the response to anxiety-provoking stimuli is similar to epinephrine effects. Emotions associated with depression and "giving up," on the other hand, may arouse a much higher level of parasympathetic response than emotions of anxiety would cause. It is likely that specific emotions have less effect than emotional arousal in general. In fact, emotional arousal and physiological changes respond to pleasant events as well as to unpleasant ones. Moreover, some psychological states that are not usually thought of as emotional states are associated with physiological activation. For instance, activation is higher when subjects are involved in social interaction than when they are not. The subject might describe himself as "involved" or "participating" rather than as "anxious" or "excited." A similar activation may accompany the feeling of being hurried, a consideration that is clearly relevant to the subject of hostages and hostage-takers.

Development (in terms of psychological complexity) of the notion of emotional specificity preoccupied psychiatrists in the 1950s and 1960s. The basic concept developed during this period, under the leadership of psychoanalyst Franz Alexander, has been called *conflict specificity*. Alexander associated different psychosomatic diseases with different intrapsychic psychological conflicts that might be manifested in different personalities. For example, his investigation of patients with peptic ulcer disease convinced him that they had dependency conflicts that could lead either to a dependent personality or to a very independent personality whose independence functioned to deny strongly felt dependency needs. Alexander and his colleagues believed that such a personality might develop in people who had dependent relationships with their mothers, often formed when the infant or child was fed as a means of alleviating frustration. Alexander pictured peptic ulcer disease as a kind of physiological regression. Thus, the frustrated adult acts as a child waiting to be fed by secreting acid and digestive enzymes that can eat holes in the stomach if no food is actually present. A layman may understand this hypothesis better if he views the mechanism as a Pavlovian conditioned reflex, in which stress serves as a conditioned stimulus for gastric secretion.

The most complex level of specificity is *personality specificity*. In the late 1930s, Dunbar found that people with different diseases had different personalities. For example, men with coronary heart disease seemed to be hard-driving, achievement-oriented people. Because Dunbar had methodological problems, including difficulty getting random samples of patients, her work was criticized, but in recent years some of her ideas have been vindicated in studies with sounder methodological bases. Friedman and Rosenman have described a coronary-prone behavior pattern as the "Type A personality." People with this pattern are competitive, very pressured by time, very deeply involved in their work, and have difficulty relaxing. They do not complain of anxiety and cannot be labeled as neurotic. They are active doers and not brooders. In a prospective study of 3,400 men, free of coronary heart disease, the presence of the Type A personality pattern was associated with a much greater risk of heart attack or other symptoms of coronary heart disease in the 39- to 49-year-old group. From a physiological standpoint, we might expect these people to be constantly manifesting stress-related changes even though they are generally happy with their lives and find the stress exciting and pleasing, if they notice it at all. Rosenman and Friedman have shown that this personality pattern is accompanied by elevated cholesterol, triglycerides, and decreased blood clotting time, all of which are physiological changes that can plausibly lead to coronary heart disease.[14]

Probably the best example of how these different kinds of specificity interact to produce actual disease is the well-known study by Weiner and his coworkers. Subjects in this experiment were army recruits undergoing basic training, an experience generally acknowledged as stressful and also one which, like terrorist incidents, assembles people of diverse backgrounds and exposes them to a shared stressor. In this experiment the investigators screened 2,073 inductees into the U.S. Army to find those with serum pepsinogen levels in the upper 15 percent range and the lower 9 percent range. These 120 subjects were given a battery of psychological tests and a series of X-rays of the upper gastrointestinal (GI) tract. The subjects received a second upper GI series between their eighth and sixteenth week of basic training. In the first examination, three men had healed ulcers, and one man had an active ulcer. Five more recruits had developed active ulcers by the time of the second examination. The study showed that both the level of serum pepsinogen and the psychological test results successfully predicted who would get ulcers, but that these two predictors were not independent of each other. All nine people who got ulcers were in the high serum pepsinogen group. Also, seven of the nine were among ten men selected by the experimenters on the basis of psychological testing to be most likely to develop peptic ulcer disease because of psychological conflict. They had been selected before either the men or the experimenters knew they had ulcers. These results show that both physiological differences and psychological differences are important in determining the development of peptic ulcer disease. They also reveal that predisposing physical and psychological factors may be correlated.[15] In terms of the previous discussion, these results indicate that response specificity and conflict specificity interact to produce ulcer disease. In this, and in other so-called "psychosomatic" diseases, stress can have either an etiological or a modulating influence, depending on the individual and on the intensity of the stress response.

Psychological Defenses and Physiological Response

Although we have categorized some of the sources of variability in physiological response to stressors, the psychological aspects of this categorization remain superficial. Personality and conflicts cannot easily be compartmentalized. Personality tests can be misleading. For example, numerous studies have shown that a person's self-rating of anxiety in a personality test bears little relationship to the physiological reactivity shown in an anxiety-provoking laboratory situation. One of the many reasons for this is that physiological changes are more closely related to the emotional state during physiological recording than to a general personality trait of anxiety-proneness. Specific aspects of a situation may determine a person's emotional reaction to stress more than the fact that the situation itself is stressful to a hypothetic "average" person.

For a situation to be stressful, the individual must find it threatening, and that evaluation depends on the subject's past experiences, attitudes, and psychological defenses. Defenses function to make a situation that is perceived as threatening at some level more benign through intrapsychic mechanisms. The physiological impact of psychological defense is illustrated in some of Lazarus's studies. He presented subjects with films of aboriginal puberty rites involving mutilation of the penis. The films had various sound tracks. If the sound track promoted *denial* that there was any pain or discomfort involved, or *intellectualization* by presenting a theoretical sociological explanation of what was going on, a viewer's heart rate and skin conductance response was less than when no sound track was used.[16]

One of the persistent ideas in psychosomatic medicine is that defenses that lead to repression of emotion result in greater eventual physiological expression. This theory is often derived from earlier Freudian postulations that emotional stimuli increase psychic energy, which has to be discharged by emotional expression, lest it become dammed up and find outlets in somatic symptoms. Originally, somatic symptoms were considered to be symbolic expressions of conflict. They were labeled as "functional" rather than organic: that is, there was no organic physical pathology underlying the disability or complaint. Later there was a tendency to believe that dammed-up emotional energy could also be discharged in activity of the autonomic nervous system or in other physiological systems. These ideas are not currently confined to psychoanalytically-oriented psychiatrists. In California, at least, there is a fairly widespread belief among the lay public that failure to express feelings can lead to psychosomatic illness. On the other hand, the findings of Lazarus and others contradict this belief; their research indicates that defenses that prevent emotional expression also result in less somatic disturbance, at least in the physiological systems tested. Other experiments suggest that emotionally expressive people show more autonomic lability or instability than less expressive people.

Because most laboratory situations are, by definition, artificial, the stress they produce is considerably less than that experienced by victims of any terrorist incident. Epstein and Fenz have done an interesting series of experiments that explore the relationship of performance, defense, and physiological response in a "real life" situation that is less artificial and more intense than that found in most laboratories. These investigators have measured psychological and physiological responses of sport-parachutists prior to flight, during the flight up to the moment of jumping, and after landing. Their results show that experienced parachutists are clearly different from novices in the timing of their physiological and psychological responses. In the early phases of the jump sequence (for example, immediately after getting into the airplane) experts and novices were equally fearful and equally physiologically activated. As the moment of the jump approached, however, the experts' physiological and psychological fear response decreased, while the novices' increased right up to the last moment. In some way, experienced parachutists can "turn off" their fear response as the moment of the jump approaches. If each of the two groups is subdivided on the basis of performance ratings, the good performers at each level of experience have a decrease in physiological activation in the last parts of the jump sequence. Among experts, the mean heart rate at the time of jump for the poorer performers was 120 and for the better performers, 85. These findings confirm the inverted "U" relationship between arousal and performance by showing that very high levels of arousal are associated with disruption of performance in this particular task.

In these studies, denial was the more frequent defense among the novice group. For example, one novice jumper said, "I was not afraid at all, until I looked down and saw my knees trembling. Then I realized how scared I really was." Thematic apperception test cards of parachuting scenes were presented to novice and expert jumpers in order to learn more about their defense mechanisms. In the novices' stories, the hero was usually either completely calm or intensely fearful. The heroes in the stories told by experienced jumpers concentrated on the task of jumping and seemed to be oriented toward taking in sensory information relevant to the task. Although they did not insert denials of fear in their stories, they generally avoided expression of emotion. We can infer from these results that the novices unsuccessfully attempted to control their fear by denial, whereas the experienced group, having less fear to control because they were more familiar with the tasks, could control what fear remained by not thinking about their feelings.[17] These studies revealed that both physiological and psychological reactions depend both on the efficiency of the defense and the strength of the emotion being defended against. They also emphasize the important effects of training on stress response. While this particular variable may have little relevance for the average citizen, who may nonetheless become a victim of terrorists he or she has never heard of, it does have considerable relevance to groups who are at "high risk" from either a geographical or professional standpoint.

Another defense mechanism operates in certain individuals during periods of intense emotion. It is the experience of *depersonalization* or *derealization*. Depersonalization is the feeling that the self or mind is out-side the body, and derealization is the feeling that although the mind is within the body, the outside world is unreal or remote. These two ex-periences are not completely distinct and only represent some of the possible ways of splitting apart parts of the mind, the body, and the ex-ternal world. Arthur Koestler describes one of these experiences in his book *The Invisible Writing*. He had been captured and imprisoned dur-ing the Spanish Civil War. He writes:

> On the day when Sir Peter and I were arrested, there had been three occa-sions when I believed my execution was imminent. On all three occasions I had benefited from the well-known phenomenon of split consciousness, a dream-like, dazed self-estrangement, which separated the conscious self from the acting self—the former becoming a detached observer, the latter an automaton, while the air hums in one's ears as in the hollow of a sea shell.[18]

This experience does not always alleviate anxiety; it can be accom-panied by continued psychic distress as in the anxiety-depersonalization syndrome described by Martin Roth.[19] This experience is especially in-teresting in that there seems to be a kind of physiological truth in the feel-ing that the relationship between the mind and the body has changed. Lader has reported a case of an anxious woman who intermittently ex-perienced intense panic and depersonalization. When this patient ex-perienced depersonalization, the skin conductance indicators of anxiety showed decreased activation.[20] This mechanism may be seen as a kind of safety valve that prevents the organism from being overwhelmed by panic and keeps important physiological systems from going too far from equilibrium.

Conclusions

The descriptions of the experience of being held captive by terrorists provided by surviving victims leave no doubt that most hostages undergo a physiological stress response of some kind. We have reviewed evidence suggesting that if such a response is intense enough or prolonged enough it can have important health consequences. Although the duration of the stress situation of terrorist captivity may only be a few hours or a few days, the situation is much more threatening than most events in ordinary life and certainly much more so than any situa-tion that has been orchestrated in laboratory research studies. Being cap-tured by terrorists is not on the Rahe list of "significant life events" because of its low frequency for the general population, but it certainly represents a very significant event for anyone who has experienced it. People's patterns of life reportedly change significantly following captivity: the stress of the event reaches far beyond the actual period of captivity. Such changes are known to have health implications, either through the mechanisms of the primary physiological stress response or through secondary mechanisms such as increased use of alcohol and other drugs, accident-proneness, and other covert or overt self-destructive behaviors.

The extent of the health disability in victims of terrorism needs to be specifically investigated. In this chapter we have presented several conceptual systems that deal with the human stress response and its effects on health. These systems may provide useful perspectives for examining the specific consequences of terrorist victimization. It is impossible to draw quantitative conclusions on the basis of research done on stressors of a different magnitude or duration. Nevertheless, two features that future research on psychosomatic implications of terrorist captivity must have are implicit. First, because individuals vary so much in their response to stress it will be necessary to examine a fairly large number of cases to draw any definite conclusions. These cases should be examined for a variety of physical illnesses and not limited to the few traditionally "psychosomatic" ones. Thorough physical examinations will be necessary to distinguish between complaints of sickness and demonstrable physical disease. Second, a control group is essential to provide a baseline rate for illness so that valid inferences may be made. This control group should be as similar in age, sex distribution, and social background to the group exposed to the terrorist victimization as is feasible.

The nature of modern terrorist tactics, particularly the hijacking of aircraft, meets many of the requirements for empirical research. Some of the complicating factors that have most plagued psychosomatic investigations of prison camp survivors are absent. First, comparable control groups are readily available. Since the victims have only a symbolic significance, it makes little difference to most terrorists which particular airplane is hijacked. Passengers on an airplane that is not hijacked can be our comparison group. Second, air travelers tend to be more representative of the general population than prisoners of war. (Although those who travel in airplanes are an economically select group, prisoners of war often come from a group composed largely of physically healthy young men.) Thus, the results of investigations of skyjacking victims may be more readily generalized to the population at large. Third, the stressors in terrorist captivity situations are largely psychological.

Physical hardship or torture is the exception rather than the rule. In the case of prisoners of war and concentration camp victims, it has been difficult to separate the long-term effects of psychological and physiological trauma, since the prisoners have often been malnourished, mishandled, and exposed to infections. Fourth, the psychological stress in terrorist victimization is well-defined in nature and in timing. Prisoners of war and concentration camp victims underwent profoundly stressful situations even well before capture. For example, soldiers have usually been in combat, and the captured Jews had seen their world gradually destroyed. The victims of terrorism, on the other hand, are usually caught by surprise and the onset of the stressor can be timed to the minute. Although reactions to the event of being captured will vary from person to person, at least the stressor is externally similar for everyone, so that investigations of different coping mechanisms are simplified.

Objective research on the issue of psychosomatic implications of terrorism is essential to resolve the extent of damage to the victim. We cannot be satisfied with mere speculation, however plausible it may be. As far as I know, there is no hard evidence that short-term stressors have the consequences I have argued that they could have. The body has remarkable homeostatic mechanisms and recuperative powers, and there is no reason to add unfounded hypochondriacal worries to the many others the victim has. Well-controlled medical and psychological investigations of these victims need to be undertaken in order to answer the questions and satisfy the needs of clinicians, researchers, and policymakers.

Notes

1. Selye, H.: *The Stress of Life*. New York, McGraw-Hill, 1956.

2. Stroop, J. R.: "Studies of interference in serial verbal reactions." *J. Exp. Psychol.* 18:643-662, 1935.

3. Eysenck, H. J.: *The Biological Basis of Personality*. Springfield, Ill.: Charles C. Thomas, 1967.

4. Herbert, C. C., and Mead, N. E. in *The Physiology of Emotions*. Edited by Simon, A.; Herbert, C. C.; and Straus, R. Springfield, Ill.: Charles C. Thomas, 1961, pp. 187-209.

5. Ibid., p. 190.

6. Rahe, R. H.: "Life-change measurement as a predictor of illness." *Proc. R. Soc. Med.* 61:1124-1126, 1968.

7. Phillips, D. P., and Feldman, K. A.: "A dip in deaths before ceremonial occasions: Some new relationships between social integration and mortality." *Am. Soc. Rev.* 38:678-696, 1973.

8. Roth, W. T.; Tinklenberg, J. R.; Doyle, C. M.; Horvath, T. B.; and Kopell, B. S.: "Mood states and 24-hour cardiac monitoring." *J. Psychosom. Res.* 20:179–186, 1976.

9. Richter, C. P.: "On the phenomenon of sudden death in animals and man." *Psychosom. Med.* 19:190–198, 1957.

10. Dimsdale, J. E.: "Emotional causes of sudden death." *Am. J. Psychiat.* 134:1361–1366, 1977.

11. Lown, B.; DeSilva, R. A.; Reich, P.; and Murawski, B. J.: "Psychophysiologic factors in sudden cardiac death." *Am J. Psychiat.* 137:1325–1335, 1980.

12. Engel, G. L.: "Sudden and rapid death during psychological stress. Folklore or folk wisdom?" *Ann. Intern. Med.* 74:771–782, 1971.

13. Greene, W. A.; Goldstein, S.; and Moss, A. J.: "Psychosocial aspects of sudden death." *Arch. Int. Med.* 129:725–731, 1972.

14. Friedman, M.: *Pathogenesis of Coronary Artery Disease.* New York: McGraw-Hill, 1969.

15. Weiner, H.; Thaler, M.; Reiser, M. F.; Mirsky, I. A.: "Etiology of duodenal ulcer. 1. Relation of specific psychological characteristics to rate of gastric secretion (serum pepsinogen)." *Psychosom. Med.* 19:1–10, 1957.

16. Lazarus, R. S.: "*Psychological Stress and the Coping Process.*" New York: McGraw-Hill, 1966.

17. Fenz, W. D.: "Strategies for coping with stress." In *Stress and Anxiety,* Vol. 2. Edited by Sarason, I. G., Spielberger, C. D. New York: Hemisphere (Wiley), 1975, pp. 305–336.

18. Koestler, A.: *The Invisible Writing.* London: Hamish Hamilton, 1954.

19. Roth, M.: "The phobic anxiety-depersonalization syndrome and some general aetiological problems in psychiatry." *J. Neuropsychiat.* 1:293–306, 1960.

20. Lader, M.: *The Psychophysiology of Mental Illness.* London: Routledge and Kegan Paul, 1975, pp. 192–193.

3
Coping with
Terrorist Victimization

Jared Tinklenberg

Introduction

There is a growing conviction that specific steps must be taken to assess and deal with the unusual plight of the victim of terrorism. Those who are charged with the responsibility for containing and resolving terrorist incidents as well as for protecting the victim are increasingly concerned with the development of a deeper understanding of the psychological mechanisms at work in the hostage as well as in the captor. Since both are likely to exhibit certain predictable behaviors under the stress of a terrorist incident, an understanding of these behaviors and the mechanisms underlying them is crucial to any program of intervention and control. In addition, this understanding can be extended to the development of theories and techniques that may be applied by hostages to reduce anxiety and maximize the chances for survival. The present chapter focuses on adaptive behaviors people use to cope with the severe stress of being a hostage during a terrorist incident. The discussion has been extended to include examples from similarly threatening situations requiring many of the same psychological mechanisms. Several examples of defense and coping mechanisms are drawn from information on the severely stressful experiences of prisoners of war and concentration camp inmates.

We should begin with a definition of crucial terms, since there is considerable overlap in the use and meaning of such words as "adaptation," "defense," and "coping." In accordance with Robert White's system, we will consider *adaptation* as the superordinate category under which the terms *defense mechanisms* and *coping* are subsumed.[1]

Adaptation includes all the responses and strategies a hostage may make or use in order to reduce stress and maximize his chances of survival. For the purposes of this chapter, defense mechanisms are narrowly defined as the essentially unconscious psychological adjustments that the individual makes to a present danger and its attendant anxiety. They are largely influenced by the personality of the individual and are often characteristic of his response in many different situations. Coping refers to an ongoing, active process used to meet the task requirements of adapting to a relatively difficult situation. Coping involves innovative, rather than routine, behaviors and differs from defense in that it is not restricted to unconscious psychological mechanisms, but also involves conscious, deliberate behaviors as well. For clarity, under the general concept of adaptation we will first discuss defense mechanisms and then coping strategies. It should be noted, however, that these mechanisms do not operate singly, or necessarily in any particular order, but often work simultaneously or in clusters. The repertoire of adaptive mechanisms is extensive and varies among individuals. In addition, strategies change over time and with circumstances; mechanisms overlap and may even be contradictory. For instance, the victim may simultaneously deny the reality of the experience and hope that things will come out all right.

Although the systematic study of terrorism and of victimology is relatively new, many of the victims' responses to their captors and to the stress of captivity come from the same repertoire of behavior that people have used to adapt in other stressful situations. Thus, the observations gained by psychiatrists and other behavioral scientists in a variety of contexts can be usefully applied to victim responses in the terrorist situation.

The problem of predicting successful adaptive behavior in a terrorist situation is complicated by several basic factors that alter the characteristics of the situation and may have a profound influence on the outcome:

Temporal Dimensions

The range of responses available to an individual confronted with severe anxiety is determined to some extent by the duration as well as the severity of the stress. Victims of prolonged captivity will utilize different adaptive behaviors at different rates of progression than victims who are confronted by a terrifying, but relatively brief, threat. Indeed, unless adaptive behavior is adjusted to the temporal duration of the threat, an individual may not be able to withstand the physical and emotional stress. Initially, stress usually induces sustained and directed activity, increased vigilance, and greater alertness to outside events as the body prepares for strenuous activity. However, Selye and others have noted that individuals cannot maintain this response over a prolonged period of time.[2] Unless he adopts other adaptive behaviors, persistent threat will cause an individual's thought and judgment to deteriorate, somatic disturbances to appear, and, often, erratic and impulsive behavior. The individual may become undiscriminating and emotionally and behaviorally labile; he may even panic. Obviously a panic response is not useful for survival since it is followed by the collapse of mechanisms that serve survival itself: body control, attention, and alertness to reality testing.[3] Victims of brief terrorist encounters may be well served by an initial, brief, intense physiological arousal. Victims of a prolonged threat, such as the hostages held in the U.S. embassy in Tehran, are in an essentially different situation; they must find other ways to adapt to the extended temporal demands of long-term captivity.

Prior Life Experiences and Personality Factors

Victims of terrorism vary both in their life experiences before the incident and in the behavioral response repertoire that they bring to it. Some individuals, such as military or diplomatic personnel, may have had prior training that enables them to mobilize a wide range of conscious adaptive behaviors in addition to unconscious defense mechanisms. Presumably they might have better adaptive advantages in a terrorist situation compared with individuals who have had little or no prior experience. One contributor to the relatively low level of psychopathology manifested by the American hostages in Iran may have been their prior experiences and training in the foreign service and military fields.

Personality type is another important factor determining coping behaviors. Studies of prisoner of war (POW) and concentration camp survivors have shown that certain personality types adapt more successfully than others under identical circumstances. As an example, Ford and Spaulding psychiatrically evaluated the 82 surviving USS Pueblo crew members who were captured and imprisoned in North Korea for 11 months in 1968. Those men who adapted poorly to the prolonged stress were frequently evaluated as being passive-dependent, whereas those who coped well with the stress most often had personality diagnoses of healthy or schizoid.[4] Thus, individual behavior will vary depending upon previous experience and personality type.

The Terrorists' "Set"

The outcome for the victim is obviously dependent upon the terrorists' particular "set," that is, on their motives, goals, and the actions they are willing to take. Motives may range broadly from simple monetary gain to obtaining publicity for a specific political cause. Since the victim may not know what the motives, expectations, and tactics of the terrorists will be at the outset, they can only institute adaptive behaviors as they perceive and evaluate new information. Fortunately, a detailed review of terrorist incidents in recent years indicates that in virtually all cases the motives and tactics of terrorists are not focused on simply killing the hostages but are more complex, and thus amenable to psychological manipulation. Only a small percentage of the total number of hostages held in international incidents have been killed in cold blood by their captors; a greater number have died in the crossfire during rescue attempts. Even when hostages have been executed, as in the Moluccan hostage incident described by Gerard Vaders elsewhere in this book, psychological factors in the hostages and in the hostage-takers may still play a decisive part in determining the choice of victims and how many are eventually murdered. Thus, the personalities and life experiences of the terrorists, their motives, and their objectives will also determine which adaptive behaviors will be most useful in any given hostage incident.

The defense and coping mechanisms outlined below represent only a few of the various adaptive behaviors available to the individual. They will be discussed at length because they seem to be the most salient behaviors used to adapt to hostage incidents.

Psychological Defense Mechanisms

When an individual is suddenly confronted with a severe threat he frequently employs an initial psychological defense of *denial* or a *counterphobic mechanism*. Denial is said to occur when an individual partially or totally refutes the reality of an experience, the emotion associated with it, or the memory of the experience. This common defense mechanism helps the individual reduce the shock of the experience to a manageable level and may in some instances inhibit precipitous action, such as excessive reflex "heroism." However, denial can be employed only so long as it can coexist with reality testing.[5] Too much denial, or denial that is too prolonged, may lead to psychosis. As the stressful situation continues and progressively more information concerning "reality" impinges on the individual, it is increasingly difficult to deny the experience. Thus denial is a time-limited defense that generally loses its effectiveness after a short period. Anxiety levels actually rise with sustained denial of perceived reality. Optimally, the defensive denial gradually lessens as the hostage assimilates the reality of the situation in emotionally acceptable degrees and adopts other adaptive behaviors.

An articulate report of denial has been provided by an American woman who was among 149 passengers and 9 crew members who were skyjacked to the Jordanian desert and held captive for a week by the

Popular Front for the Liberation of Palestine. She vividly described the initial response of several passengers as stunned refusal to believe that a skyjacking was actually taking place.[6] Gerard Vaders reported how an elderly woman among the hostages held on a train by South Moluccan terrorists responded with massive denial when one of the terrorists said he was expecting the anti-terrorist police unit to attack and told hostages to lie on the floor if there was a shoot-out. When she heard this instruction she responded, "I'm not going to do that—my dress will get dirty."

Thus, a hostage's first response might be, "I don't believe this" or "this can't be happening" or other statements that seem to assume that the real situation does not exist. These statements are psychologically true; the individual unconsciously and automatically refuses to comprehend the situation. For brief periods denial helps. It permits time to lapse and protects the individual from physical collapse. Panic reactions are forestalled or made less likely. The temporizing effects of denial give the victim an opportunity to gradually assess the situation and perhaps formulate coping strategies. Extreme forms of denial may increase risk, of course. An individual might not follow the captors' demands or might try to push a gun away. Unless the denial is extreme, however, it can act as an unconsciously self-constructed buffer mechanism that protects the psychological balance of the individual and permits him to gradually and constructively assimilate a dangerous and threatening reality.

The individual who utilizes *counter-phobic mechanisms* reduces stress and anxiety by excessive and sometimes precipitous responses that actually oppose his basic inclinations in a threatening situation. A simple example would be the case of a man with a fear of heights who insists on peering over the edge of a cliff. Counter-phobic psychological defenses may serve the individual well in some stress situations, but in violent circumstances such as a hostage incident, counter-phobic behavior often, if not always, is maladaptive. Acted-out counter-phobic behavior in these situations is sometimes termed "macho" or "machismo," and often increases the chances that the victim will be injured or killed.

In our own investigations in the California prison system of adolescent assailants and their victims, we found several examples of this negative outcome. Our data clearly indicate that counter-phobic responses in potentially violent situations are frequently futile and dangerous. An unfortunately common example is the robbery victim who, while the assailant is pointing a gun at him, reaches under the counter to get his own weapon. The assailant immediately shoots and kills him. Other victims have defiantly dared the assailant to shoot, or have threatened to kill the assailant although they were unarmed and knew that the assailant had a loaded gun. In the Moluccan train situation described by

Gerard Vaders, it is difficult to speculate on the psychological motivations of persons other than Vaders himself. Early in his account, however, Vaders describes how "the others on the train were either sitting still or following orders. The Moluccans had us tape paper over the windows and many were doing that. One man seemed a little too aggressive. That was Mr. de Groot." Although Vaders did not make this connection directly, it is not surprising that Mr. de Groot was selected as one of the three hostages to be executed. Fortunately, de Groot managed to escape. We can cite more examples of this type of behavior, but the point is that for a victim of terrorism to survive, the counter-phobic mechanism usually is not a good immediate adaptive response.

Closely related to counter-phobic mechanisms are those that are usually described as *reaction formation* and *identification with the aggressor*. These usually occur over longer periods of time and thus involve later phases of hostage incidents. Reaction formation may be described as an adaptive process in which an individual adopts attitudes and behaviors that are, in fact, opposite to the impulses he harbors either consciously or unconsciously. For example, fear of the terrorist is transformed into approval or admiration. In a situation where one person is victimized by another, this process may extend to identification with the aggressor. When observed in the victims of terrorists the process may be described by different terms, such as "identification with the captor," or "identification with the controller." The victim unconsciously incorporates the characteristics of the feared person and becomes psychologically allied with him. By transforming himself from the person threatened into the person who makes the threat, the victim reduces his anxiety.[5]

Obvious examples of this process can be drawn from Nazi concentration camp experiences, during which some inmates mimicked their captors to the point of wearing swastikas to cover their Star of David insignia and walking with a goose step. These mechanisms may have been salient in the highly publicized case of Patricia Hearst. In brief, Hearst, then an 18-year-old newspaper heiress, was abducted from her Berkeley apartment in February of 1974 by a gang of terrorists who called themselves the Symbionese Liberation Army. She was held hostage and subjected to severe stress for a prolonged period of time. Subsequently, she appeared to join her captors and identified with them to the degree of participating in some of their violent activities and assuming the "revolutionary name" of Tanya. Although before her abduction Hearst had limited or no experience with guns, three months after her capture she carried a gun and attempted to provide covering fire when her companions, William and Emily Harris, were challenged by a storekeeper for shoplifting. She also took part in bank robberies. The court's decision in the Hearst case reflected the psychological complexity of these events, assigning culpability with a guilty verdict, yet adding extenuating circumstances in granting conviction with probation.

Whatever conceptual model is used to explain this phenomenon, shifting allegiances between victims and their captors is a factor that must be considered when dealing with hostage situations. The unconscious defense mechanisms of reaction formation and identification with the aggressor represent one such conceptual framework. Others are explored in Chapter 6 by Drs. Soskis and Ochberg and in Chapter 8 by Thomas Strentz.

The defense mechanisms mentioned up to this point, often associated with neurotic symptoms even in otherwise psychologically healthy persons, are generally considered to be on the less adaptive end of the scale. It is important to remember that they *are* unconscious and that hostages who have used them to adapt to the severe stress of terrorist incidents may experience considerable guilt about having done so after the incident is over. If this guilt is more than transient, or if it interferes with function, it must be treated.

Unconscious psychological defense mechanisms at the other end of the scale include *intellectualization, creative elaboration,* and *humor.* These mechanisms are generally considered more "healthy" or "mature" than the others, and some of them shade into the processes described in this chapter as coping strategies. Often, they are combined in varying proportions in one behavioral response. Intellectualization is a psychological process that reduces stress by taking the threatening situation into the sphere of the intellect, thus divesting it of its emotional and personal meanings. The threat can then be worked on as a cognitive problem with the conceptual tools of philosophy, religion, political theory, science, and so on. An example from the incident reported by Gerard Vaders would be the time spent by several hostages wondering if they would be eligible for compensation for enduring a period of high stress and immediate threat to life. This response occurred at the same time the elderly woman quoted earlier was utilizing denial. The way that Gerard Vaders carefully thought through his personal existential position when he believed he was about to be executed may also have entailed some intellectualization.

Creative elaboration is a related psychological process by which the victim elaborates on specific situations, sometimes in disguised form—in dreams, stories, imagery, or fantasy. Hostages on the train spent time planning meals they would eat when they were free. In the *Pueblo* incident, one captive U.S. crew member spent a great part of his time mentally designing and building a complex computer, while another—a chef—mentally planned elaborate meals. Still another crew member fantasized in detail about specific tactics that U.S. troops would use to mount a massive retaliatory raid upon the North Koreans.[7,8] A physician member of the team that cared for the American hostages in Iran after their release listed fantasy as the most common coping behavior. Freedom and food were the most frequent subjects.[9] The compensatory as well as distracting role these fantasies can play for people trapped in a hostage situation are clear.

In the context of an ongoing terrorist incident the humor that arises is clearly of a "gallows" type. Nevertheless, this defense mechanism can have an extremely adaptive function in reducing anxiety. Some of the captives aboard the skyjacked airplane that was held in the Jordanian desert had been inmates of Nazi concentration camps. These veterans of Nazi internment joked about the others' complaints, saying that compared with what they had already lived through, the plane was a "Hilton Hotel."[6] Gerard Vaders utilized humor at the very beginning of his captivity as he mused over not having to write "Santa Claus poems" that year, since he would have a good excuse (the hostage incident occurred during the Christmas season). Later, the hostages told jokes to each other to pass time. It is clear that these defense mechanisms, unlike those described earlier, have a more adaptive role for the victim of terrorism in a hostage situation; their positive intrapsychic benefits are not offset by excessive escape from or inappropriate handling of the reality situation.

Initial Coping Strategies

Although defense mechanisms and coping strategies overlap considerably, the term "coping" generally refers to using more conscious, deliberate methods to reduce stress while attempting to meet the demands of the situation or to achieve specific goals. Coping generally denotes creative as opposed to routine actions, and reflective as opposed to reflexive behavior. There are a wide variety of coping mechanisms, but we will focus only on those that are most salient for victims of terrorism.

Earlier we noted that denial and counter-phobic mechanisms are the techniques that many people initially use in frightening situations. Denial is generally limited to the beginning stages of the unexpected threat and usually dissipates as the individual gradually assimilates the reality of the experience. Our studies in the California prison system on victim and assailant interactions, especially in violent situations, indicate that continued denial is often associated with injury or death. In other words, the refusal to relinquish control to a clearly dominant assailant increases the victim's danger. To date, the victim's most useful coping strategy in the initial stages of a terrorist episode has been to consciously accept that he must at least temporarily *relinquish control* to his captor. When propitious, the victim should tacitly or explicitly acknowledge that he accepts the terrorist's dominance. Relinquishing control in this fashion serves two purposes: it emphasizes the reality of the situation for both the terrorist and the victim, and it reduces the possibility of precipitous violent action on the part of the terrorist. In interviews with California kidnappers whose victims were killed, a recurrent theme was, "He didn't know who was boss," or irrational comments such as "he would have hurt me if I had let him." It is important to remember that assailants are anxious and fearful too, especially in the initial phase of an aggressive interaction, so it is very likely that a terrorist will overreact if his victim is nonsubmissive. The treatment Gerard Vaders received when he took notes openly clearly illustrated this principle; so does de Groot's being chosen for execution after he acted "a little too aggressive."

Thus, the victim's most prudent initial strategy appears to be to leave resistance and intervention to law enforcement or military professionals who have been specifically trained in appropriate strategies and tactics for the use of force. Even if the terrorists are assaulted, victims are advised not to interfere, but instead to seek cover and maintain a submissive posture as much as possible.

In order to relinquish control the victim must be aware of his own emotions in the situation. In addition to fear, victims of terrorism commonly experience rage, frustration, and humiliation. However, because it is usually counterproductive to act on these powerful feelings, it is important that the victim be attuned to his internal state and learn to control his emotions and actions. The ability to relinquish control as an adaptive coping mechanism is a companion to the ability to *maintain control over one's own emotional responses*.

As we said earlier, unconscious defense mechanisms will often inhibit initial action; the next adaptive step is often to replace this unconsciously determined inhibition with a conscious, deliberate inaction during which the victim focuses on whatever self-relaxation is possible so that he can adjust his behavior to the situation. Some victims have found it useful to concentrate on their immediate environment, not letting their imagination wander through all the negative possibilities. Others have directed their thoughts toward neutral subjects or pondered comforting, sustaining themes such as religion. Assuming familiar roles and doing tasks that are easily mastered have also helped victims reduce anxiety and maintain self-control. Gerard Vaders used this coping strategy when he decided to take notes at the beginning of the Moluccan terrorist attack, thus functioning in his familiar role as journalist, and so did Betty Neal, an office worker on the staff of B'nai B'rith, who assumed the role of secretary to the Hanafi Muslim leader in the Washington, D.C., hostage incident. Dr. Eitinger develops this point in relationship to the experience of members of the helping professions in long-term captivity situations.

In many stressful situations there are warning periods during which individuals can rehearse their roles and formulate appropriate coping behaviors. Although most victims of terrorism have had no prior warning or training, certain geographically or occupationally high-risk populations are now informally or formally discussing the possibility of terrorist captivity. Ideally, such programs should actively rehearse a captive situation so that the potential victim can see how he would react emotionally under threat and learn how to deal with it. It is important in this context to understand that calm inaction in the face of severe threat is in fact "doing something." For people in Western societies, who value active control over their destinies, such passivity is especially difficult to value or to practice. Being aware that inactivity is often the best initial strategy for ultimate survival is important; it can help victims to maintain self-esteem, a crucial component in reducing immediate stress and facilitating successful adjustment after the terrorist episode.

Extended Coping Strategies

Following the initial coping strategies of, first, consciously relinquishing control to the terrorists, and then maintaining passive emotional self-control, victims can begin to use adaptive maneuvers that are more appropriate for long-term captivity. Some of these strategies include gathering information, establishing positive bonds with the terrorists, establishing affiliations with other victims, focusing on survival for some purpose, and maintaining the will to live.

Gathering information about the environment, the physical layout, the circumstances of fellow victims, and most importantly about the "set" of the terrorists has adaptive value and can significantly reduce stress. For example, in all three sites of the Hanafi siege in Washington, D.C., the women hostages were treated much more gently than the men.[10] These differences in treatment seemed to stem from the religious beliefs of the Hanafi. This assessment alleviated some of the captives' anxiety (especially that of the women) as it suggested that execution was not the paramount intent of the terrorists. In the *Pueblo* incident cited earlier, one crew member reported that he had been certain that the North Koreans would eventually release them because he observed that although the guards beat them severely, they were careful to avoid visible disfigurement.[4]

It is important to realize that, just as it takes a while for initial denial to dissipate, there is an optimal rate at which information can be assimilated. Receiving either too much or too little information can often increase stress and its symptoms. If possible, therefore, the individual should adjust his interactions with the terrorists or with other sources of information according to his ability to control his emotions.

In general, it is adaptive for hostages to attempt to *establish positive bonds with the terrorists.* Whether the terrorist and the victim should communicate remains a controversial issue. The U.S. Task Force on Disorders and Terrorism recommends that victims attempt to establish dialogue with the terrorists, taking care to express serious, noncontentious interest in their personal and political beliefs; attempt to persuade them to alternatives; avoid giving information; and seek to elicit information that would help apprehend the terrorists.[11] In contrast, some clinicians who have worked extensively with hostage survivors recommend that the victim not attempt to establish any contact with the captor unless and until the captor initiates the communication.[12] A reasonable position on this issue is that victims should be prepared to take full advantage of whatever opportunities the terrorists offer for contact. The important goal of this contact is to induce the terrorists to develop positive emotional bonds with their captives. Hostages should vigilantly seek such bonds and respond quickly and sincerely, since greater human awareness of each other generally reduces the possibility of violence. An example is the experience of Betty Neal, who acted as secretary to the Hanafi leader and assisted him in his negotiations by handling the phone communications. She later reported that the leader gave her advice on where to hide and how to protect her life should violence erupt, a far cry from his threats to cut off the heads of other captives.[10] The Moluccan terrorists' decision not to execute Gerard Vaders after they had heard a detailed account of his family problems appears to have been at least partially determined by a similar process of "humanization."

In terrorist episodes, positive affective bonds between captor and victims are usually enhanced over time. This psychological process has been reflected in many situations where the terrorists' brutality and violence decreased during the episode. A U.S. expert on terrorism, Darrell Trent of the Hoover Institute at Stanford, has collected evidence indicating that if the victims have not been harmed in the first three days, their chances of surviving unharmed progressively increase.[13]

Another extremely useful coping strategy after the initial phases is for victims to *establish group affiliation with other victims.* This process has repeatedly proven to be adaptive, even where only a few other victims have been involved. The feeling of common adversity, of "all being in the same boat" has been convincingly documented as a stress-reducing psychological process. This tactic was absolutely essential among concentration camp survivors; having even a single friend meant the difference between either going on or giving up and dying.[13] The U.S. Task Force on Disorders and Terrorism recommends that victims take every safe opportunity to discuss and evaluate their situation with an emphasis on what they can do to help each other.[11] Group interaction also provides an environment where leadership may arise both to benefit morale and to ameliorate some of the conditions of captivity. Benefits of this strategy were seen among members of the *Pueblo* crew who were billeted together several to a room. Spontaneous leaders who arose were very helpful in reducing the guilt experienced by many men after their forced confessions.[7] In her account of the skyjacking to the Jordanian desert, Jacobson reported that after all the men had been removed from the plane, the women who remained established a self-policing and self-assisting solidarity system.[6]

The final coping strategies that we will discuss reach beyond the terrorist incident itself. The ability to *focus on survival for some purpose* may take a wide variety of forms. Some concentration camp survivors have reported that they were determined to survive because they felt desperately needed by other members of their families.[14] This strategy may also take the form of faith in something bigger, something that transcends the human condition. The transcendental view evidently has great positive value for anxiety reduction and survival, whether it be commitment to a religious faith, devotion to a cause or art form, or the positive value of carrying on certain interests to which one is deeply attached. Many captives at the Islamic Center site of the Hanafi siege, where several individuals read the Koran during the incident,[15] reported that religion was useful, and similar positive effects of religious practice and belief were described by several of the Americans held captive in Tehran. A deep and abiding faith in mankind or in one's colleagues may also serve as a positive focus. The *Pueblo* crew members who fared relatively well during captivity reported that they *knew* they would not be abandoned.[4] Among concentration camp survivors, many sustained themselves with the firm conviction that the bulk of humanity would not tolerate such atrocities.[14]

Although it is related to the strategy of survival for a purpose, *the will to live* refers to a more primitive commitment to life itself, with or without special purpose. It may consciously take the form of a deep and total decision to live no matter what and on any terms: to choose life for its own sake. Survivors of long-term imprisonment have reported that they decided to live at some point during the early months of captivity and credit that decision for their survival.[16] Among concentration camp inmates the will to live often became the entire motivation of the individual, overwhelming all others; on the other hand, "give-up-itis" was one of the major causes of nondeliberate death.[14] Another example of this psychological mechanism's force is in *Pueblo* Commander Bucher's report that at one specific time, repeated beatings, exhaustion, and pain had made him contemplate suicide. But instead, as the next beating approached, he stood up, drawing upon "prayer and a fundamental will to live and prevail over these beasts."[8] Although most terrorist incidents have been more time-limited than prisoner of war or concentration camp captivity, this fundamental decision to survive may be a focal point around which hostages can organize other coping strategies.

The adaptive behaviors that we have reviewed in this chapter have been repeatedly demonstrated by victims of terrorism. They have also been used in various other life-threatening situations to reduce anxiety and to make positive outcomes more likely. Although we have been addressing some of the worst events that can happen to a person, the focus on adaptation, and especially on coping, conforms to more general views of this human process. Perhaps the most comprehensive brief analysis of the positive goals of adaptive behavior has been provided by David Hamburg: First, whatever stress is currently being faced is met and brought to the best possible resolution; second, anxiety is kept within tolerable limits; third, self-esteem is maintained; and fourth, relationships with significant others are made or preserved.[17]

Notes

1. White, R. W.: "Strategies of adaptation: An attempt at systematic description." In Coelho, G.; Hamburg, D.; and Adams, J. (eds.): *Coping and Adaptation*. New York: Basic Books, 1974, pp. 47–68.

2. Selye, H.: *The Stress of Life*. New York: McGraw Hill, 1956.

3. White, R. W.: *The Abnormal Personality*. New York: The Ronald Press Company, 1956.

4. Ford, C. V., and Spaulding, R. C.: "The Pueblo incident: A comparison of factors related to coping with extreme stress." *Archives of General Psychiatry* 29:340–343, September 1973.

5. Freud, A.: *The Ego and the Mechanisms of Defense*. New York: International Universities Press, Inc., 1966.

6. Jacobson, S. R.: "Individual and group responses to confinement in a skyjacked plane." *American Journal of Orthopsychiatry* 43(3):459–469, April 1973.

7. Spaulding, R. C., and Ford, C. V.: "The Pueblo incident: Psychological reactions to the stresses of imprisonment and repatriation." *American Journal of Psychiatry* 129(1):17–26, July 1972.

8. Bucher, L.: *Bucher: My Story*. Garden City, New York: Doubleday and Company, 1970.

9. Johnson, R. E.: quoted in *American Medical News*, February 13, 1981.

10. *The New York Times*, March 12, 1977.

11. National Advisory Committee on Criminal Justice Standards and Goals, Report of the Task Force on Disorders and Terrorism: *Disorders and Terrorism*. Washington, D.C.: U.S. Government Printing Office, 1976.

12. Dr. Calvin Frederick, National Institute of Mental Health: quoted in *The Washington Post*, March 12, 1977.

13. Trent, D.: personal communication, Hoover Institute, Stanford University, May 1977.

14. Dimsdale, J. E.: "The coping behavior of Nazi concentration camp survivors." *American Journal of Psychiatry* 131(7):792–797, July 1974.

15. *The Washington Post*, March 11, 1977.

16. Segal, J.; Hunter, E. J.; and Segal, Z.: "Universal consequences of captivity: Stress reactions among divergent populations of prisoners of war and their families." *International Social Science Journal* 28(3):593–609, 1976.

17. Hamburg, D. A.: Seminar in Coping, Stanford University, 1969. See also Hamburg, D. A.; Coelho, G. V.; and Adams, J. E.: "Coping and adaptation: Steps toward a synthesis of biological and social perspectives," in Coelho, G.; Hamburg, D.; and Adams, J. (eds.): *Coping and Adaptation*. New York: Basic Books, 1974, pp. 403–440.

4
The Effects of Captivity

Leo Eitinger

The word "captivity" has many different meanings. Even if we look only at the very practical ones, they cover a wide range, from the open prisons in Sweden, where the inmates commute daily to work in their own cars and return "home" to prison in the evening, to the captivity of the hostage as described dramatically in Dr. Guy Richmond's memoirs:

> An officer was held hostage by determined men who had a grievance relating to their treatment by the courts. They were appealing their conviction and wanted publicity. They seized an officer and held him in the barber's chair with a razor at his throat. It was impossible to rescue him in spite of officers posted with rifles at strategic points. To shoot would have been to shoot the officer. I mobilized all available medical services and requested our consulting surgeon to stand by with a reserve of blood plasma. If they cut Ernie's [the hostage's] throat, there might still be a chance of saving his life. The historic culmination was a special edition of the *Sun* within an hour or two of the interview with the men concerned. They held the officer until they had seen a newspaper report of their grievances. On his release he was in shock and exhausted.[1]

Between these two extremes lies a whole range of captivity stress situations and reactions. All share certain features, including loss or limitation of freedom, loss of power over one's fate, some kind of relationship to one's incarcerator, and usually some effort to relate to one's family and/or society. Attempts to cope with the stresses of captivity necessarily differ over the short term, where immediate survival is the issue, and over the long term, where numerous psychological adjustments have to be made.

Finally, the long-term effects of the stress of captivity, not only on the victims themselves but also on the families to which they return, are just beginning to be explored and understood. While the people involved may react in somewhat different ways, both psychologically and physically, certain features seem to be common to all, or nearly all, experiences of captivity.

Aspects of Captivity

Deprivation of Freedom

The core of any form of captivity is the loss of freedom to move freely "around in the world." The most extreme restraint, which is often applied against hostages, can produce anxiety leading to panic with few or no possibilities for movement or action. Hostages often accurately perceive that they are in danger of losing their lives. The tragic history of a significant number of the hostages captured by either ordinary criminals or political terrorists proves that the assessment of the situation as life-threatening can be correct.

Deprivation of freedom may be exacerbated by a high degree of physical restraint. The Nazis systematically tortured certain victims by means of confinement in the so-called "Stehbunker," a cubicle so small that it was impossible to lie down or even sit down properly. Making the situation even more intolerable, the height of the bunker was so low that crouching was the only possible position. Interestingly enough, the extreme leftist terrorists captured in Stockholm in March/April of 1977 had learned their lesson rather well from their fascist counterparts. They had prepared a box for one of the hostages in which he could neither sit nor stand completely erect.

Another only slightly less disagreeable Nazi torture forced prisoners to stand between two rows of electrically charged barbed wire for at least twenty-four hours, usually to reduce their powers of resistance before an interrogation. I remember very well the overwhelming temptation to lean against the barbed wire and to very simply end the torture of restraint, of sleep, food, and water deprivation on a hot summer day. Only with a very strong will to survive could one resist the temptation to take the easy way out. Solitary confinement with more or less pronounced sensory deprivation may be considered the next level of deprivation of freedom. From the experiments of Heron, Hebb, and McGill and those of Lilly at the National Institute of Mental Health (NIMH) in Bethesda, as well as the later works of many others, we know the results of extreme sensory deprivation.[2] It is also well-documented that these studies have been used as the basis for extreme torture in different forms and modifications, practiced even by very "civilized" nations. Still lesser degrees of deprivation are solitary confinement with or without the possibility of working, so-called normal prisons, and then camps with relatively ample possibility to move around, to meet people, and to speak to them.

A lesser, yet still intolerable, degree of imprisonment is where the prisoners are constantly observed behind bars. To be on display for twenty-four hours a day with no privacy at any time, to stay behind bars, like an animal in the zoo, is without a doubt a deep insult to human dignity and a serious blow to self-esteem.

In her outstanding personal report on individual and group responses to confinement in a skyjacked plane, Sylvia Jacobson[3] reflected on the effect of constant observation: "By afternoon, armed men of various North African armies began to pass through the plane in a steady stream, hour after hour, staring curiously at its interior and its occupants. This aroused feelings of revulsion, degradation, dehumanization, and vague threat. Distinctly we felt impotent, confined, constricted, and like animals in a zoo. Even the adolescents resented the feeling of being on display. Divisiveness was subdued. Despite differences of nationality, religion, race, sorrows, needs, values, resentments, and fears, there was a unity in a showing of proud indifference, aloofness, and disdain to the inquisitive stares." It is questionable how long this attitude of proud indifference and aloofness can be maintained. Most likely it would eventually give way to contempt toward the whole world, including oneself.

Restriction of movement is only one factor in captivity, albeit the most salient one; it interacts with other aspects of the victim's environment. Isser Harel's book on Eichmann[4] describes a captive who was restricted in his movements but otherwise lived under relatively good material conditions. He was kept with one leg chained to a bed, had to wear dark glasses, and had little opportunity to talk with others. On the other hand, he was under constant medical supervision and had specially prepared vitamin-rich food and regular exercise. Any kind of abuse was strictly forbidden. His very cooperative and appreciative attitude proves to a certain extent that even a relatively extreme degree of restriction on freedom can be tolerated with only a few negative reactions, provided that the other material and psychological conditions are acceptable or at least not too stressful. Even so, we know from the concentration camps that the freedom of movement in some camps, and the possibility of visiting others in different blocks or barracks, did not benefit most of the inmates. They were far too tired, after twelve hours of hard labor and the many additional hours of standing at attention in the endless roll calls, and far too hungry to move around more than was absolutely necessary.

Power over One's Fate

Responsibility for One's Fate. The captive's total attitude toward the loss of freedom tends to be influenced by the way he experienced its causes. The "normal" criminal prisoner is a captive for very complex reasons. Society asks both for atonement for the crime and for "justified" punishment, while at least giving lip service to the reeducation of the criminal. Where education is not feasible, the rationale of imprisonment is to prevent crime or to protect society. In theory, although not always in practice, the criminal is somebody one attempts to change and thus "a person of importance." In addition, he is seen as having been master of his own destiny at one time, so that his loss of freedom is self-inflicted. These views vary widely in different captivity situations.

The kidnapping victim is a prize that is seized in order to be exchanged for something else. His importance lies only in this exchange value, so that he is considered essentially as an object snatched randomly or by location or, occasionally, because of some connection with wealth, family, or business. Victims of hijackings or hostage incidents are often simply regarded as symbols—without personality or individual value. The question, "Why me?" is often unanswerable.

Prisoners of war, on the other hand, are taken to reduce the fighting potential of the enemy. Although they have no individual value, they count as masses. Even though prisoners of war can rarely influence their fate, on the whole they will accept it as part of the game, even if the game itself is considered meaningless.

Dissenters and political prisoners in totalitarian regimes are perceived as people who, as intolerable threats to the state, must be crushed. In such a setting, responsibility for one's own imprisonment may be attributed to integrity and heroism. Although the most common treatment of such prisoners is interrogation and torture, later incarceration in labor and other camps may lead to loss of individuality and personality and an identification only as part of a large resource. In the combined concentration and extermination camp, victims were virtually worthless and unable to understand their situation. They arrived in huge transports by the thousands and only a very few were brought to areas where the last remnants of their working capacity could be used. After that, they went the same way as the others before them—into the gas chambers and crematoriums. They were humiliated and debased to the utmost degree. Their individuality was, of course, of no importance. They were numbers only, an idea accentuated by the numbers tattooed on their arms. Their working capacity was a "quantité négligible," and the ashes of their corpses were even used as fertilizer.

Having to deal with this meaninglessness and lack of identity often affected the prisoners' ability to cope with conditions in the camp. Among the millions imprisoned, there were political and religious groups who of course did not consent to the rationale, such as it was, of their arrest. Unlike prisoners of war, they did not accept the Nazis' right to put them in camps; once arrested, they identified themselves with the cause for which they were imprisoned, thus gaining a certain degree of self-respect and coping capability. To become the object of completely meaningless events, however, is detrimental not only to one's dignity, but also to one's ability to deal rationally with the ongoing situation. Those who cannot identify themselves in any way with other prisoners fare much less well, as we will discuss later.

Predictability of Fate. Lack of power over one's fate makes any prediction for the future uncertain and any feeling of security impossible. On the other hand, knowledge of imminent and inexorable death presents an equally intolerable stress. In this respect "normal" criminal prisoners are actually well off. They have a defined sentence and, in many countries, can calculate precisely the day of release. Hostages are at the other extreme of the spectrum, particularly hostages of terrorists who are members of various "liberation movements." Nobody actually knows what they will demand or if it will be possible to appease them at all. When hostages depend on an immunity that terrorists do not recognize, as in the case of the American diplomats held in Iran, their previous sources of security are undermined. Skyjacked victims, who do not even know who the skyjackers are or where the aircraft is going to land, experience this insecurity most painfully. This has been demonstrated by the many accounts of the Entebbe victims, as well as by Sylvia Jacobson. She noted that the fourteen college students on her plane, in their first attempt at coping, started scanning the seat pocket maps and speculating among themselves about their eventual destination.

Prisoners sentenced to life imprisonment or to death with suspended death sentences are a case of predictability. Panton[5] investigated 34 male prison inmates who were sentenced to be executed relative to a representative prison population sample of 2,550 male inmates; his psychological tests indicated that there were behavior disorders among the Death Row inmates. Further evaluation of these prisoners revealed feelings of resentment, hopelessness, failure, frustration, and social isolation or, in other words, signs associated with the situational stress of awaiting execution.

These results are hardly surprising. In Nazi concentration camps, non-Jewish prisoners would say that their stay in the camp was a race between their ability to survive and the duration of the war. The Jewish prisoners, however, knew that they were sentenced to death, as were all Jews deported to the camps, and that those who continued to live were only being used for their working capacity to the last possible moment. They experienced every day of life as a new gift. Sometimes the gift was rather difficult to bear, but nevertheless, it was always considered a gift from heaven.

Relationship to the Incarcerator

The "normal" criminal prisoner and his warden see each other as representing different social systems and values. They meet in a sort of "modus vivendi" in their daily work, but seldom bridge the gap that society has placed between them. Their relationships are institutionalized with relatively few possibilities of variation. Individual preferences of the wardens and of the captives do exist, naturally enough, and there are differences in the degree of humanity and understanding the prisoner encounters, but it is mainly the regulations of the institution that determine interpersonal relationships in those settings.

At the opposite extreme, in the concentration camps, the SS soldiers were tormentors, educated to this aim. The SS guards considered people in the camps to be subhuman ("Untermenschen"); those of "Aryan" background had some chance of being "reeducated," but the others were considered lost. Only in very rare cases (especially at the end of World War II when the SS soldiers were replaced by old, partly incapacitated reserves) did relationships of interpersonal understanding evolve.

The relationships between hostage-takers, including kidnappers, skyjackers, and terrorists, and their victims are more complicated and have often been difficult for liberators to understand or to accept. Symonds[6] has stated that there is a special psychological relationship between the kidnapper and his victim. In most crimes, the interest of the criminal is to remain as anonymous as possible. In the crimes of kidnappings and hostage-taking, the criminal must have contact not only with the victim, but also with others. He uses the capture and custody of the victim as a lever to force the family, the police, or the government to fulfill his goal. To sustain his leverage, the criminal must make sure that the victim remains alive or create the illusion that this is so. A paradox ensues. Ochberg[7] has discussed this phenomenon, called the "Stockholm Syndrome," which is named after the young women hostages in a Stockholm bank robbery who, after the incident was concluded, attacked the police and defended the criminals. In such situations, the victim perceives the criminal as his protector and believes that his family and the police, by their behavior or refusal to accede to the criminal's demands, are the ones who are endangering his life. Under such conditions, when anxiety and terror are overwhelming, the victim easily distorts reality and may actively view the family and the police as the enemy.

The situation of political terrorists and their hostages is even more complex. In the beginning of an action, hostages experience the real danger of being killed. As time passes and the threat of immediate death diminishes, the hostages feel a certain relief that opens the way for communication and usually some effort to understand the terrorist. He may be perceived as an "underdog" (socially) or a "poor guy" forced to such extreme action because of a political situation or because no other ways are open for his "righteous goals." The victims thus unconsciously accept to a certain extent the hostage-taker's presentation of himself, viewing him as a human being with personal traits and problems deserving of sympathy. The hostage-takers reinforce this feeling when they stress that they "have nothing against the hostages personally" and treat them humanely. The next rapprochement comes when the hostage-takers and their victims have to solve new problems in the ensuing situations. Group feelings and interpersonal relationships evolve in and among both parties, and they no longer consider each other as anonymous enemies, but rather as individual human beings and members of a group. According to Geoffrey Jackson,[8] experienced hostage-takers like the Tupamaros in Uruguay try to avoid these situations. During his entire captivity, Jackson was met by "faceless beings" only—hooded captors whose faces he never was allowed to see. Nevertheless, feelings of sympathy emerged and the jailers were changed continuously.

In spite of this apparent conciliation, the deep-seated fear of death is constantly present in most hostages. When they finally are liberated, their immediate gratitude turns toward those who did *not* kill them, in spite of what the victims actually *expected* during their whole ordeal. This extreme feeling of relief will thus very often be expressed in the form of gratitude toward the captors because they did not implement the worst expectations of the victims, did not abuse them and kill them, but let them survive. It is understandable that emotional reactions like these can be misinterpreted by the liberators and be considered as "identification with the aggressor."

None of these coping mechanisms surfaced in the Entebbe victims, mostly because they lacked the opportunity for interpersonal contact. The hostages were treated as personal enemies of the captors and were handled and moved around according to well-prepared plans. Captors and captives had no common problems to solve, and established very few interpersonal relationships. Thus, none of the hostages expressed any warm feelings of gratitude toward the terrorists. The antagonism between the hostages and the terrorists was obvious and the negative reactions of the hostages entirely predictable.

It is easy to understand that "neutral" victims of a politically motivated skyjacking are more concerned about their lives than about political principles or the struggle between their captors and their political adversaries. Victims of this kind are much more ready to establish interpersonal relationships with the hostage-takers, to try to understand their cause, and to consider them as individuals when group formation takes place. This process will be facilitated, even exaggerated, if the hostages lack a clear concept of what is right or wrong in a given situation. Their readiness to identify with the terrorists' cause will be enhanced by diffuse and unclear ideas about the social and/or political injustice the kidnappers are allegedly attempting to combat. The mass media, by trying to understand and accept the aims of all "liberation" movements, no matter what methods are used to attain them, have created some confusion among the public concerning means and ends. Consequently, many hostages are easy prey for the intensive social/political/national propaganda of the kidnappers, who insist that their action is not only absolutely necessary, but also "correct, righteous, moral, and acceptable." Even the kidnapped British ambassador to Uruguay, Geoffrey Jackson, who made a very deliberate and successful attempt to cope with this sort of reaction in himself, felt it important to formulate a "Four-Point Plan," the last two points of which dealt with this issue: "(3) There is no reason to hate these people (my hosts). Nor however, may I be sentimental about them. I must therefore, make no concession to them and give them no satisfaction. (4) These people, however objective I force myself to be, have done my family, my government and my country an immense injury. . . ."[8] Those who are less well prepared and less capable of thinking deliberately and objectively are more likely to fall into the propaganda trap of the terrorist; this is so because of the increasing moral confusion resulting from the media's distortion of the criminal nature of many politically motivated acts.

Relationship to Family and Society

The family of the normal criminal prisoner often shares his sentence in the sense of suffering poverty, deprivation, failure, and shame. The amount and intensity of shame may depend on where they live, and in some settings, a certain emotional support may be available. They are just as likely, however, to be shunned and isolated. At the same time, they are expected to visit and support the prisoner, whom they may now despise. They do, at least, know where he is and how he is and can maintain contact as they wish.

Hostages are cut off from any connection with the outside, and their families are ignorant of their fate. The families are helpless to do anything but band together and try to exert pressure on those who might have some power to ameliorate the situation. Hostages desperately want to make some sort of contact with those they love. This situation occurs frequently with victims in a skyjacked plane, who know that their families are waiting at the airport. What will they think? How will they react? What will the airline company, the radio, or the news tell them? Sylvia Jacobson remembers it thus:

> Around what would have ordinarily been the time of landing at Kennedy Airport, self-orientation and self-concern shifted to expressions of alarm for the expectantly awaiting families. How shocked they would be on learning that this plane would not land. Seatmates and passengers within whispering reach of one another allied themselves, exchanging names and addresses, making promises that survivors would somehow notify the next of kin of those who might not make it.[3]

The desire for contact with the outside is not just an expression of strong family ties, but also of an overwhelming need in human beings not to disappear without a trace. Messages in bottles thrown into the sea are a phenomenon known through centuries and are an attempt to fulfill this purpose. In modern times, thousands of victims from the ghettos and concentration camps have testified to this need. People who knew that their families were destroyed, who had seen their parents or children perish in the gas chambers, who knew that they themselves had no chance whatsoever of surviving, have all been eager to leave some trace, some report of what had happened to them. The most famous reports are the historical "Ringelblum Archives," found in the Warsaw Ghetto in September 1946. Equally significant are papers describing the work of a group of medical doctors who, until their last day, conscientiously and scientifically registered all their observations on diseases produced by famine in the ghetto.[9,10] Their work demonstrated that their will to remain human, through scientific interest, was a good in itself. Still more moving are the papers and letters found in the ruins of Auschwitz and their surroundings. Elie Wiesel comments extensively on these documents:

> The obsession of giving testimony was permanent. And it even invaded the darkest zones of that kingdom which we call the kingdom of night. Inside hell there was a deeper hell. And in that deep, deep hell, lived the Sonderkommando, a name that would evoke fear, anguish, and death. The members of that commando would do the most cruel task that can be: they would burn the corpses. Usually their life span was two months, four months at most. Then they themselves would be burned. We heard, years ago, that some documents were written by those men, but I didn't believe it. I couldn't believe that even their people would have enough faith in language. I didn't believe either that they would have enough faith in men. And yet, some documents were discovered, not all, and if ever I come close to despair it is when I read these documents. Who were those men? Some

became mad or mute or religious, and all wrote testimony. One says for instance: "I believe that the name of Auschwitz is by now familiar to the world, but surely one gives no credence to the reports of what has been taken place here. People may take it as propaganda. What you know is but a small fragment of what really is happening. The purpose of my writing is to make sure that at least something of the truth reaches the world. I have a request to you," he says, to the person who finds the paper, "a last wish, a wish of the man who knows that his last crossroad is near, only the date is not set as yet. Here is the address of my relatives in Brooklyn. Find them, they will know, they will tell you who I am. They have pictures of myself and my family. Please publish them together with my testimony. I wish I could think that somewhere, someone will shed a tear for me and my family, for I can no longer cry."[11]

It is difficult to discuss these "documents humains" in a matter-of-fact way, but I think it is possible to regard them as the human being's deepest wish for and belief in transcendental promise, hope, and existence.

Coping with Captivity

The initial anxiety reactions to sudden, unexpected, violent attacks and initial coping efforts by victims have been described previously by Roth[12] and Tinklenberg[13] and are further developed by them in Chapters 2 and 3 of this book. In this section I will confine myself to more limited remarks emerging from my own personal experiences and research.[14]

Over the Short Term: For Immediate Survival

Coping in acute and seriously life-threatening situations usually means surviving the danger of the moment. Victims of kidnapping and hijacking confronted with an overwhelming force of armed terrorists will, naturally enough, comply with orders to keep their captors from becoming nervous and panicking and to protect themselves from greater danger of being killed. There have been several skyjacking episodes in which terrorists have immediately shot and killed victims who seemed somewhat stubborn or who seemed to express provocative feelings or intentions. Terrorists do not see their victims as individual human beings—they are only objects, a means toward achieving a goal. Any sign of human individuality in the beginning of an action disturbs this perception, and can lead to "short circuit reactions." There are, however, certain limits to complying, and if terrorists command hostages to perform a criminal act or other activity that would reduce their self-esteem to an intolerable degree, some might prefer death to extreme debasement. However, this problem usually does not arise until some time after the hyper-acute phase.

Symonds states that individual crime victims who have fought back without being hurt seem to have suffered minimal amounts of psychological trauma. They felt exhilarated and potent. Society's attitude is a typical double bind: when the victim fights back and is not hurt, he is a hero; if he is hurt, he is a reckless fool. On the whole, victims who fight back seem to receive greater social acceptance than the victims who follow society's rules and comply with the criminal.

Victims of kidnapping or skyjacking must find new mechanisms and change some of their familiar adaptation mechanisms quickly in order to cope with a situation constantly in flux. The situation will usually be complicated by the captives' heterogeneity and lack of inner cohesiveness. It is quite useful to form subgroups. Sylvia Jacobson described how rising anxiety among the hostages led non-Jews to make anti-Jewish or anti-Israeli remarks, and non-Americans to express anti-American feelings. Under extreme real danger, however, her group was able to reintegrate and organize itself.

Over the Long Term: Successful Coping

Mechanism and Value Resolutions. During sustained captivity, quite different coping goals and mechanisms come into play. The importance of this long-term perspective has been highlighted by the prolonged captivity of the American hostages in Iran. We know that there are many different value systems that may be of importance to a given individual and his psychological homeostasis. We should find a successful coping and adaptation that—provided basic minimal survival possibilities are present—tends not only to foster physical survival, but also to maintain mental health during captivity *and* during the years after liberation. In this way we could avoid value judgments about any one person's way of coping, accepting that "each individual may be saved on his own premises."

In attempting to understand the various mechanisms, it is useful to keep in mind Wilson's discussion of mental health in disaster situations,[15] in which he points out that disaster behavior in a given social unit is best predicted by understanding the norms and values that govern a group's behavior prior to the onset of disaster. Just as civilian populations and military units may be prepared for catastrophe by training and education, so individuals may be prepared to maintain their mental health during extreme situations if they can learn to cope with varieties of normal stress. Wilson advocates using an imaginative educational approach because normal training tends to groom people for a routine, while what is required is some sort of training for flexibility. He considers the greatest ally in the attempt to promote effective handling of crises the general human propensity to strive for environmental mastery, which appears to operate from earliest infancy through maturity.

Actual coping behavior varies as much with the setting as with the individual. In normal prisons, for instance, the most common and most effective coping mechanism is identification with the criminal subculture and its antiestablishment attitude. The criminal prisoner is expected to accept those values generally held in prison as his own. In addition, he must seemingly comply to a certain degree with demands from the incarcerator, and demonstrate good behavior that will be rewarded by privileges and other compensations.

In the concentration camps, however, the situation was quite different. The set of values prevailing there, on the one hand, and that of most of the inmates, on the other, were radically different and generally incompatible. Those who used the more primitive coping mechanisms of denial or creation of illusions had little chance of surviving. Others, who tried to adapt and to do anything to survive, lost both their self-esteem and their interpersonal relationships, and also usually did not succeed. The very few who did and whom I have interviewed showed deep and pathological personality change.

Those who were able to mobilize the most adequate coping mechanisms, according to my experience, were those who, for one reason or another, could retain their personality and system of values more or less intact even under conditions of nearly complete social anomie. A very remarkable example is again Geoffrey Jackson, whose book could be used as a handbook in successful coping.

Viktor Frankl[16] has correctly stressed that if a person has something to live for, the amount of suffering he can endure is practically without limits. In the camps, those who, because of their professions, could show and maintain interest in others, thus keeping their norms and values inside the camp at the same level as outside, were the best copers. Among these few fortunate ones were doctors, nurses, social workers, and priests, such as the inmates of Theresienstadt (Terezin) described by Kral.[17] Because they were more occupied with their fellow prisoners' problems than their own, they came through their trials in better mental condition than the average inmate of the camp. Only a tiny minority of prisoners, however, had this kind of resource. Most of them had to find other ways of coping, and many were not able to do so.

Group identity and cohesiveness were major factors in the ability to survive. Prisoners who were completely isolated from their family and bereft of all contact with familiar groups and relatives, very quickly abandoned themselves and their innermost values. They became overwhelmed by the notion that they had nobody and nothing to struggle for or to live for. When they became completely passive and lost their ability to retain some sort of mental activity, these prisoners easily succumbed. Their symptoms—feelings of hopelessness and giving up—could have been seen by experienced observers rather early on.

My interviews have shown that prisoners who were able to stay together with some members of their family, to remain in contact with some of their pre-war peers, or to help others and to get help, were, as shown, for instance, by Luchterhand,[18] those who resisted best. They were not deprived completely of all feelings of personal and human dignity and values in their own eyes or in the eyes of their peers. These findings are, to a certain degree, the same for ex-prisoners interviewed in Norway and Israel. The Norwegians, when asked what helped them most to survive, almost always answered "being together with some other Norwegians." In essence, the maintenance of self-esteem, a sense of human dignity, a sense of group belonging, and a feeling of being useful to others, all seemed to contribute significantly to survival in both physical and psychological terms.

In comparing the groups of survivors who mobilized coping mechanisms more or less consciously and actively with those who ascribed their survival to mere luck or chance, it appears on a statistically significant level that the former have fewer and less severe psychiatric complications than the latter. In other words, coping mechanisms that enhanced the individual's contact with the group, coping that was based on intact and positive value systems and on retaining self-respect as a human being in the best and truest sense of the words, and, finally, coping where attachment to others was of essential concern, proved not only important to ensuring immediate survival, but also to surviving without serious psychological disturbances.

Finally, there was another kind of adaptation, which all who survived had to undergo to some degree. Called "closing off" by Lifton,[19] it is described as a psychic anesthesia in the post-war literature. Lifton also discussed the changed outlook in which one could begin to accept death as a matter of course. Death became less terrifying when corpses could be seen everywhere. This changed outlook applied not only to death, but also at some level to the suffering of other inmates.

Long Term Effects of the Stress of Captivity

On Victims of Captivity

From our experience with chronic psychiatric patients we know that long-lasting institutionalization with impaired human relationships can cause deterioration not only in psychological functioning, but in biological functioning as well. We can therefore also assume that criminals held behind bars, whose self-esteem and self-respect have been reduced and abused, will suffer in similar ways, even after their release from jail. The long-term effects of such humiliation have not been investigated properly, but it is unlikely that these people will accept the social values of our society and act according to them. They are bound to feel excluded from the society and free to take action against it.

We also know relatively little about the long-range impact of short-term unexpected captivity. Symonds suggests that the general reactions of victims of crime are similar to the psychological responses of individuals who have experienced sudden and unexpected loss. When shock and denial have failed as adaptive reactions, the victim becomes frightened, and the trauma-related anxiety syndrome can persist for several years. Anxiety during the day and anxiety dreams at night, repetitive thoughts, heightened irritability, and sometimes even fright with clinging behavior, are symptoms that have been described in victims both of crime and of catastrophes. The common denominator for these victims is probably the loss of trust in their own integrity, in society's ability to protect them, or in the stability of their milieu. The most exhaustive psychological and psychiatric study of this phenomenon has probably been done on the Buffalo Creek disaster.[20] Disabling psychiatric symptoms, such as anxiety, depression, changes in character and life style, and maladjustment and developmental problems in children were evident more than two years after the disaster in more than ninety percent of the individuals interviewed. The investigators were able to rule out the possibility that the people they were examining were either presenting major symptomatology and character problems resulting from basically weak ego structure or using the disaster in order to win a large settlement from the mining company. The investigators witnessed both difficult and prolonged struggles with powerful feelings and ideas aroused by the traumatic experience of the disaster, and the survivors' very uneven attempts to reorganize themselves and rebuild their shattered coping and adaptive mechanisms. They found a definite clinical syndrome in the survivors, arising from both the immediate impact of the catastrophe on each individual and the subsequent disruption of the community. Everyone living there was affected in some way. This does not, however, mean that this psychological morbidity will increase until death. There is a constantly, but slowly progressing readjustment in this marginally adapted population. In another relevant study, Parker[21] examined the psychological morbidity that followed when cyclone Tracy, on Christmas eve of 1974, killed about fifty people, destroyed ninety percent of the housing in Darwin, and resulted in the evacuation of 30,000 people to cities in southern Australia. His samples are rather small, but he tries to demonstrate that there are two different reaction types. Victims who perceived the disaster as a salient threat to their mortality were most likely to show immediate psychological dysfunction, whereas those who perceived that the disaster would involve a greater relocation stress were more likely to exhibit psychological dysfunction later on.

It would be of great practical, therapeutic, and scientific interest to investigate whether a similar differentiation could be found in victims of hostage taking and other forms of individual crimes.

The most comprehensive literature is that dealing with captivity in prisoners in POW camps and concentration camps and how they continue to be affected. In spite of the diversity of the populations investigated, and the differences in cultural backgrounds and theoretical orientations of the investigators, certain consistent patterns of chronic changes emerge. These patterns, however, are superceded by the victims' common experience of feeling alone with their problems and sufferings: "There is a lot of pain in the world that people have, but physical pain is not the worst. The worst pain is the pain of loss, when you have nothing, no family, no home, no ties, you have nothing—that is the worst pain in the world."[22]

Julius Segal and his colleagues are quoting an American captive after his return from Vietnam in 1973. But this captive returned as "a hero nearly." The nation, or in any case a part of it, was expecting him, and the total social organization of the U.S. Armed Forces and of the Veteran's Administration were at his disposal. Nevertheless, he experienced this deep feeling of distress and hopelessness, of loss and isolation. This feeling of total despair and isolation was, naturally enough, much more obvious in the few Jews who survived the concentration camps. Their families had been killed, their cultural backgrounds obliterated, their homes and milieu destroyed. Their world lay in ruins. The few whom the extermination machinery had not managed to completely crush had been subjected to both the most extreme psychophysical trauma and the total destruction of their anchorage in this world.

There are a wealth of studies of this group that meticulously scrutinize all anamnestic data and can describe symptoms found in each single case. Comparing these, it is possible to find relationships between special forms of traumatization and their pathological results. Strøm and our team[23] could, for instance, not only correlate the incidence of diarrhea at the follow-up investigation of ex-prisoners with the higher incidence of the same condition during imprisonment, but could also show that diarrhea was more prevalent among those who had been in captivity for more than two years, who had lost more than one-third of their body weight, or who had experienced psychic disturbances or marked anxiety phenomena during imprisonment. Similar correlations were found between diseases of other organs both during and after imprisonment. Anxiety reactions, on the other hand, were more common among those arrested before the age of twenty-five and among those who had suffered from mental illness prior to their arrest. Anxiety was also more prevalent among those who had suffered repeated head injury and weight loss of more than thirty percent, and especially among those who had reacted with mental disturbances during their imprisonment.

Other studies have been concerned with the after-effects of malnutrition and starvation in relation to infections and other diseases. The high mortality rate among the survivors is more persuasive evidence of the impact of long-lasting and stressful captivity. This was evident in American and Canadian POWs who had been held in Japan and Korea, and in West German POWs who had been imprisoned in Russia.

Eitinger and Strøm[24] could show that Norwegian concentration camp survivors had an abnormally high death rate during all the years after liberation. Given the number and age of the ex-prisoners, 608 deaths might have been expected between 1945 and 1965, whereas the observed number was 719—a ratio of 1.18 for all prisoners. For prisoners who were under the most difficult situations, the ratio was 1.5, much higher than that for the other prisoners. The prisoners' mortality ratio was particularly high during the first years after liberation, but it was also above 1.0 in all the later periods. A high death rate was found in all age groups of ex-prisoners, but it was most marked in the younger age groups. They were the ones most affected by tuberculosis, and their resulting mortality rate was very high during the first few years after their liberation.

In the 1950s and 1960s, when the first extensive report of investigations on concentration camp survivors started to appear, there was a certain discrepancy between the Scandinavian and American results. The former stressed somatic and neurological findings, whereas the latter were more concerned with the psychodynamics of traumatization and its psychological effects. Today this seems to be a rather useless distinction. We know, on the one hand, about the extreme physical hardships of forced labor, starvation, and other massive somatic traumatizations, and on the other, about the terror, persecution, defamation, family dissolution, isolation, and the universal psychological stress that was imposed. These psychophysical stresses and traumatizations occurred simultaneously and were directed against the same individuals; therefore, it is nearly meaningless to attempt to distinguish the relative importance of a single factor in later reactions. To see only the one or the other side of this complex picture only demonstrates the observer's one-sidedness, and says little about the nature of the pathological finding. Studies that have shown that survivors' general morbidity is higher than that of control groups can most easily be explained by the fact that excessive stresses lowered the ex-prisoners' resistance to infection and lessened their ability to adjust to environmental changes. The effects of captivity are so deep that the vulnerability of the victims remains heightened, and full recovery does not appear to be possible. Finally, there is the newly published work by Höpker,[25] who investigated 1,098 postmortem protocols of former German POWs and compared them with matched controls (2,875 protocols in all). The study was very thorough and its conclusions drawn with great caution. One very clear finding was that there are more internal hydrocephalus and degenerative changes in the brain tissue among the POWs. Clinically, this means that the changes that occurred can be compared with the deterioration, or diminished efficiency, that one sees in senility. Such patients tire more readily, have less initiative, and are duller in comprehension. Tasks that they could formerly accomplish with ease become increasingly difficult and finally pass completely beyond their capabilities. Failures of memory—at first, especially, for names—are very common, and restlessness and irritability can complicate the picture.

On Families of Captives

The victim of captivity is not the only person who may suffer long-term adverse effects. The effects on a family of having a captive member may be severe and extensive. As mentioned, families of normal criminal prisoners suffer on several fronts; the combination of economic deprivation, parental loss, social stigma, and added stresses can be expected to have very harmful effects on spouses and children.

To date there is practically no available material on the families of hostages, even those who were held on a long-term basis. Whatever studies have been done have dealt mainly with families of other captives who have eventually been allowed to return. However, until recently the effects of the POWs' experience on their families have been largely overlooked, according to Julius Segal et al. McCubbin et al.[26] highlighted adjustment problems that were found among the families of American men returning from captivity in Vietnam and confirmed that family reunions among POWs are indeed stressful. The effect that the absent and returning POW father has on children has only recently begun to be studied, but from parallel situations rather disturbing results are well known.

Most studies have dealt with families of concentration camp survivors. These investigations have provided ample evidence that the problems of these survivors probably do not die with them. Barocas[27] has suggested that children of concentration camp survivors may become the transferential recipients of their parents' unconscious and unexpressed rage. The survivors, terrified of their own aggression and their inability to express it, may explicitly or implicitly direct their children to act it out, vicariously gratifying their parents' wishes. This would explain the explosive and aggressive behavior of the children that Niederland described.[28] The severe depressive reactions that Rakoff et al.[29] observed in the children of survivors may reflect intense parental restraints, culminating in an internalization of the anger. The process by which the concentration camp syndrome may be transmitted to the children thus seems to be very complex.

Similarly, John Sigal[30] reviewed in 1976 the effects of paternal exposure to prolonged stress on the mental health of the spouse and the children. He quoted an unpublished dissertation by Karr, who found that the children of both (or one) parents who were concentration camp survivors have significant difficulties in impulse control. They have a tendency to anxiety and depression, feel overprotected, and have a strongly ambivalent feeling of hostility and of guilt toward their parents. These findings were more or less the same as those Sigal and his group had encountered earlier in children of concentration camp survivors. A comparison of concentration camp survivors with Canadian POWs who had been in Japanese camps for forty-four months showed practically no differences in the later results. The extreme stresses these two groups had been exposed to were sufficient to erase cultural and ethnic differences and to result in a final common path of symptomatology. The effect on their offspring, however, seems to be somewhat different. Although the observations were only preliminary and tentative and the sampling incomplete, it is interesting to note that only the oldest female child seems to be affected. Her symptoms are depressive affect, disruptiveness, and quick temperedness. She may be difficult to manage or rather timid, withdrawn, and excessively dependent. Alternatively, she may develop a more conventional psychological disorder. This depression in the oldest female child seems to result from identification with a distressed—sometimes clinically depressed—mother who has witnessed her husband's depletion and deterioration every day. Russel[31] actually treated thirty-six families of concentration camp survivors, and found that in spite of his own very guarded expectations, family therapy with this group proved to be "difficult, but possible." The prognosis, however, is poor. He found the following problems: Mothers felt unable to nurture children; they felt that any child born of them could not be healthy or normal. Fathers tended to be weak, withdrawn, quiet, and passive. Both parents had largely exaggerated expectations regarding their children's scholastic achievements. The limits they set for their children were too rigid or they set no limits at all, resulting in chaos. Even more than might be expected, these family units presented many types of dysfunctional communication patterns. Families sought help because the child who became the identified patient was uncontrollable. They had an isolated family life with no real commitment to or deep involvement in the real world. Survivor guilt was found in almost all adults of the sample. On the whole, the picture given by the different Canadian investigators is a gloomy one.[32,33,34]

Rabkin[35] has tried to explain this pessimism by pointing to the countertransference reactions in therapists working with "survivor families." According to Rabkin, the therapist shares the role of survivor with the parents—with one important difference: The therapist has passively survived, the parents are witnesses. The ambiguity of this identification creates a discomforting ambivalence because the therapist can defend himself against painful anxiety and guilt by denying his oneness with the parent-survivors. Ordinary men do not wish to be reminded of their guilt or their vulnerability. The therapist, as one of these ordinary men, does not unequivocally want to be privy to the survivor's experience. Therefore he both seeks and shuns the witness; his desire to hear the truth is countered by his need to ignore it.

It is far too early to predict long-range results for victims of crimes, skyjacking, and so on. How the second generation in these groups will be affected is even more uncertain. Unfortunately, the recent rash of hostage incidents around the world may provide a wealth of material for long-term studies. Currently there is enough knowledge about other related serious psychic traumatizations and their long-term effects on the victims and their families to make us take the captive experience very seriously as a source of great and lasting damage both to the victim and to those around him. We must take every measure possible to prevent both these traumas and their deleterious results.

Notes

1. Richmond, G.: *Prison Doctor.* Surrey (Canada): Nursaga Publ., 1975.

2. Zubek, J. P. (ed.): *Sensory Deprivation: Fifteen Years of Research.* New York: Appleton & Meredith, 1969.

3. Jacobson, S. R.: "Individual and group responses to confinement in a skyjacked plane." *Am. J. Orthopsychiat* 43:459–469, 1973.

4. Harel, I.: *The House on Garibaldi Street*. Toronto, New York, London: Bantam Books, 1975.

5. Panton, James H.: "Personality characteristics of deathrow prison inmates." *J. Clin. Psychol.* 32:306–309, 1976.

6. Symonds, M.: "Victims of violence: Psychological effects and after-effects." *Am. J. Psychoanal.* 35:19–26, 1975.

7. Ochberg, F.: "The victim of terrorism: Psychiatric considerations." Paper given at the Fourth Seminar on Terrorism. The International Center for Comparative Criminology, Evian, 1977.

8. Jackson, G.: *People's Prison*. London: Faber & Faber, 1973.

9. Lenski, M.: *Problems of Disease in the Warsaw Ghetto*. Jerusalem: Yad Vashem Studies III (I–IV), 1957–1960.

10. *Maladie de la Famine*. Edit.: Comité de Redaction I.D.C. Warsaw, 1946.

11. Wiesel, E.: "The author and his responsibility." Paper given in Oslo, 1976.

12. Roth, T.: "Stress: Psychological considerations." Paper given at the Fourth Seminar on Terrorism. The International Center for Comparative Criminology, Evian, 1977.

13. Tinklenberg, J.: "Coping." Paper given at the Fourth Seminar on Terrorism. The International Center for Comparative Criminology, Evian, 1977.

14. Eitinger, L.: *Concentration Camp Survivors in Norway and Israel*. Oslo: Universitetsforlaget, 1964. (Mart. Nijhoff, The Hague, 1972.)

15. Wilson, R. N.: "Disaster and mental health," in Baker, G. W., and Chapman, D. W.: *Man and Society in Disaster*. New York: Basic Books, 1962.

16. Frankl, V. E.: *From Death Camp to Existentialism*. Boston: Beacon Press, 1959.

17. Kral, V. A.: "Psychiatric observations under severe chronic stress." *Am. J. Psychiat.* 108:185–192, 1951.

18. Luchterhand, E.: "Prisoner behaviour and social system in the Nazi concentration camps." *Int. J. Soc. Psychiat.* 13:245–264, 1967.

19. Lifton, R. J.: *Death in Life: Survivors of Hiroshima*. New York: Random House, 1967.

20. Lifton, R. J., and Olson, E.: "The human meaning of total disaster: The Buffalo Creek experience." *Psychiatry* 39:1–18, 1976.

21. Parker, G.: "Cyclone Tracy and Darwin evacuées: On the restoration of species." *Brit. J. Psychiat.* 130:548–555, 1977.

22. Segal, J.; Hunter, E.; and Segal, Z.: "Universal consequences of captivity." *Int. Soc. Sci. J.* 28:593–606, 1976.

23. Strøm, A. (ed.): *Norwegian Concentration Camp Survivors*. Oslo: Universitetsforlaget, 1968.

24. Eitinger, L. and Strøm, A.: *Mortality and Morbidity after Excessive Stress*. Oslo: Universitetsforlaget, 1973.

25. Höpker, W. W.: *Spätfolgen extremer Lebensverhältnisse*. Berlin, Heidelberg, New York: Springer, 1974.

26. McCubbin, H. I.; Dahl, B. B.; Metres, P. J.; Hunter, E.; and Plag, J. A.: *Family Separation and Reunion: Families of Prisoners of War and Servicemen Missing in Action 1974*. Center for Prisoners of War Studies. Naval Health Research Center Report, No. 74-70.

27. Barocas, H. A., and Barocas, C. B.: "Manifestations of concentration camp effects on the second generation." *Am. J. Psychiat.* 130:820–821, 1973.

28. Niederland, W.: "The problem of the survivor.' *J. Hillside Hosp.* 10:233–247, 1961.

29. Rakoff, V.; Sigal, J. J.; and Epstein, N. B.: "Children and families of concentration camp survivors." *Canad. Mental Health* 14:22–26, 1966.

30. Sigal, J., and Rakoff, V.: "Concentration camp survival: A pilot study of effects on the second generation." *Canad. Psychiat. Assn. J.* 16:393–397, 1971.

31. Russel, A.: "Late psychosocial consequences in concentration camp survivor families." *Am. J. Orthopsychiat.* 44:611–619, 1974.

32. Sigal, J., et al.: "Some second-generation effects of survival of the Nazi persecution." *Am. J. Orthopsychiat.* 43:320–327, 1973.

33. Sigal, J.: "Effects of paternal exposure to prolonged stress on the mental health of the spouse and children." *Canad. Psychiat. Assn. J.* 21:169–172, 1976.

34. Trossman, B.: "Adolescent children of concentration camp survivors." *Canad. Psychiat. Assn. J.* 13:121–123, 1968.

35. Rabkin, L. Y.: "Countertransference in the extreme situation: The family therapy of survivor families." In Wolberg, L. R., and M. L. Aronson (eds.): *Group Therapy.* New York: Shalton, 1975.

5
Victim Responses to Terror: Understanding and Treatment

Martin Symonds

In this chapter I plan to share my knowledge and experience of victims' responses to criminally induced terror. I have derived much of my understanding from evaluating and treating victims of sudden unexpected criminal violence.[1] It is my hope and belief that the insights gained from the unfortunate experiences of these victims can be effectively used to understand the responses of victims of terrorists.

When I first began to study victims of sudden, unexpected violent crime in 1971, I included victims from three different groups. First, I studied victims of crimes in which there was generally no contact with the criminal, such as a burglary. Any violence that did occur was generally limited to property and not to person. Second, I reviewed cases of sudden, unexpected violent crime in which there was minimal contact with the criminal, such as street assault and robbery—popularly known as "mugging." Finally, I studied those sudden, unexpected violent crimes in which there was prolonged contact with the criminal, such as rape, robbery, kidnapping, and hostage-taking.

After reviewing the victims' behavior I became aware that all of their responses regularly followed certain sequential phases regardless of what type of crime was involved. Only the duration and intensity of each phase was influenced by the nature and quality of contact with the criminal. Briefly, all victims of sudden, unexpected violent crime—no matter what kind—initially respond with shock and disbelief. This first phase is "denial." This is quickly followed by phase two, when denial is overwhelmed by "reality." These two phases form the acute response to sudden, unexpected violence.

After varying periods of time the individual enters into phase three, "traumatic depression." It is characterized by circular bouts of apathy, anger, resignation, irritability, "constipated" rage, insomnia, startle reactions, and replay of the traumatic events through dreams, fantasies, and nightmares. It is also the phase of self-recrimination. Phase three can also be called the "I am stupid" phase, since the victim replays and evaluates the traumatic events under peacetime conditions—after the event is over and the criminal is gone, and not under the conditions of criminal-induced terror.

Under the conditions of extensive contact with the criminal (such as prolonged hostage-taking) it is highly unlikely that any significant phase three behavior would take place. These hostages would, in the active presence of criminal terror, still respond as if they were in phase two. (I will develop victims' responses in phase two in detail later in this chapter.) It is in phase three that the prior specific personality patterns and traits primarily influence victim behavior. Those individuals who are excessively love-oriented and dependent on others seem to be more prone to develop constricting depressive behavior. Their fears increase, phobic responses develop, and they often form hostile, dependent relationships with family and friends. Individuals who are predominantly freedom-oriented and detached from others, or who are power-oriented and aggressive, tend to increase their prior behavior. They may become more removed from people, develop reclusiveness, or manifest "short-fuse" irritability. In effect they have said, "The world is a jungle and to hell with Mr. Goodguy." Phase three is similar to the "Survivor Syndrome" described by Niederland.[2]

As an individual attempts to integrate and adapt the traumatic experience into future behavior and life style, he can be said to enter phase four, "resolution and integration." In this phase the individual increasingly develops defensive alert patterns to minimize or prevent future victimization. He profoundly and permanently revises his values and his attitudes toward possessions and other people in this last phase. People whose homes have been burglarized exemplify this revision. They sometimes reduce their personal investment and involvement in property, jewelry, watches, TV sets, and the like. These items now become objects that can be replaced. In this response pattern, the individuals no longer allow themselves to be painfully vulnerable to loss by investing a personal sense of self in property. They hope never to exhibit the emotions or behavior of the woman who ran down the aisle of a plane that was just about to take off, screaming, "Stop, stop the plane, I left my purse in the airport. Everything is in my purse. My life is in my purse."

These individuals are unable or unwilling to accept their victimization and to integrate it into their future life style. They experience their victimization as a personal affront to their pride, compounded by perceived indifference to their plight. They tenaciously hold on to their feelings of rage and injustice, seeking only reparations and revenge for their victimization and thus remaining psychologically disabled.[3]

This chapter focuses on the acute psychological responses of victims to those crimes in which there is prolonged contact with the criminal, and thus where the victims' acute responses occur in the criminal's presence. These are the crimes of rape, robbery, kidnapping, and hostage-taking. I will particularly focus on how victims respond when they are used as instruments to pressure third parties to satisfy criminals' demands. These are the crimes of kidnapping and hostage-taking.

Criminals use violence, or dramatic threats of violence to induce extreme fright or terror in victims so that they will be rendered helpless, powerless, and totally submissive. To fully understand how victims respond to criminally induced terror, it is helpful to explore people's reactions to terror in general. The dictionary defines terror as extreme fright. This year I asked a number of social acquaintances and colleagues whether they had ever experienced terror and if so, when and how they had dealt with it. Everyone I asked, numbering close to 100, had been terrified at some time in their lives, more so by unpredictable, frightening events than by people. Examples included waking up in a room filled with smoke, and developing a leg cramp while swimming and feeling unable to get back to shore. One person was on a flight to England during World War II, when the pilot announced that the plane was on fire and he didn't think he would be able to land it successfully. Thirty-seven years later, this man vividly recalled sitting still, reviewing his life, and hoping that he would die suddenly and not suffer.

The popular concept that individuals respond to the terror of sudden, overwhelming danger by panic, with screaming, with running, or in a mindless, catatonic state is not supported by actual victim behavior, nor by the literature on catastrophes and disasters, whether man-made or natural. Some individuals do respond with mindless running or acts of desperation, but such "panic terror" behavior generally occurs when the person's physical movement is not completely impeded and escape seems possible, whether it really is or not. During prolonged captivity an individual may commit desperate, even suicidal acts if he feels hopeless about release. Some examples of this reaction include jumping out of burning buildings, frenzied behavior of a driver who discovers a bee in the car, or feeling hopeless and running into electrified barbed wire in concentration camps. The criminal terrorist deliberately induces terror when he holds victims captive and prevents any possibility of their escape. In situations where the terrorized victims feel trapped, they respond to the sudden, overwhelming danger to their lives by a paralysis of affect that I call "frozen fright."

Years ago I became aware of the phenomena of frozen fright when I interviewed an 8½-year-old incest victim. During our interview, she was bright, vivacious, talkative, and very cooperative. Afterwards, when I said she could go, this youngster took a deep breath, sighed heavily, and said, "I thought I would never get out of here alive." At that time, and even years later after further reflection, I did not see any evidence at all of fright bordering on terror. Since that time, almost twenty years ago, and after interviewing numerous victims of violent crime, I've been able to identify and confirm the phenomena of frozen fright in these individuals. Superficially, it appears that cooperative and friendly behavior confuses even the victim, and certainly the criminal, the family and friends of the victim, the police, and society in general. I must emphasize this point. Terrorized captives, whose only perceived hope of survival depends on the criminal, will exhibit the "cooperative behavior of frozen fright."

Most people exhibit this paralysis of affect, with its pseudo calm behavior, when they are terrified. Sometimes youngsters or immature, dependent, and histrionic individuals will continually cry, shake, cling, and tremble when they feel threatened by overwhelming danger. Despite the active dramatic behavior, the victim's affect is frozen and unresponsive to any change except the external removal of danger. A tragic example occurred when a youngster in a robbery cried, cried, and cried. When she persisted despite the efforts of her fellow victims and the robbers to shut her up, one of the robbers shot her to death. An example from animal behavior is one that dog owners commonly experience—their pet's response to thunder. Many dogs shiver, shake, moan, and cling during a thunderstorm. No amount of reassurance seems to allay their response; only when the thunder ceases does the dog calm down.

Although the affect of terrorized victims is frozen, their motor and cognitive functions are not. This dissociative phenomenon normally seen in terrorized victims differs from the separation of affect from cognitive and motor functions seen in people involved in dangerous, high-risk work, such as undercover agents. Such individuals, who voluntarily accept exceptionally hazardous work, have a suspension of affect that allows for hyperawareness and hyperalertness. In terrorized individuals the sudden threat to life causes an acute dissociative response. A paralysis of affect occurs, with narrow constriction of cognitive and motor functions to serve purely one function, namely survival. In their frozen fright, victims narrowly focus all their energy on survival, exclusively concentrating on the terrorist. The criminal terrorist's effort to totally dominate the victim reinforces this reaction. By creating a hostile environment, the terrorist thwarts any efforts that would reduce this domination; the victim feels isolated from others, powerless, and helpless.

The triad of being in a hostile environment, feeling isolated, and feeling helpless produces a profound reaction that Karen Horney called "basic anxiety." Under conditions of terror, basic anxiety causes adults to set aside recently learned experience and to respond instead with the early adaptive behavior of childhood for survival. I have called this response "traumatic psychological infantilism."

Traumatic infantilism compels victims to cling to the very person who is endangering their life. It accounts for the obedient, placid, compliant, and submissive behavior seen in frozen fright. Even remembering terror, when the criminal is no longer present, can precipitate traumatic psychological infantilism.

A supermarket manager, for example, was held up by criminals and placed in a meat freezer. Four hours later he was released by the police. Six weeks following the incident, the manager's assailant called him at work and said, "Charlie, I am the cat that put you in the freezer. Do you want me to put you in there again?" Charlie said, "No." The criminal said, "O.K. You're a good boy, I want you to take the money from the safe and put it into a brown paper bag. Put it on the take-out counter. I'll pick it up. Charlie, remember the freezer." The manager, a battle-honored World War II veteran, did just that. The detectives couldn't understand how someone could be robbed by telephone. Charlie, the manager, said, "You don't know what it is like to be locked in a freezer and feel you are going to die."

If the atmosphere of terror still persists and the psychologically traumatized victim perceives that the terrorist, who has the power of life and death over him, is letting him live, then profound and persistent attitudinal and behavioral changes occur. He now sees the criminal as the "good guy." This phenomenon is called "pathological transference." I have seen this reaction repeatedly in men, women, and children under conditions of perceived extreme threat to life. The following two examples are drawn from the experiences of police officers.

In one case, a narcotics undercover agent was held captive for three and a half hours while a criminal gang deliberated whether to "waste him or not." However, the leader of the gang said, "No." Finally the agent's backup team figured out where he was and rescued him. When I interviewed this man two months later, he kept telling me what a good guy the leader was. For two hours he repeatedly stated, "He could have killed me and didn't." His superiors, who were present, kept yelling about what a "mean bastard" that crook was, but the undercover agent persisted in defending the criminal.

In another situation, an off-duty detective was captured when he interrupted a robbery. When they learned he was a detective, two of the gunmen said, "We'll waste you, you mother-fucker." Then they placed a bag over his head and made him kneel down. The detective later stated, "Silly as it may seem, I was glad it was going to be in the head because I thought it would be quick." Instead, he heard the robbers discuss him and then leave. He wasn't shot. Months later, one of the robbers was caught. Jerry, the detective, was involved in his capture, and the robber said to him, "You owe me something. I saved your life." Subsequently Jerry visited the man many times. A close relationship developed and the detective told the robber, "If you need me, I'm there for you because you were there for me at the time." When the second robber was caught, the detective told his superior, "Chief, this guy has really changed," and went out and bought lunch for the second robber. The third robber is still at large. The detective fantasizes this conversation with him: "Listen Otis, what went down, went down; turn yourself in. Believe me I'll work with you. I'm not looking for revenge."

Pathological transference only occurs when someone threatens a person's life, deliberates, and then does not kill him. The victim doesn't dwell on the threat, but rather the feeling that the criminal let him live. Pathological transference does not occur (or if it does, it instantly evaporates) when the criminal shoots at the victim.

Pathological transference is consistently found in individuals held hostage by criminal terrorists. Hostage victims are essentially instrumental victims. They are used and exploited by their captors as leverage to force a third party (the family, police, or the government) to accede to the captors' demands. The captors threaten extreme violence to the victim, primarily in their communications to the third party, if their demands are not met. This suggests to the victim that the terrorists will not harm him if the third party gives in to the captors' demands. This use of the victim as leverage lays the grounds for intense pathological transference. This transference is both accelerated and heightened when the hostage has already been psychologically traumatized by terror. These two components, traumatic psychological infantilism and pathological transference, form the crucial elements in what has been called the Stockholm Syndrome.

The Stockholm Syndrome has often been viewed as simply identifying with the terrorist, but that concept does not adequately explain hostage behavior. It seems more useful to see how the hostages' attempts to relate to those who have first captured and terrified them, and then used them as instruments to obtain their objectives from a third party, have affected their behavior.

The suffering of the victim is the leverage used for negotiations with a third party. Hostages, in their psychologically traumatized state, never view negotiations for their release as benevolent, because they would immediately give anything for their release. The hostage interprets and experiences any negotiations as endangering him. He therefore perceives negotiations, especially protracted ones, as evidence of indifference, hostility, and rejection, so that the very people who are negotiating for his release seem to be unloving and life-threatening. This reinforces the pathological transference already developed by prolonged exposure to the terrorist.

So far I have discussed the behavioral psychodynamics of victims held captive by criminal terror. Understanding these dynamics is essential for the effective treatment of hostages from the moment of release. Since 1974, the Karen Horney Victim Treatment Center has utilized the following principles of "Psychological First Aid for Victims of Violent Crime." They aim to reduce the feelings of isolation, helplessness, and powerlessness that criminal terror induces:

1. Restoring power to victims early on by asking permission to interview them: "Is this a good time to talk to you?" "Do you mind if I ask you some questions?"
2. Reducing isolation by providing nurturing behavior, thus diminishing the experience of the hostile environment the victim was subjected to.
3. Diminishing the helpless, hopeless feelings of the victim by giving him the experience of determining his present and future behavior in terms of space and time.
4. Reducing the feelings of being subjected to the dominant behavior of the terrorist by having the counselor identify himself to the victim's satisfaction, ask for permission to sit down in the victim's presence or to smoke, etc.

The foregoing approaches to the victim are based on undoing and reversing the factors that brought about traumatic psychological infantilism.

The rescuers must remember that the sudden release of the victims reproduces an acute phase of crying, clinging, and submissive behavior. The victims still are in the grips of traumatic infantilism. Using methods like those listed above to help nurture and restore power is crucial to prevent the rescuers from causing even more injury to the victim. It also is important to allow the victim to clean up before being restored to familiar surroundings, to delay debriefing, and to give the victim privacy without isolation.

It is important in the treatment of acute responses after release and especially in the treatment of delayed responses, to recognize the victims' need to ventilate. They must be allowed and encouraged to express their feelings of hostility toward the individuals involved in negotiations for their release, as well as any feelings of pathological transference they may have toward the terrorist.

During the siege, while the victim is still being held hostage, it is important not to disturb the development of pathological transference. It must be left alone. Disturbing pathological transference while the victim is held hostage would only reactivate the victim's terror and could produce a hopelessness that might result in panic terror behavior. This could lead to desperate acts such as running out, even into death. Negotiators must try to reinforce any pseudo-helping efforts that the terrorists make for the victims. Rescuers must not expect the victims' cooperation in any escape plans. They must remember that to victims of terror, "An open door is not perceived as an open door."

Once the victim has been released, pathological transference persists; the victim is reluctant to either express negative feelings toward his captors or even to participate in their later prosecution. It takes a while, often months, for this reaction to subside.

I believe that the persistence of pathological transference in the victim long after his release is based on a primitive fear that any expression of negative feelings or behavior toward his former captors may bring awesome retaliation. Yet the victim is also aware of the captors' predatory use of his suffering to obtain their demands. This accounts for the persistent, impotent, "constipated" rage often seen in victims of violent crime. This rage is common among concentration camp victims who know that they cannot get revenge, or even reparations, from the Nazis for their suffering. Based on my experiences with concentration camp survivors, I have encouraged other victims to come to terms with this rage by adopting the attitude that "Survival, living without fear, is getting even."

Finally, I feel it is important to constantly reassure victims of terror that their behavior during captivity was fully acceptable. "As long as they are alive, they did the right thing." They did nothing wrong, and we should welcome them back as we would a loved one who had recovered from a frightening and painful illness.

Notes

1. Symonds, M.: "Victims of violence: Psychological effects and aftereffects." *American Journal of Psychoanalysis* 35:19–26, 1975.
2. Niederland, W.: "Post traumatic symptomatology." In Krystal, H. (ed.): *Massive Psychic Trauma*. New York: International Universities Press, 1968, pp. 60–70.
3. Symonds, M.: "The 'second injury' to victims." *Evaluation and Change*, Special Issue, Spring 1980, pp. 36–38.

6
Concepts of Terrorist Victimization

David A. Soskis
Frank M. Ochberg

Introduction

When the time for healing finally comes, when our anger and grief and fascination have subsided, we must search out and use the tools of healing. If these tools do not fit the task, we must reshape them; if they do not exist we must make them. The helping and healing professions have accumulated many technologies and techniques for rapidly evaluating, transporting, and treating victims who are physically injured during a terrorist attack. These techniques, whose development and refinement are one of the few positive outcomes of war, are applied in natural disasters and conventional criminal incidents as well as in the more limited terrorist context. But terrorism, insofar as it injures the spirit or mind, and insofar as this injury is partly a result of the differences between terrorism and war, produces wounds that call for psychological concepts and techniques adapted to its own special nature.

Several of these concepts and techniques, including the general theories of stress, defense mechanisms, and coping techniques, and the accumulated experience with human responses in a wide variety of captivity situations have been discussed in the previous chapters. We have chosen to pursue these perspectives because we believe they are the most useful approaches currently available for dealing with terrorist victimization. In our discussion we will pursue a more theoretical and speculative course in an attempt to explore other concepts that may prove useful in helping the victims of terrorism. These concepts will, in a way, bracket those presented earlier. On the one hand, we will be considering extremely basic issues of definition and meaning for terms like "victim," terms that are used, if not understood, in all discourse in this area. On the other hand, we will be extending some of the concepts developed by

Drs. Roth,Tinklenberg, and Eitinger in some speculative ways we feel are relevant to the problem of terrorism.

The Concept of "Victim"

Terrorists frequently assert that in their struggle, "there are no innocent victims." We would emphatically disagree and counter that it is exactly in the human creation of victims that the evil in terrorism resides. Many more lives may be lost in natural disasters, epidemics, or accidents, but these unfortunate people are not victims of evil. Evil is the human creation of a victim.

If one takes this, or any other, moral position on terrorism it is important to define one's terms. In our own thinking, and in this work, "victim" is the central term. A concept like "victim" has well-developed semantic and social meanings; it cannot be defined as we please if our inquiry is to lead beyond ourselves. Surprisingly, the dictionary defines "victim" in several ways that may prove enlightening even to those who use the term often.

Both *Webster's New Twentieth Century Dictionary of the English Language* and the *Concise Oxford Dictionary of Current English* give three different meanings for the word "victim." First, "a living being sacrificed to a deity or in the performance of a religious rite."[1] This corresponds to the word's Latin root, *victima*, which means a beast for sacrifice. Similarly, both the Hebrew and Arabic words for victim originate in the term "korban," a sacrificial offering (as described in the Bible). The connotations involve the setting apart of an individual who will be consecrated through some kind of religiously justified harm. Although the historical development of Judaism, Christianity, and Islam has generally moved away from literally sacrificial practices, this sense of victim is right on target for the systems of explanation and meaning used by most contemporary political terrorists. It can help us to understand why the terrorist does not profess guilt or shame for his or her acts, or concern that something bad has happened to the victim. After all, there are worse things that can happen to you (or so the terrorist feels) than to be an offering for a noble cause. This also helps us understand the feeling that former hostages have of being different, set apart, separated from all other human beings.

The second definition involves "a person or thing injured or destroyed in pursuit of an object, in gratification of a passion, or as a result of event or circumstance."[1] This is what we usually mean when we speak of victims of terrorism. Imbedded in this definition are what we would consider the two necessary conditions for calling a person a victim: that he or she has suffered harm, and that this harm is attributable to some cause. Note that two of the causal phrases in this definition ("in pursuit of an object, in gratification of a passion") retain some of the sacrifical sense of the first definition: the victim is an expendable means to an end.

Superficially, the final dictionary definition is farthest from our present context: "a person who suffers some loss, especially by being swindled, a dupe."[2] This definition's slightly negative connotation, i.e., of a "sucker," however, is one of the central psychological elements in the reaction of people to victims, and is one to which we shall return later in this chapter. In all of these definitions, there is a pervasive sense of the victim's powerlessness to prevent the events that victimize her or him; this should not, however, be confused with inability to actively cope with these events and with their aftermath.

Now, we can narrow our conception of victimhood to coincide with the terrorist context. One necessary element of this conception is that a human assault is committed by someone who is bigger, stronger, or better armed than the victim. Because the interaction is aggressive, the victim feels fearful and less powerful—in essence, he or she has been knocked down several rungs on a dominance hierarchy. Ultimately, therefore, the victim can only respond with resignation or rage.

Presuppositions in the Modern Terrorist Context

Although this conception of what it means to be a victim is somewhat narrow, it would apply to many forms of personal crime and to some war-related victimization. To understand terrorist victimization, we must be more specific. On an obvious, descriptive level, we have the external characteristics of modern terrorism, described in the introduction to this volume (disregard for the rules of war, emphasis on publicity, passionate cause, and the like) and discussed extensively elsewhere. Here we will focus on several often unspoken presuppositions that pervade the terrorist context and have a profound impact on its victims.

The most fundamental of these presuppositions is that human life has value. Commitment to this value binds together terrorist, victim, and audience in the triadic relationship that characterizes modern terrorism and makes activities like hostage negotiation possible. Where the aim is solely to kill, we have assassination. Where the victim does not value his own life, we have suicide; where he values it less than something else (his principles, the survival of the state) we have martyrdom; where he sees himself as a soldier who accepts the risks of combat, we have a prisoner of war—but not a hostage. And, finally, where the object of terrorist blackmail—its intended audience—does not value individual human life, where in Arthur Koestler's phrase, the individual is "a multitude of one million divided by one million,"[3] or where cruelty reigns, there is simply nothing to negotiate—no game. Thus terrorism is not a problem in totalitarian states; small countries like Holland and Israel, which are conspicuous for the value they place on life and individual rights, have figured disproportionately in the history of modern terrorism. The United States also values individual human lives and was forced, in the Iranian hostage situation, to face the consequences of these values.

A second, and debated, presupposition is that terrorist violence is limited. This presupposition does not always hold. When one incident starts a chain reaction of massive retaliatory measures, both anti-government terrorism and democracy soon disappear. Where the societal restraints on violence, or the very structure of government, are weakened (as in Lebanon and Northern Ireland) what began as terrorism becomes insurrection and then civil war, taking on a different psychology with enduring tragic consequences. Paradoxically, in some Western target states where the presupposition that violence is limited does hold, a low tolerance for violence can work in favor of terrorists and against victims. The gradual evolution of our criminal justice system away from a focus on restorative measures to victims and toward punishment for the perpetrator has partially been based on a view of the criminal as offending the state, disturbing the "King's Peace." This emphasis on keeping the peace can shift to a position of "don't make waves." When this happens, when we seek peace at any cost, the situation is ripe for the terrorist's bargain: "What will you do, or ignore, so that we will leave you alone?"

So far we have emphasized that terrorism as we know it can exist only when and where retributive violence is limited in scope or space. There is an unfortunate negative aspect of this proposition, however, that plays a major role in contributing to the problem of terrorism today: whereas revenge is limited in space, it is almost limitless in time. The haunting vision of 10-year-olds being trained in hand-to-hand combat in Palestinian camps or of the children's gangs of Belfast make it clear that vengeance must be reckoned in terms of generations and centuries, not only in years. The endurance of revenge and of movements based on vengeance are a major source of discouragement for those who must plan responses to the phenomenon of terrorism. This inheritance of vendettas evokes emotions of frustration, helplessness, and hopelessness and tempts us to ignore the problem or to think in terms of appeasement or of barbaric "final solutions."

Models for Terrorist Victimization

In addition to the effort to directly specify presuppositions that shape events, it is also helpful to describe one or more related events that can serve as models. Models that can be usefully related to terrorist victimization include grief, death imagery, encounters with bloody or terrible events, and the experience of rape victims. Each of these is distinct from terrorist victimization, but related to and sometimes combined with it. The consideration of each of these traumas also gives us access to a diverse range of well-developed research literature and to a perspective that may prove illuminating.

Grief, as opposed to victimization, is the psychological reaction to the loss of a loved one, of a cherished goal, or of a cherished aspect of one's life. The most universal grief experiences surround the loss from death of a parent or spouse, or, more rarely, of a child—someone whom you have loved and been very close to is no longer there. The human response is one of sadness and it often shares many features with a group of illnesses we call depressions. There are differences, however, between grief and depression: grief is more limited in time and does not generally include a significant element of lowered self-esteem. In other respects they may be difficult to distinguish, and grief responses may precipitate depressive illness in predisposed individuals. Grief is a human and proper reaction, as is the process of mourning, but grief does not always proceed normally. If there is no real experience of pain, or if numbness and denial persist too long, we may have what is called "pathological grief"—a festering, unconscious reaction that interferes with health until it is worked through and resolved.[4,5]

Grief and mourning experience may be very much involved in terrorist victimization. We know that victims of terrorism can be badly beaten or injured, possibly maimed, and suffer the rage we have previously described as associated with being knocked down in a dominance hierarchy, with being made suddenly less powerful. However, they can also grieve, and grieve deeply, for the loss of an image of themselves—whether that image was as potent, as in control, or as whole. This grieving may be accompanied by the depressed feelings that accompany other grief reactions and may also precipitate depressive illnesses in predisposed individuals.

Research work on and folk wisdom about grief remind us that the mourning process has a timetable of its own that should not be rushed—even if it does not coincide with the convenience of the helpers or with the convenience of the victim. In traditional Jewish practice, for example, this timetable is expressed simply in a series of well-structured changes in status. During the first week after the loss, bereaved observant Jews "sit shiva." They are expected to be unable to work and are cared for at home by family and friends. They are not expected to put up a front and the gift you bring to such persons is food, expressing their dependency and your permission for them to concentrate on their internal work of mourning.

When these seven days have passed, a less restrictive period of one month (Shaloshim) ensues: the person returns to work, but a significant part of his time is occupied with prayers related to the lost loved one. The best known of these is the mourner's Kaddish, which is recited three times daily during the first year. When reciting this prayer, the mourners rise as a group and the rest of the congregation, seated, responds with short phrases at intervals through the prayer. After the first month the intensity of the mourning process continues to decrease through the first year. Now the person is getting back to his old self and is expected to seek out the world he had left behind. Still, one does not remarry during this period—new relationships should be free of the old ones. The process is punctuated by the unveiling of the grave stone, which in Jewish practice usually occurs after the year of Kaddish has been completed and is accompanied by a clear recognition that the dead person is gone. After this year-long period, the loved one is remembered on each anniversary of his death through a recitation of the Kaddish. Other religious and cultural systems have similar time tables for the work of mourning, although the emotional displays considered proper may vary from a "stiff upper lip" to demonstrative wailing or some form of celebration.

The experience of terrorist victimization often represents as significant a trauma as bereavement and is not infrequently combined with it. Yet how often do official helping systems provide this kind of structured caring over time? We believe that such traditional practices should represent a standard for the nature and duration of helping programs. They also remind us that each phase has a phase-specific behavior that is discovered through the observation of many individuals over time. What is pathological in one phase may be entirely normal in another; people may get stuck in one phase of recovery or have to return to issues or experiences that have been incompletely dealt with psychologically.

The human reaction to *death imagery* and its psychological importance have been explored in detail by Robert Lifton.[6] This phenomenon is strikingly illustrated by the comments of a woman who survived one of the worst air disasters in history, in which 600 people were killed. One of a handful of survivors, she stated a year after the tragedy, "The problem is, I know I am going to die." This was not, she explained, a feeling of fear that this would happen soon: "No, I just know I am going to die." This young woman was expressing that she no longer possessed the protective veil that keeps most of us from having to constantly visualize and be aware of our mortality. For her, this veil was suddenly pulled back, and the vision was an alarming, almost devastating one to live with. Victims of terrorism are also forcefully exposed to images of death, although in fewer numbers. The duration and quality of their exposure, however, is similar in intensity to the experience of air-disaster victims. There is no better image for this experience than Gerard Vaders, tied as a living curtain between two sections of the train so that he faced the baggage compartment where the legs of the murdered engineer protruded in a pool of blood.

A third and related model is also part of the experience of natural and man-made disaster victims, as well as of the experience of the victims of terrorism and war: the *inescapable encounter with bloody or terrible events*. It is the experience of the stewardess as she wandered among the bodies at Tenerife, or of the father who was forced to watch an SS man swing his 2-year-old daughter by her feet and smash her head against a wall. Dori Laub, a psychiatrist who has worked extensively with Holocaust victims and their children, has pointed out the unique importance of such terrible events, which are too powerful to be tied to the ego or to objects—the terrible events themselves become the foci of symptoms and of identifications.[7] Those of us fortunate enough to lead normal lives are not, and cannot be, fully prepared to encounter such events. The gory and grotesque elements in children's fairy tales and the violent or horror movies we go to see may be our attempts to desensitize ourselves to such events through small doses that we can control. For most people, encountering the real thing is so shocking and the images so overburdening that they flood the conscious and unconscious mind, sweeping past usually effective defense mechanisms and coping strategies. In their aftermath, they haunt a person when he is awake and poison his dreams for years on end. Sometimes, sadly, efforts to forget or even to simply go on with life fail.

If excessive exposure to bloody events can overwhelm us, the complete absence of visible injury can be a surprisingly troublesome source of difficulty for the victim of war, crime, or any aggressive interaction. If there is no visible wound, no blood, how is anyone, including ourselves, to know that we have truly been wounded? Clinicians familiar with the problems of crime victims have noted that the victim who has escaped physical injury is likely to encounter significantly more problems in getting help after the crime and to suffer more crime-related, inappropriate guilt.[8] This observation has been corroborated in a different context by the research of psychiatrist William Sledge and his colleagues on American prisoners of war in the Vietnam conflict. Their research will be discussed in greater detail later in this chapter. In his study of what he calls the "benefited response" of former prisoners who reported significant *positive* mental changes, Sledge found these men significantly more likely to have been injured during captivity.[9] Thus, the invisible wound may extract an added toll just because it is invisible.

The final model for terrorist victimization is the *experience of rape victims.* Although terrorists use murder or the threat of murder as their basic coercive technique, the crime of murder is not as good a model as rape for terrorist victimization. First, by definition, all murder victims are killed; most hostages are not. Second, a significant number of murder victims have had, before being murdered, a prolonged and/or intimate relationship with the person who killed them; this is less true in rape, and seldom true in terrorist acts.

The crime of rape can serve as a model for terrorist victimization in other ways. In the introduction to this volume, we quote a Palestinian terrorist who labeled his actions as a "severe entry into their minds." The verbal analogy to the act of rape is obvious. Beyond this, both rape and hostage-taking coerce the participation of the victim and compel our attention (if not our understanding). The analogy may be extended to the spectrum of perpetrators in rape and in terrorism. In both crimes, the act itself is apparently a final common pathway that gives reward, meaning, or relief to a diverse group of deviant personality types. There are no ideological extremists or idealists in the ranks of rapists, but two other personality types are found quite frequently in both groups that interact in important ways with victims in the course of an incident.

First is the predatory, psychopathic rapist who takes people casually as things to be used for pleasure, gain, or stimulation. These individuals often have long histories of antisocial or criminal behavior, sometimes dating back to childhood, and rape or terrorism are far from the only violent activities in which they have been involved. They show their victims little mercy and feel almost no remorse or guilt for what they have done, although they may profess a conventional emotional response if they feel it will be to their advantage to do so. The second personality type is one who has experienced repeated social or occupational failures and who uses rape as a shortcut to something that at least resembles sexuality or uses terrorism as a shortcut to something that resembles success and attention from the world. These inadequate individuals use rape to coerce the intimacy or sex that they crave. They are more likely than other rapists to prey on children, since children are less able than adults to realize and communicate the inadequacy of their assailants. The same type of person strives for involvement in a meaningful cause or vocation or seeks status within an organization through the deviant pathway of membership in a terrorist group. These are the "gofers" who are assigned most of the drudgery and much of the danger in ongoing terrorist operations. Thomas Strentz of the Federal Bureau of Investigation (FBI) has developed this concept of the interaction of deviant personality types in the structure of terrorist organizations.[10]

After the Severe Entry: Isolation of the Victim

The special usefulness of the experience of rape victims as a model for the victim of terrorism is clearest when one considers the negative consequences of victimization that have nothing to do directly with what the offender does to the victim. The most serious and far-reaching of these consequences is the victim's isolation, and we will examine this phenomenon in some detail. Both hostages and rape victims are isolated by their own feelings of guilt and shame: guilt over whether they perhaps should have resisted at the cost of their lives, and shame at having been taken, used, damaged, or defiled. This makes it harder for victims to share their experiences with others and to work them through psychologically by themselves on a constructive, conscious level—both the subject matter and the emotions make avoidance or denial likely defenses. Since the experience of these victims touches upon areas in which most people have some unfinished psychological business, it is not surprising that some of the guilt and shame has an unreal or unrealistic character when viewed by outsiders. This lack of "objective" reality does not, unfortunately, diminish the punitive force of the emotions themselves. Friends or relatives who try to comfort victims are often angered and saddened as they find out quickly that the guilt or shame does not go away as soon as the well-meaning helper demonstrates that, from a rational point of view, it doesn't make sense.

Even more agonizing in these situations is the possibility that guilt may be *real* and *justified*. Psychiatrist Dori Laub has described a patient whose life is crippled by multiple phobias, living alone in a large American city. During the Holocaust he and his family were transported by cattle car to a place where they were to undergo mass execution. As the door opened and the guards ordered the prisoners out, the patient ran and managed to escape. The last he heard of his family was his young son yelling, "Daddy, don't leave me!" Laub points out that this man has been irreversibly scarred by his *real* abandonment of his son.[7] It will *not* do to say, "Who knows what I would have done," or, "You did the only thing you could," although both statements may be true. Determining what *will* do in such cases is something we have only just begun to struggle with. Perhaps in situations like these it is necessary first to acknowledge the reality of guilt before we can expect real forgiveness from ourselves or from others, along with the possibility of effective atonement and healing. The need to consider guilt as an emotion that is not always pathological may be applicable to situations less extreme than the Holocaust or international terrorism. Psychoanalyst Willard Gaylin has found that individual guilt can have positive aspects; it can be a constructive emotional response that signals a departure from our ego ideal and that may impel us to constructive as well as to destructive behavior.[11]

In terrorist incidents, realistic guilt is most likely to become a problem when some hostages have been released before others or when persons with military or law-enforcement backgrounds have not resisted the hostage-takers with force. Such situations have occurred in many terrorist incidents, such as the one at Entebbe or the Moluccan incident described by Gerard Vaders, in which a Chinese man and pregnant woman were released before the other hostages. In the Tehran hostage situation, both factors were relevant to the Marine embassy guards who were among those released by the terrorists early in the incident. The fact that they were released because they were black only adds to their conflict, since it undercut the ideal of American solidarity that this incident rekindled. Again, the temptation at all levels to avoid the real moral and psychological issues involved is powerful. Certainly, the guards had not been adequately prepared for what was to happen. We will discuss the question of whether, and how, people can or should be prepared for the worst in the final chapter of this volume.

In addition to being isolated by his or her own psychological reactions, the victim of rape or terrorism faces a further and related process of isolation by others. These two processes often interact in a negative spiral with more social isolation leading to more unrealistic thinking, and so on. Social isolation is particularly tragic, since friends or relatives sometimes pull away at the very time when they are most needed. This distancing is often a product of the discomfort caused by the issues of brute violence or sexuality that the incident itself raises, even if the victim tries to protect friends and relatives by not talking about it. Mixed with this is often a fear or suspicion that the victim has somehow been contaminated or changed irreversibly for the worse. The female victim of rape may be treated by a friend, lover, or spouse, sometimes unconsciously, as "damaged goods."

Early observers of terrorist incidents were not adequately prepared for the possibility of this kind of social isolation, especially in light of the expressed public support and publicity the hostages seemed to be getting. The hostages also were poorly prepared, since they had felt that their ordeal was finally over. Yet, as we have seen, Gerard Vaders suffered from a period of official suspicion and overt hostility that could have easily exacerbated any tendencies he had toward guilt or shame and which certainly complicated his recovery. Brian Jenkins, who has conducted extensive studies on terrorist incidents at the Rand Corporation, has described a similar and subtle, yet debilitating problem in American executives and diplomats released after terrorist captivity. It is expressed in official reports in phrases like, "He acquitted himself well, to the best of our knowledge, during the course of his long captivity." Former hostages themselves have described such suspicion and distancing among their friends and colleagues as if they were feared as a source of contamination.[12]

What is this need to distance, and often to go beyond distancing to actually blame or condemn the victim? What are the dimensions of this phenomenon, and what controls it? What makes it increase and what makes it decrease or go away? We have already mentioned several factors that bear on this issue—those that lead to realistic or unrealistic guilt and shame on the part of the victim. It is well known that in social interactions we tend to signal to others how we feel about ourselves and that they, in turn, often use these cues to guide their behavior toward us. These cues are often nonverbal or paraverbal (in tone, pauses, or inflections) and may be noticeable only with careful observation of a videotaped communication, where the interaction can be repeated or stopped as desired. In addition to being non-verbal, the signals are often unconscious or unexamined; people are often amazed when they first realize what they have been communicating about themselves to others.

There are dimensions of victim-blaming, however, that do not necessarily respond to encouraging victim cues. Surrounding all victim experiences is the aura of victim as loser, with the negative connotation that this term implies. As a nation with a relatively recent frontier tradition, we place a heavy emphasis on standing on our own two feet, fighting for ourselves, and winning. Those who do not win are often left behind and there is frequently a not too subtle note of negative moral evaluation added: it is not just unappealing to lose, it is wrong. Morton Bard and Dawn Sangrey have emphasized the pernicious role of this identification of victims with losers and of losing with being undesirable or bad in the experience of many conventional crime victims.[13]

Psychologist Melvin Lerner articulated and explored another extremely useful perspective on this phenomenon in a series of careful and creative experiments that helped formulate what is known as the "just world theory." Although his theory was not originally developed to explain terrorist victimization, it has been applied to rape victims and offers one of the most useful psychological perspectives on this issue. Lerner's work deals directly with why and how observers, and even friends and helping professionals, can add insult and blame to the injury of a victim of terrorism. Lerner postulates that human beings *need* to believe in an orderly world where people can, and do, get what they deserve. Evidence of undeserved harm and suffering, such as that undergone by a victim of a terrorist incident who had no previous relationship with the terrorists or to their cause, seriously threatens this belief. In such situations people are impelled to help, to effect a just outcome and thus reestablish justice. However, if the observer is unable or unwilling to act (out of fear for his safety, his supply of gasoline, or his untroubled existence) he still has an alternative that will maintain his belief-system intact: he may alter his view of what has happened—of the event itself—to one that lets him believe that the harm or suffering was in some sense the victim's own fault, or that the victim deserved it because of the kind of person he was. In general, when confronted with an apparently blameless victim, observers will prefer an explanation that involves postulating a misdeed to one that involves constructing enduring negative personal qualities for the victim.

The "just world theory" emerged from a long series of similar experiments. The typical experiment involved a group of observers who watched a victim receiving uncomfortable but not dangerous electric shocks. The observers and victim did not communicate directly with each other and were unaware of the true nature of the experiment. (They may have been told, for instance, that it was a study of physiological reactions or learning.) The observers were either given power to help the victim (by voting to compensate her) or given no such opportunity. When given the opportunity, observers voted to compensate the victim and expressed no negative evaluations of her. When they were not given the opportunity to help, when there was no expectation that she would be compensated, they made negative evaluations of the victim's personal worth, attractiveness, and other personal traits. When the conditions of the experiment were varied to produce a longer duration of suffering and a more "noble" appearing victim, the condemnation of the victim *increased*.[14] These findings have been replicated and extended to observers from diverse geographical and social backgrounds and to several different types of victimization.[15]

When the experimental situation is made more like real-life victimization, the findings become more complex. In a study by Jones and

Aronson relating to rape victims, a simulated jury in a rape case was presented with different degrees of "respectability" of the victim. In general, they tended to recommend harsher sentences to offenders who had raped more respectable victims. This finding confirms that justice is not blind and may be far from equal, but the trend still appears logical. Yet only Lerner's postulated need for a "just world" view or a similar model explains another finding in this same study: when a high degree of respectability in the victim was *fixed*, the subjects in the simulated jury were inclined to attribute some behavioral responsibility for the rape to the victim herself.[16] For the highly respectable victim, the true "innocent," the jurors were unable to accept the reality of undeserved suffering and recreated their just world by distorting the event they were supposed to be judging objectively—only here, the logic of the unequal justice went *against* the respectable victim.

Does Lerner's model take us beyond predicting when a victim will be blamed and offer any perspectives useful for helping? We believe that it does. A crucial contribution of this series of experiments depends upon the researchers' ability to manipulate various parts of the model and study the effects on the occurrence and strength of negative evaluation of the victim. Summarizing the results of these manipulations, condemnation is increased by identification with the harm-doer. More to the point of discovering ways to help victims is the finding that condemnation can be significantly lessened by *any* procedure that causes the observers to identify with the victim. This does not have to be on a real economic or political basis; the effect of lessening condemnation can be produced by instructions simply to "imagine yourself in the victim's place."[17] This is not easy to do (we have discussed factors that make people pull away from victims of violent crime) but it is not impossible, and several well-developed clinical and educational techniques for achieving this iden-tification already exist. Many traditional ethical systems have enjoined us never to judge a man until we have "walked a mile in his moccasins" or stood in his shoes. Lerner's work rephrases these categorical im-peratives as hypothetical: *if* you want people to evaluate and work with victims of terrorism fairly, *then* you should formulate explicit procedures to increase their identification with these victims. It is not enough to assume that people will naturally be fair—in fact, the case is just the opposite.

Cognitive Factors in Terrorist Victimization

What is lost or missing when a victim is isolated either during or after a terrorist incident? There are many approaches to answering this ques-tion, and our initial starting point will play a major role in determining our conclusion. A useful way to conceptualize situations like these is in terms of basic human needs that may be denied in such a process or setting. This approach has been developed most fully by Abraham Maslow, who has outlined five basic groups of needs: physiological needs, safety needs, belongingness and love needs, esteem needs, and the need for self-actualization.[18] Of course, safety needs are threatened in all terrorist contexts. The need that the process of isolation interferes with the most, however, is that for belongingness and love. The deleterious effects of social isolation on people at every social and psychological level have been well-documented. Here, however, we will explore another aspect of the isolation of victims of terrorism that can be related to a group of needs that Maslow indicates may also be basic to human nature: the need for understanding, explanation and meaning.[19] We believe it is useful to include these needs in a balanced view of human experience and behavior. Through isolation and restricted communication, victims of terrorism are deprived of information. When information is withheld from people, the needs for explanation and meaning are frustrated; when information is manipulated, these needs are exploited.

The need for explanation begins with the onset of a terrorist incident; it involves the impulse to grasp what is going on, to place it in some familiar context. For Gerard Vaders, a professional at handling information, this task was relatively easy—he was helped through the early phases of the incident by his ability to place himself back in the war and to gather relevant cues (from the colors on their guns) as to the identity of the enemy.

For other victims of terrorism and of undeserved adversity, this absence of explanation and information has constituted one of the greatest stressors of the incident. Job cries out in his undeserved suffering, "Behold my desire is that the Almighty would answer me and that my adversary had written a book. Surely I would take it upon my shoulder, and bind it as a crown to me."[20] The Hebrew word "book" here connotes an indictment: Job *wants* a formal charge; he would treasure it. Not to have one, as many victims of terrorism within and outside of the state know, is one of the most painful aspects of this experience. In the absence of a formal indictment that makes sense, of an articulated explanation, the victim of terrorism turns to his only source of explanation—the terrorist. As Gerard Vaders said, every movement a terrorist makes is studied for its meaning.

In his or her role as controller or manipulator of information, the terrorist may have a more profound impact on the victim than through any physical abuse. Gerard Vaders showed how this manipulation occurs when he reported that one of the Moluccans, protesting that he did not hate the Dutch people, added that his wife was Dutch. One can see how this would weaken the hostages' ability to remain hostile toward the terrorist. The crucial point about this human interest story is that the statement about having a Dutch wife was a lie! Whether originated as part of an organized group effort to manipulate the information given to the hostages or as an individual terrorist's means of communicating comfortably with his captives, the creation of a fact to fit a need remains just that and constitutes a definite danger to the hostages. This same process occurred with the American hostages in Tehran (for example, one was falsely told that his mother had died) and is clearly facilitated in a totalitarian political or religious context.

It is crucial that terrorist groups control sources of information if they want to function effectively. Within these groups, which may be cohabiting and which are usually small and isolated, a logic of terrorism that is often incomprehensible to outside observers emerges. Those familiar with the unique dynamics of small groups as exemplified in the intense cognitive and emotional experiences that occur in therapy and encounter groups are better prepared to deal with the compelling truth that some of these beliefs hold for their believers.

In articulating a theoretical model for this creation of fact the social psychology of small groups, rather than individual psychodynamics, provides the most useful perspectives. An example is the work of psychologist Solomon Asch, who established both the extreme potency of this phenomenon and the factors that limit it. His studies are all the more remarkable since they dealt with *truly* factual perceptions such as the relative length of two lines. In a typical experiment, a naive subject was asked to evaluate which of two lines was longer and to give his evaluation aloud along with a group of subjects who were really confederates of the experimenter. The real subject always gave his opinion last. When *all* the confederates gave the wrong response, the true subject, despite the obvious incorrectness of the reply and often with real reluctance and discomfort, would go along with the majority fully one-third of the time. Asch systematically varied the size of the majority from zero (subject alone) up to sixteen. He found that increasing the size of the majority from zero up to three produced a significant and proportional increase in this phenomenon, but that beyond a majority of three there was no further consistent increase. Even more significant for the victim of terrorism, he found that no matter how large the majority, the presence of even one dissenter who "told it like it was" greatly decreased or eliminated the unrealistic influence of the majority on the subject.[21]

These studies would suggest that a group of four is the size that will maximize the efficiency of control by a terrorist group in case information or opinions that vary from the "party line" leak in. Many terrorist groups, in fact, operate day to day in cells of three or four individuals, and it is probable that this cognitive factor is one of the things that determine this size, in addition to the ability of the larger group to survive the destruction of one such cell. On the positive side, Asch's findings reaffirm an individual's power to influence the beliefs and opinions of a group no matter how large the group or how "far out" the opinions may be. In fact, this "far-out," obviously unrealistic quality that is present in so much terrorist rhetoric may signal an even greater susceptibility to disruption by a lone dissenter. This is why Gerard Vaders was upset when the sensitive terrorist, Paul, was injured and left the group; it also explains the great role that their ability to hear occasional news broadcasts from the outside played for the hostages on the train. Even a little bit of truth may help a lot.

Terrorist group leaders fight hard to maintain absolute control over the information given to their members and hostages. Failing this, they attempt to maintain a monopoly on explanations of what has happened, a kind of tunnel vision that allows them to suppress common sense and old belief systems. This is clearly analogous to the control certain religious cults exert over their members. Some of these, as in Jonestown, have also led their followers to a violent apocalypse that seemed senseless to many who were outside of the tunnel. When we have access to the process at an earlier stage, as in hostage negotiation, it is possible to break into the overlearned, inexorable pattern and to try to show the terrorist (and, if necessary, the "converted" hostage) that one can find light by breaking out of the tunnel (which is, after all, a human construction) as well as by following it to its bloody end.

Up to this point, we have focused on cognitive distortions in the terrorist's perspectives that may work for or against the hostages. Other complementary cognitive adaptations and distortions occur in hostages and victims as well. In the case of victims of conventional crimes, these have been well reviewed by Morton Bard and Dawn Sangrey, who used the psychological concept of attribution as a unifying perspective on these efforts by victims to answer the question, "Why me?"[22] These attributions or explanations may have various degrees of objective truth, but it is their *plausibility* to those who use them that determines their instrumental effect. The philosopher Abraham Kaplan has offered a general definition of this instrumental function of explanation: When someone has been brought to accept an explanation he will generally behave differently than he would have without an explanation, or with a different one; thus the explanation itself has an effect on the person's behavior.[23]

The possible absence of objective truth, however, should not distract us from the presence of potent, scientifically measurable effects. These effects are especially important for victims, since they may support the victims' coping efforts. Bard and Sangrey quote a series of experiments by psychologist Ellen Langer on the "illusion of control," defined as "an expectancy of a personal success probability inappropriately higher than the objective probability would warrant." They interpret these studies as showing that people who *believe* they are in control of a situation, *even if they are not,* gain many of the beneficial functions of that belief in the form of personal comfort and strength to withstand pain and cope with crisis.[24] Dr. Jared Tinklenberg gave a poignant example of this process earlier in this volume: concentration camp survivors were sustained by "the firm conviction that the bulk of humanity would not tolerate such atrocities." The poignancy lies in the fact that the bulk of humanity *did* in fact tolerate such atrocities; the survivors were very few. Yet for them the belief was potent.

In Gerard Vaders's account, the minister attempted to recontextualize the terrorist incident by saying an idealistic prayer at its conclusion. We should not attack or undermine this kind of effort. The need for a plausible explanation is clearly related to Lerner's "just world theory," but there is a crucial difference from the victim's point of view: the needs of the observers to maintain their just world view lead to victim-blaming and isolation, while the instrumental function of the victim's own explanations is often positive, i.e., it leads to effective coping. In the extreme case we have a transition to what is known as the "self-fulfilling effect." As Kaplan states it, "an explanation may *become* a sound one because it is felt to be plausible by the people whom the explanation is about."[23] Here, when the process is complete, we have truth as well as potency. But even when we have the instrumental function of explanation unadorned by truth, we should respect it; victims of terrorism need all the help they can get.

The Terrorist as Victim and the Stockholm Syndrome

Still another cognitive distortion or reversal of the terrorist act is the one that labels the terrorist or his group as the real victims. Adolf Hitler was credited with the observation that people can be more easily persuaded to believe a big lie than a small one, and in that sense we have witnessed a bold attempt, often successful, by terrorist groups to turn the situations they create on their heads. Loud proclamations of victimhood should not always be taken literally.

With these considerations in mind, it is still worthwhile to explore the phenomenon of seeing the terrorist as victim. It does, in fact, occur among victims themselves and provides some valuable perspectives on the terrorist situation. Our opposition to all terrorism should not blind us to the fact that, as contrasted to terrorists from affluent portions of affluent societies (such as the Baader-Meinhof group), the terrorists in many national liberation movements (such as the South Moluccans or the Palestinians) often do come from a background of genuine exploitation, uprooting, and, sometimes, poverty. Their unfortunate situation is often highlighted both in their own eyes and for the public by their battle against countries that have higher standards of living, such as Holland or Israel. Even in relatively developed countries, terrorists may enhance the contrast between "ins" and "outs" by preying on the most fortunate or powerful members of their society—e.g., Patricia Hearst. Unfortunately for the world, unfortunate people who gain power do not automatically behave humanely when they are in control.

Gerard Vaders's account provides an excellent example of the complex reality of the terrorist as victim. This theme lurks below the surface of many of the interactions between the South Moluccans and their hostages, and occasionally breaks through: Well into the incident, after the initial flush of success had died for the terrorists, one of the hostages jokingly suggested that they order Nasi Goreng (an Indonesian dish). A terrorist responded that if they did, there would be none for the hostages, and the hostage countered, "When this is all over, I'll come eat Nasi Goreng at your place." The terrorist turned on him bitterly and replied, "Sure, in cell 580." Shortly thereafter, Djerrit (one of the terrorists) wept openly as he realized the ultimate futility of his position.

An even more explicit portrayal of the terrorists as victims and losers is presented sensitively and reflectively by Vaders in the following summary:

> You had to fight a certain feeling of compassion for the Moluccans. I know this is not natural, but in some ways they came over human. They gave us cigarettes, they gave us blankets. But we also realized that they were killers. You try to suppress that in your consciousness. And I knew I was suppressing that. I also knew that they were victims, too. In the long run they would be as much victims as we. Even more. You saw their morale crumbling. You experienced the disintegration of their personalities. The growing of despair. Things dripping through their fingers. You couldn't help but feel a certain pity. For people at the beginning with egos like gods—impregnable, invincible—they ended up small, desperate, feeling that all was in vain.

There is much of value in this eloquent passage, and many possible interpretations. Psychiatrist Frederick Hacker considers this ability to see the terrorist as victim as a crucial one, both in understanding the Stockholm Syndrome and in offering hope for the resolution of individual terrorist incidents and of the problem of modern terrorism in general. For Hacker, only such a perception can break the vicious cycle of attack and counterattack, of the creation of new generations of victims that has characterized terrorism up to now.[25] Another value of this passage by Vaders is the perspective it offers on the Stockholm Syndrome. In contrast to the excessively sexual overtones that have been attached to this phenomenon (perhaps secondary to our undue concentration on the incident for which it is named) Vaders's account is one of a balanced and mature individual. Vaders realized that he was experiencing simultaneously contradictory cognitions and emotional responses and also that he was suppressing much of what he thought and felt in the interests of survival. An entire chapter of this volume, by Thomas Strentz, is devoted to the Stockholm Syndrome and includes significant data relating to recent terrorist incidents. We will devote this discussion to some of our own observations and theoretical speculations about this central phenomenon in terrorist victimization.

The feelings of affection for the hostage-taker that compose the positive half of the Stockholm Syndrome are described in many different ways, depending on the relative ages and sexes of captor and captive. An older hostage might characterize his affection in fatherly terms; Judge Guiseppe DiGennaro talked about the terrorists who held him hostage in Rome as though they were his teenage children. Dr. Tiede Herrema used similar language to describe his feelings for Gallagher and Coyle of the IRA. Patty Hearst, on the other hand, spoke in both romantic and familial terms about her kidnappers. This syndrome, consisting of affection for the captor coupled with negative feelings toward the police, government, and sometimes the hostage's family, has been found in approximately one-half of recent terrorist hostage cases. Skilled interviewers of hostages feel that the incidence of this syndrome may in fact be considerably higher. The positive feelings toward the terrorist are often reciprocated, boding well for the ultimate outcome. The syndrome affects both sexes, all ages, and has occurred in all cultures observed. The manifestation of affection, as noted above, is determined by the age and sex of the dyad involved. Fatherly, fraternal, or romantic affection have all been described.

Since hostage victims often lose their sense of time in the initial flurry of traumatic events, the exact onset of these positive feelings is often difficult to ascertain. It is known, however, that the syndrome may begin within several hours of capture and may last several years. The intensity of feeling seems to increase during the days of captivity, stabilize in the aftermath, and eventually diminish. When Moluccan terrorists attacked another train two years later, Gerard Vaders had lost his positive feelings. When loss of affection for the captor occurs some former hostages may notice depressive symptoms. This could be a form of grief, much the same as with the loss of a loved one or with the loss of a valued fantasy.

The Stockholm Syndrome may be unfortunately named geographically, but the second part of the name, "syndrome," accurately identifies its scientific status. It is more than a unique or remarkable event, having been observed repeatedly in different settings, but far from a disease or reaction in which etiology and dynamics have been clearly specified. We feel that it is important in the interests of both scientific accuracy and therapeutic effectiveness to be able to live with some explanatory uncertainty and not try to fit individual hostages or incidents into the theoretical model with which we ourselves feel most comfortable. In fact, the true nature of the Stockholm Syndrome is far from completely understood, although many attempts have been offered to explain it. Some have seen it as a conscious determination by the hostage to befriend the terrorist. Others have focused on its similarity to the unconscious defense mechanism of "identification with the aggressor," a mechanism that was bizarrely manifested by those concentration camp victims who imitated their sadistic guards. Finally, it has been linked with the well-known halo of camaraderie and affection that surrounds many who have shared an intense group experience, be it combat, fraternity initiation, therapy, or encounter group.

Our own perspectives on the Stockholm Syndrome focus on the particular context in which it occurs and on the purposes that it serves. The context is always one of confinement and of helplessness. However mature the hostage may be, this degree of helplessness can be contextualized only within the framework of earliest childhood, before the development of adult concepts of affection and of gratitude. Gerard Vaders graphically described this recontextualization when he commented that the terrorists even set up rules for excretion, and that when this and other routines were established, feelings of safety began for the hostages. Along with this infantilization, the terrorists gave the hostages some positive "strokes" (food, cigarettes, kind words, etc.). However, they also exhibited the power and the capability to kill the hostages—and did not do it. Thus, we would identify positive gratitude for care and caring and negative gratitude for not being killed as basic emotional experiences underlying the Stockholm Syndrome. The gratitude for not being killed has no real name or referent in the lives of most people today, but the gratitude for care and caring is interpreted by the adult part of the hostage's ego as affection, or compassion, or love—emotions that differentiate slowly from the matrix of caring and love in which all infants survive and grow. When any adult is placed into a situation of threat, helplessness, and reliance on another for survival, this feeling will return if the other provides care and does not harm. In this model, the feeling and the attachment are directed to the most humane and caring of the terrorists, rather than to the most aggressive (if there is a choice).

As for the purpose the Stockholm Syndrome serves, much attention has already been given to its objective survival value for hostages and, by extension, for the terrorists themselves. For the hostages this purpose has other aspects that, we believe, encompass a basic human need—the need for hope. As with other basic human needs, people will satisfy the need for hope as best they can in the circumstances in which they find themselves, and show gratitude toward what they perceive as the source of that hope. Hope is an insufficiently studied emotion that contains definite cognitive elements. Like its negative, hopelessness, it is focused on the future and includes the possibility of its opposite. When we are completely at ease, we do not feel hope; when we cannot imagine or remember *any* help, we do not experience hopelessness, since we do not know what we are missing. People with severe depressions, of which hopelessness is a cardinal symptom, often describe an unrealistic but very real sense of terrifying immersion far from the things and people that have sustained them in the past. For the hostage, the sense of hopelessness may be realistic as well as real, and anything that lessens it and moves him toward hope will release a powerful positive emotional response.

Many people have experienced grief or depression and some of the attendant feelings of hopelessness but few, thankfully, have known the intensity of the hostage experience. This makes it difficult to provide direct analogies by which we can apprehend its meaning and furnish some justification for the validity of the Stockholm Syndrome as a unique clinical entity. Abraham Maslow pointed out two additional factors related to need-motivated behavior that further complicate our efforts at understanding; both of them apply to the hostage situation. First, only unsatisfied needs actively motivate behavior. For most of us, the basic needs for safety and hope have been well satisfied, so that we do not have an extensive background of experiences or behaviors related to their severe deprivation. We are not really prepared to transact emotionally or intellectually with these primitive needs. Second, Maslow points out, much behavior is not in fact caused by the basic needs of the individual, but by features of the "external field" or environment. In hostage incidents these situational determinants may be particularly potent and interfere with a clear perspective on the causative role of individual psychodynamics. For example, if everyone in a room is tied up, it will not be immediately apparent that some of the hostages characteristically utilize motoric activity to move toward others in pursuit of their needs for love and belongingness.[26]

Despite its great positive value in the hostage situation, the Stockholm Syndrome also has a negative side. In mild form it may consist of impressions among hostages during the incident, as expressed by Gerard Vaders, that "the authorities are mishandling the situation." A more serious danger occurs when law enforcement and military personnel trying to manage such incidents warn hostages about liberation plans (they may share the warnings with their captors). Although mature and sophisticated hostages like Vaders may be aware of their irrationality, most hostages cannot and should not resist the alien but profound, affectionate feelings and related resentments that emerge from the well of their unconscious.

Once an incident is resolved, the effects of the Stockholm Syndrome often become most dramatic. The star witness for the prosecution may be irrationally, yet tenaciously, attached to the terrorist who threatened his life. The victim, who in the aftermath of a notorious terrorist event has a world audience at his disposal, may preach leniency toward the outlaw group. All of these attitudes and behaviors may be based less on a realistic appreciation of the merits of the terrorist cause than on the Stockholm Syndrome. Despite all of these negative aspects, most former hostages would agree with the current practice of encouraging the development of the Stockholm Syndrome rather than combating it; the bond of affection between captive and captor improves the chances of survival for both.

Positive Coping Techniques:
Making the Best of the Worst

If the victim of terrorism could have what he wanted, he would want not to have been a victim of terrorism. This fantasy or wish is all the more poignant in the case of terrorism since there has hardly ever been any real human relationship between the terrorist and his victim before the act that brought them together—and in the case of random bombings, even during the act. "If only I had been in a different store that day!" But this wish cannot be fulfilled other than in fantasy, and it remains to be determined how helpful such fantasies are to victims. We are left with the victims' need to adapt to the event that has occurred as best they can, and the desire of family, friends, and professionals to help them. In the final section of this chapter, we will explore another possibility, one that may seem almost contradictory—that victims can derive positive outcomes from the terrorist experience.

We believe this possibility is a real one, and our belief has grown from our contacts with victims. Our discussion presupposes everything we have said in earlier sections of this chapter, and we should keep these other perspectives in mind if the search for positive outcomes is not to degenerate into a self-deluding rationalization that comfortingly concludes the terrible story with a fabricated happy ending. Fortunately, we have a paradigmatic example of "positive coping" readily at hand in Gerard Vaders's account at the beginning of this volume, and we will repeatedly use it to illustrate specific points. One of this account's greatest values is its ability to place the concepts of positive coping techniques and positive outcomes where they belong—in the realistic context of the victim's and his family's lives. In this context, it is clear that the events on the train in December 1975 took a heavy toll from both Gerard Vaders and his family despite his relatively successful efforts to cope and despite any positive outcomes that may have emerged.

We have not been alone in our efforts to explore possible positive aspects of terrible experiences, and the efforts of other researchers in this area can provide a useful perspective. In his Foreword to this volume, Dr. David Hamburg has commented that "the clinical literature on life-threatening situations is long on stress and short on coping." Dr. Hamburg's own work in this area[27] has helped correct this imbalance, and Dr. Jared Tinklenberg has referred to this work earlier in this volume. Another leading researcher in this field has been Dr. Gerald Caplan, who has described a type of response to stress which he calls "mastery." Drawing on the work of R. B. White, he defines this response as "behavior by the individual that (1) results in reducing to tolerable limits physiological and psychological manifestations of emotional arousal during and shortly after the stressful event and also (2) mobilizes the individual's internal and external resources and develops new capabilities in him that lead to his changing his environment or his relation to it, so that he reduces the threat or finds alternate sources of satisfaction for what is lost."[28] Caplan emphasizes that social support systems play a crucial role in facilitating mastery of severe stress.

Research efforts to understand and learn from the experience of prisoners of war in the recent Vietnam conflict have provided an opportunity to focus on these positive aspects of coping. Psychologist Margaret Thaler Singer has noted recently that several of these efforts (to which we will refer in the final chapter of this volume) have made significant additions to "the study of personality resiliency and of positive personality growth potentials in adults who have been severely stressed."[29] An example from this group of studies is the report of Dr. William H. Sledge, Dr. James A. Boydstun, and Alton J. Rabe on a group of former Air Force prisoners of war. Of the 221 prisoners of war who responded to their questionnaire 61 percent indicated that significant favorable mental changes had resulted from their captivity experience. In contrast, only 32 percent of a non-prisoner control group of pilots and navigators with similar combat histories reported these favorable changes. Individuals in the "benefited" group of former prisoners reported that generally they "felt more optimistic, believed they had more insight into self, and felt better able to differentiate the important from the trivial. Interpersonally, they felt they got along better with others and claimed greater patience, human understanding, and appreciation of communication with others."[30] Members of this benefited group were also more likely to have been injured during captivity, to have been in conflict with their captors over physical treatment, and showed a divorce rate twice as high as that of the other prisoners of war. Thus, the correlates of a positive subjective evaluation of the effects of a prisoner of war experience are certainly not all positive ones.

It is important to emphasize here that we accept the validity of a victim's own value judgment of his or her experience. This does not prevent us from also gathering objective data amenable to the criterion of inter-subjectivity (such as divorce rates or hospital admissions). But this second type of behavioral data, although it can be agreed upon by different observers, should not be confused with the victim's own evaluation of the experience. In the case of terrorist victimization, it is doubly important not to substitute our own evaluations for the victim's, since such substitution or recontextualization is exactly what terrorists do when they tell the victims, "We do not hurt you because we hate you," or, "You are really part of our struggle for freedom." Let the victim decide.

If we are to be open to the possibility of positive responses, we must also drop or at least curb our prejudices about which defenses or coping styles are inherently healthy or constructive. In his chapter on stress earlier in this volume, Dr. Walton Roth has already explored the prevalent prejudices against using denial as a defense mechanism and the research evidence that in some crisis situations it may indeed be quite adaptive. Psychiatrist Arnold Beisser (himself a victim of postpolio-myelitis quadriplegia) has recently introduced a useful broadening of the perspective from which one may view the use of denial or other defense and coping mechanisms by victims. He feels that previously unexamined psychological factors that act to promote a positive view of health and of life *outside* the medical context may help explain the positive outcomes in seriously ill patients and other victims who utilize denial. Beisser says we must consider denial and affirmation of *both* illness *and* health:

> A patient is more than an illness. Indeed, the patient may have an illness, but his or her life would be of little value if that were all the patient had. To

assess the value of affirming or denying illness or of affirming or denying factors for health, the primary issue is the patient's psychic economy and at what expense (to self and to personal functioning) he or she must adhere to a particular view. The physician, in order to make such an assessment with the patient, needs to be aware of all the aspects of the situation, both from his or her own perspective and that of the patient.[31]

In our own view this perspective can be usefully applied to the situation of the victim and potential victim of terrorism. It is a particularly valuable perspective for members of the helping and healing professions, who tend to concentrate on what they have studied—pathology. That is because observation of the ongoing lives of victims of terrorism in countries like Israel, Northern Ireland, or Lebanon mostly reveals an affirmation of life, not death. People don't want to live *for* fear, even if they must live part of their lives *in* fear. You know where the shelters are, but mostly you ignore them. You stay in your home as long as you can and you adjust as you have to; if you are forced to, you leave. The mother in a Lebanese family of professionals whose Beirut home was heavily damaged by rocket fire insisted on remaining there for months despite protests from her family. Her behavior and its value for her own health is better explained by understanding what she was affirming ("This is my home and nobody can make me leave it"), rather than what she was denying ("There is physical danger to me now in Beirut").

What positive values, traits, or experiences can victims achieve or enhance? The range of possibilities is as wide as the range of victimization and of victims, and we will concentrate here on two broad groupings: the first involving interpersonal relationships of sharing and helping, and the second involving intrapersonal processes that can be labeled as stoicism or courage.

An example of the value of sharing and helping during a terrorist incident is in Gerard Vaders's relationship with Prins, the group's "doctor." Prins made up for his lack of formal medical training by an intuitive abundance of personal healing. He cut through the social and age differences between himself and Vaders by the simple but deeply powerful act of physical caring—he massaged Vaders's arms after Vaders had been suspended between compartments for hours as a "living shield." Vaders immediately recognized the great value of this contact and tried to maintain it after that. Later in the account, Prins also cared for other hostages and helped to gradually develop a caring-sharing culture in this small group of victims. The physical directness of some of the acts (such as warming food between their legs for one of the elderly hostages) is well-adapted to a setting where ambiguous verbal communications may prove too abstract. The way the group disapproved of a hostage who hoarded later in the incident indicates that the culture of sharing had developed some sanctions of its own.

The sharing and helping between Vaders and Prins was more than physical. When Vaders thought he was to be executed he shared all the details, including the unpleasant ones, of his domestic situation with Prins. Rather than giving a precise and rigid set of instructions on who is to be told what, Vaders wisely chose to provide Prins with the human context Prins needed to decide what should and should not be communicated. Paradoxically, this totally open sharing may have saved Vaders's life by disarming the stereotyped views that defended the Moluccans' resolve to kill.

Instances of sharing and helping like those described above have occurred among the victims of many different terrorist incidents, including the recent captivity of Americans in Iran. They do not always follow the lines of preexisting professional roles (for example, not all hostage teachers help their students); instead, natural helpers and leaders often emerge. Ofra Ayalon observed this process among the Israeli victims of Palestinian terrorists when children as well as adults surprised themselves and others by their abilities to help.[32] For these helpers, as for Gerard Vaders, the act of sharing and helping made *them* stronger and seemed to offer some protection against the harmful effects of their terrorist captivity. Sharing and helping represent active responses in a setting in which passivity prevails and in which other forms of action may be fatal. Especially when they are direct and physical, these responses can also retain their positive moral valence and thus preserve esteem in a situation filled with uncertainty and doubt.

In the aftermath of the incident, this positive effect can continue as helping victims take the opportunity to coach and counsel other victims and to join (as Vaders and Prins did) in official efforts to cope with subsequent terrorist attacks. We believe that such involvement has the potential to initiate an upward spiral of helping and health for former victims. The victims' energies may thus be used to capitalize on the expertise they have gained rather than to attempt to escape and deny. This is a constructive form of "working through" that may be especially valuable when few helping professionals can truthfully say, "I know exactly what it must have been like." The positive effects of this process go beyond purging the psyche of overwhelming trauma, however. Abraham Maslow, in his analysis of basic human needs, pointed out the inherent reciprocity of the human needs for belongingness and love—the need is to both receive and to give love.[33] It is the same for caring and being cared for; terrible situations may serve to rekindle an extinguished human flame.

In this final part of the chapter, we will explore the positive intrapersonal dimensions of terrorist victimization that can be described as stoicism or courage. Serious and rational discussions of these dimensions have been relatively infrequent in the recent history of terrorism. Instead, we have often had excessive rhetoric in which cold-blooded murderers of children are described by themselves and their admirers as "heroes of the revolution," and equally hyperbolic counter-responses label all victims of terrorism as heroes without giving any specific evidence that they did anything other than lie down or stand up when they were told to. Perhaps we are unable to cope with the fact that terrorists are indeed much more willing to give up their lives than are victims or the governments that try to help victims. There is a kernel of truth here, despite examples of self-sacrificing heroism like that of the engineer on the train captured by the Moluccans. There *have* been relatively few incidents of hostages trying to overpower their captors—even when they may have had a reasonable chance to succeed, and including instances when the hostages have had military or law enforcement backgrounds. Part of the explanation is obvious: only those who are prepared to die carry out terrorist acts, while those who ride airplanes or eat in restaurants tend to value their lives and are rarely prepared for immediate death. Beyond this, however, we must recognize that giving up one's life is in fact far from synonymous with courage, rationality, or even strength—as a study of the varieties of suicide plainly shows.

Clearly we must again consider what some of these basic concepts actually mean and apply them appropriately to the terrorist context. This is not an academic exercise in metaphysics, especially for potential victims in high-risk situations; an adversary with a commitment that is stronger than life can be met only by counter-extremism, which we hope we will eschew, or by a personality strengthened through education and understanding.

One of the most graphic, explicit, and helpful formulations of these issues can be found in the writings of Vice Admiral James Bond Stockdale, a former president of the Naval War College. In September of 1965 his Skyhawk jet was shot down over North Vietnam, and he spent the next seven and one half years as a prisoner of war, mostly in solitary confinement. Amid his efforts to cope with the injuries he had sustained, with isolation, and with torture, Stockdale conducted a unique process of discovery that gradually centered on the domain of values:

I was to spend years searching through and refining my bag of memories, looking for useful tools, things of value. The values were there, but they were all mixed up with technology, bureaucracy, and expediency, and had to be brought out into the open.[34]

The memories that helped this man most were those associated with the classical and historical aspects of his education rather than with the technical or practical ones. Especially useful to Stockdale was a brief treatise by the Stoic philosopher Epictetus, called the *Enchiridion*. Epictetus was born a Greek slave and, like Stockdale, had to cope with the handicap of lameness, which he labeled "an impediment to the body but not to the will." When we read Epictetus, it is not hard to see why Stockdale found him so relevant:

> It is not the things themselves that disturb men, but their judgments about these things. For example, death is nothing dreadful, or else Socrates too would have thought so, but the judgment that death is dreadful, *this* is the dreadful thing. When, therefore, we are hindered, or disturbed, or grieved, let us never blame anyone but ourselves, that means, our own judgments. It is the part of an uneducated person to blame others where he himself fares ill; to blame himself is the part of one whose education has begun; to blame neither another nor his own self is the part of one whose education is already complete.[35]

This Stoic perspective is far from the conventional psychological wisdom of coping, but this may merely indicate how far away conventional psychology is from the wisdom that will allow victims of terrorism to cope positively or even to transcend their experiences. In the terrorist context, values strongly held *are* central, and moral actions directed toward intrinsic consequences are more easily distinguishable than usual from prudence directed toward extrinsic outcomes. Stockdale recognized this in his own "extortion environment":

> In 1965, I was crippled and I was alone. I realized that they had all the power. I couldn't see how I was ever going to get out with my honor and self-respect. The one thing I came to realize was that if you don't lose integrity you can't be had and you can't be hurt.[36]

Stockdale's courage, and his perspective on courage, are useful because they are not naive. Clearly, he and the men he led *were* had and hurt, in many senses of these words ("They would slam you into the ropes and make you scream in pain like a baby"). The key to this kind of positive coping is those senses in which he could *not* be had and hurt, the things over which we, in our own natures, have the most control. It is this kind of liberty, rather than the freedom to leave when we want to or to do as we please, to which Thomas Jefferson was referring when he said:

"The God who gave us life, gave us liberty at the same time: the hand of force may destroy, but cannot disjoin them."[37] Viktor Frankl, also a survivor of inhumane captivity, makes the same point when he asserts the possibility of affirming attitudinal values even in the most hopeless situations of captivity and disease.[38]

Stockdale's classical education also helped him to construct a concept of courage that could withstand the test because it was realistic. Plato, he had learned, defined courage as "endurance of the soul." Stockdale elaborates: "Both Plato and Aristotle specified that courage had to be exercised in the presence of fear. Aristotle described courage as the measure of a man's ability to handle fear." Aristotle also explicitly said that because courage "is a moral virtue, involving feelings as well as reason, one achieves it by avoiding the pitfalls of excess (rashness) or defect (cowardice)."[39]

A source of strength, then, for the victim of terrorism lies not merely in the possibilities of escape and of coping with stress, but in the possibility of finding the best in the midst of the worst, in the presence of fear, and with the memory and possibility of failure. It is Gerard Vaders saying: "I still have guilt over the war. I did nothing bad, but not enough good. Not enough for the Jews. My sister did more and was in Dachau. Then I chose not to take too many risks. But on the train I did risk. I decided to write and to do it openly." When we are speaking of an experience that most people have never had, it is well to conclude with the words of one who has gone through it. There is no better way to affirm the possibility of positive coping with terrorist victimization than to demonstrate that it has been a reality. As a mature and balanced person with an unusual gift for expression, Gerard Vaders was able to sum up, as he faced execution, the organic intermingling of realism, stoicism, and courage that we have been describing:

> I was preparing for execution. Making up a balance. My life philosophy is that there is some plus and some minus and everyone ends up close to zero. Some say that is pessimistic. I think it is realistic. I was 50 years old. It had not been a bad life. I'm not happy with my life, but satisfied. I had everything that makes life human.

Notes

1. *Concise Oxford Dictionary of Current English.* 6th ed. Oxford, England: Oxford University Press, 1976.

2. *Webster's New Twentieth Century Dictionary of the English Language.* Unabridged, 2nd edition. New York: Simon and Schuster, 1980.

3. Koestler, A.: *Darkness at Noon.* New York: Modern Library, 1941, p. 257.

4. Mendelson, M.: *Psychoanalytic Concepts of Depression*. 2nd ed. Flushing, New York: Spectrum Publications, 1974, pp. 121–130.

5. Parkes, C. M.: *Bereavement: Studies of Grief in Adult Life*. London: Tavistock, 1972.

6. Lifton, R. J.; Kato, S.; and Reich, M. R.: *Six Lives/Six Deaths: Portraits from Modern Japan*. New Haven: Yale University Press, 1979.

7. Laub, D.: "The traumatic neurosis revisited: Traumas experienced during the Yom Kippur War by children of concentration camp survivors." Paper presented to the Association for Mental Health Affiliation with Israel, Eastern Pennsylvania Chapter, Elkins Park, Pa., May 20, 1979.

8. Bard, M., and Sangrey, D.: *The Crime Victim's Book*. New York: Basic Books, 1979, p. 80.

9. Sledge, W. H.; Boydstun, J. A.; and Rabe, A. J.: "Self-concept changes related to war captivity." *Archives of General Psychiatry*. 37:430–443, 1980.

10. Strentz, T.: "A terrorist organizational profile: A psychological role model." In Alexander, Y., and J. Gleason (eds.): *Behavioral and Quantitative Perspectives on Terrorism*. New York: Pergamon Press, 1981.

11. Gaylin, W.: "On feeling guilty." *The Atlantic*. 243(1):78–82, January 1979.

12. Jenkins, B.: "World overview of research: Areas of consensus and of ignorance." Paper presented at the American Psychiatric Association Symposium on Psychiatric Aspects of Terrorism, sponsored by the Law Enforcement Assistance Administration, Baltimore, Md., September 17, 1979.

13. Bard, M., and Sangrey, D.: *op. cit.*, pp. 76–102.

14. Lerner, M. J.: "The desire for justice and the reactions to victims." In Macaulay, J. and L. Berkowitz (eds.): *Altruism and Helping Behavior*. New York: Academic Press, 1970.

15. Lerner, M. J.: "Social psychology of justice and interpersonal attraction." In Huston, T. (ed.): *Perspectives On Interpersonal Attraction*. New York: Academic Press, 1974.

16. Jones, C., and Aronson, E.: "Attribution of fault to a rape victim as a function of respectability of the victim." *Journal of Personality and Social Psychology*. 26:415–419, 1973.

17. Lerner, M. J.; Miller, D. T.; and Holmes, J. G.: "Deserving and the emergence of forms of justice." In Walster, E. and L. Berkowitz (eds.): *Advances In Experimental Social Psychology* (Vol. 9). New York: Academic Press, 1976. The studies on which the "just world theory" are based and the relationship of this theory to concepts of attribution and cognitive dissonance are explored in Lerner, M.: "Just world theory." In Wolman, B. B. (ed.): *International Encyclopedia of Psychiatry, Psychology, Psychoanalysis and Neurology*. New York: Aesculapius Publishers, 1977.

18. Maslow, A. H.: *Motivation and Personality*. 2nd ed. New York: Harper and Row, 1970, pp. 24–60.

19. *Ibid.*, pp. 48–50.

20. The Book of Job. Chapter 31, verses 35–36.

21. Asch, S. E.: "Studies of independence and conformity: I. A minority of

one against a unanimous majority." *Psychological Monographs.* 70(9), Whole No. 416, 1956.

22. Bard, M. and Sangrey, D.: *op. cit.,* pp. 52–75.

23. Kaplan, A.: *The Conduct of Inquiry: Methodology for Behavioral Science.* New York: Harper and Row, 1968, pp. 356–357.

24. Cited in Bard, M. and Sangrey, D.: *op. cit.,* p. 62. The experiments are described in Langer, E. J.: "The illusion of control." *Journal of Personality and Social Psychology.* 32(2):311–328, 1975.

25. Hacker, F. J.: *Crusaders, Criminals, Crazies: Terror and Terrorism in Our Time.* New York: W. W. Norton, 1976, p. 118.

26. Maslow, A.: *op. cit.,* p. 55.

27. Hamburg, D. A.: "Coping behavior in life-threatening circumstances." *Psychotherapy and Psychosomatics.* 23:13–25, 1974.

28. Caplan, G.: "Mastery of stress: psychosocial aspects." *American Journal of Psychiatry.* 138:413–420, 1981.

29. Singer, M. T.: "Viet Nam prisoners of war, stress, and personality resiliency" (editorial). *American Journal of Psychiatry.* 138:345–346, 1981.

30. Sledge, W. H.; Boydstun, J. A.; and Rabe, A. J.: *op. cit.,* p. 443.

31. Beisser, A. R.: "Denial and affirmation in illness and health." *American Journal of Psychiatry.* 136:1026–1030, 1979.

32. Ayalon, O.: "Coping with terrorism: The Israeli case." In Meichenbaum, D. and M. Jaremko (eds.): *Stress Prevention and Management: A Cognitive-Behavioral Approach.* New York: Plenum Press, 1980.

33. Maslow, A.: *op. cit.,* p. 45.

34. Stockdale, J. B.: "The world of Epictetus: Reflections on survival and leadership." *The Atlantic.* 241(4):98–106, April 1978, p. 99.

35. Epictetus: *The Enchiridion.* 5. Translated by Oldfather, W. A. Cambridge, Mass.: Harvard University Press, 1966, vol. 2, pp. 487–489.

36. Stockdale, J. B.: *op. cit.,* p. 105.

37. Jefferson, T.: "A summary view of the rights of British America, 1774." In Koch, A. and W. Peden (eds.): *The Life and Selected Writings of Thomas Jefferson.* New York: The Modern Library, 1944, p. 311.

38. Frankl, V. E.: *The Doctor and the Soul: From Psychotherapy to Logotherapy.* New York: Alfred A. Knopf, 1955.

39. Stockdale, J. B.: "Taking Stock." *Naval War College Review.* Winter 1979, pp. 1–2.

7
Research on the
Victims of Terrorism

Rona M. Fields

Terror and terrorism have seldom been studied empirically for a number of substantial, if not sound, reasons, including inadequate baseline data, limited access to victims, poor documentation, and lack of funding.

There have been a few studies, including some empirical ones, which are discussed elsewhere in this book. My own research has focused on the experiences of child and adolescent torture victims and hostages, particularly in Northern Ireland and in Israel. In this chapter I will discuss the problems of defining and carrying out research on terrorism and then will describe briefly some results of research on children in Northern Ireland over a seven-year period.

A Few Definitions

The actual process of terrorization is the exertion of irresistible strength with the threat of annihilation. It is accompanied by unpredictability and received with the physical and psychological shock of any severe trauma. Terrorization is the application of this force, overwhelming the victims' capacity for willing their own behavior. The fear of imminent destruction is accompanied by a sense of powerlessness and unpredictability. There are four basic threats that induce the stress response and they are all present in terrorization: threat to life, threat to bodily integrity, threat to security, and threat to self-image.[1] The consensus among laboratory and field researchers is that appraisal of a stimulus as one or more of these kinds of threats brings about a stress reaction with both physical and psychological proportions.

Response to the threat and its sequelae comprise the coping mechanisms and are a product of ameliorating and exacerbating factors in individuals' total environments, such as their biopsychological and social past and present and their anticipations of future being. Coping styles include physiological responses such as psychosomatic disorders, immobility, channeled activity, stereotyping or scapegoating, regression, and capacity for and orientation toward intimate relationships. The chapter by Jared Tinklenberg in the present volume discusses some of these coping mechanisms extensively. Clinical research on victims asks who is terrorized, what happens during the process of terrorization, what the immediate and lasting effects are, and how damage can be limited and coping enhanced. While there has been some writing and research in areas other than clinical, such as historic, cultural, legal, and tactical concerns, I have chosen to deal specifically here only with the victims' experience of and reactions to terrorization.

Before turning to a discussion of research, however, I would like to emphasize that the direction from which terrorism comes cannot always be determined. Terrorization of large groups of people can and has been effected by governments, by guerrilla organizations, by lone, deranged individuals, by military forces, by paramilitary organizations, and even by entertainers, such as Orson Welles in his Martian landing broadcast of 1938.

The British White Paper of May 1948 referred to an "irresistible wave of terrorism" sweeping the then Palestine mandate and "defying the force of 84,000 troops." Yet there is evidence that for several years the civilian population of that place had been terrorized by the sudden and unprovoked attacks of military forces ostensibly searching for "illegals" in their midst. Two years before the White Paper, in an incident similar and parallel to a 1972 action in Derry, Northern Ireland, the British Parachute regiment fired randomly in the main thoroughfare of Tel Aviv, wounding and killing passersby and shopkeepers. In Palestine and in Northern Ireland (and perhaps in other places as well) terrorization of the civilian population by military and other organs of government antedated the organization of guerrilla groups and the utilization of guerrilla terror tactics against the civilian population.

One of the main differences, however, between a military or guerrilla operation and the actions of relatively isolated, fringe-type "terror squads" or criminal groups like bank robbers derives from the idiosyncratic targeting characteristic of the latter kind of group. The military or guerrilla terrorist attacks an unsuspecting civilian population and usually exerts maximal force immediately, i.e., bombing or shooting first and taking hostages or prisoners secondarily. Also, the military or guerrilla group takes prisoners or hostages for purposes other than bargaining, although bargaining or negotiating may ensue. These "war" tactics are undertaken to demoralize the larger target population. The objective of the criminal or deviant/revenge kind of group is to take a particular prisoner or prisoners for purposes of vengeance on a specific part of the population. These gradations and subtleties sometimes make a difference in the kind of threat posed to the terrorized; consequently, the sequelae, including the responses and coping styles of the hostages, may also differ.

Previous Research

The study of terrorization is related to that of stress, particularly trauma-induced stress. There is little enough agreement in the literature about what constitutes stress itself, and even less material on field studies of stress that would be most relevant to terrorization. Roth, in his chapter, discusses the concept of stress as it is understood by researchers today. In addition, for purposes of comparison, studies tend to lump together victims of several kinds of captivity experiences—terrorism, torture, lengthy incarceration, and concentration camps—with few attempts to differentiate among the experiences and their sequelae.

Deception studies, while somewhat more useful, are highly controversial because of fear of harm to the subjects. We do have important evidence from the studies of Stanley Milgram on obedience to authority. In a much-reported experiment, he told each subject that he would be participating in a "learning experiment," and had him administer increasingly strong electric shocks to a "learner" in the next room in response to the "learner's" mistakes. In spite of agonized screams, pleas to stop, and the visible (although falsified) anguish of the learner behind the glass, many subjects, in great conflict, found themselves unable to disobey the orders of an authority figure who insisted that the shocks must continue.[2]

In a simulation study that emulated real life even more closely than the experimentor himself had anticipated, Zimbardo had Stanford students spend several days in a mock prison situation—some as jailers, others as prisoners. He found that the stress of captivity was apparent in the behaviors of the volunteer prison inmates within a day or two of their incarceration and that within less than a week it was impossible to continue the experiment because the simulated situation had evoked genuine maladies. In addition, the setting elicited cruel and vicious behavior from some of the volunteer jailers.[3]

Other research includes retrospective studies of torture victims or, as they are also called, victims of brainwashing, who had been prisoners of war in North Korea.[4,5,6] In addition, Robert Lifton developed interesting clinical material on other victims of "thought reform" from China.[7] His work was one of the first serious considerations of the mental health implications of this kind of psychological torture. Later studies, however, did not have the same kind of baseline data and were of limited comparative value. These include examination of prisoners of war in Vietnam and the classic studies of concentration camp survivors.[8-12] Eitinger, whose chapter in this book discusses these latter studies, did find that individuals who had suffered earlier psychiatric symptoms or repeated trauma seemed to have more permanent and disabling damage. He and his colleagues also found that the effects of their experience resulted, for the concentration camp survivors, in premature morbidity and mortality.

Finally, there have been occasional studies of victims of natural disasters, also discussed in Eitinger's chapter. Hardly any of these studies, however, even those of a specific researcher, have used the same instruments and measurements on each subject and at appropriate reexamination intervals, so consistent estimates of change are almost nonexistent.

Recent studies by Vasquez and Ryczynzki,[13] carried out in France on Chilean refugees who had been tortured, indicate neurological damage with considerable other effects on blood chemistry, cardiac function and perceptions. Their studies have focused as extensively on the medical as on the psychological aspects of the effects.

Barriers to Research

A major difficulty in obtaining representative data on the effects of trauma-induced stress is the lack of opportunity for detailed, empirical studies of the victims of disasters, both natural and man-made. Unlike some areas of social psychological or health service related research, there have been no accumulated data on victims because the situations have not been dealt with epidemiologically. In places such as the Netherlands and Israel, where treatment of hostage victims has been documented, these data are still maintained as confidential and not reported in professional journals.

Often, neither the victims nor the health professionals who treat them afterwards are aware of the existing data on the different effects, so neither of them suggest or routinely perform any particular kinds of evaluative examinations. Since there has been so little investigation of the effects, there has also been no generalizable information on treatment prospects. More important, data are lost because of lack of knowledge about the symptoms and pathologies connected with these experiences.

There is also the problem of obtaining the data. Not every research assistant (even when funded) is eager to fly off to a war zone and, in grubby little houses and smelly alleyways, try to do psychological tests on subjects whose names, addresses, and appointment schedules are as vaporous as the mists on the Irish sea.

It is also difficult, if not impossible, to obtain trust, merit that trust, and also maintain tidy records for scientific interpretation. Hostages and kidnap victims frequently have either political or organizational reasons for anonymity and rapid reabsorption into a mundane routine. The U.S. Foreign Service personnel who have been political captives are hardly accessible for evaluation outside of the security network, and the same factors prevail in Israel and other countries as well.

These difficulties are compounded by the very nature of the requisite investigation. Such research, taking into account a multiplicity of variables, must be cumulative in order to constitute a large enough sample for multivariate analysis. This is very costly research unless it is already built into a health maintenance organization or governmental health agency. Psychological evaluations would have to become a standardized procedure as part of a medical evaluation, as well as long-term study and reevaluation at specific intervals. The U.S. government has not to date invested major support for systematic studies of terrorist victims by independent researchers. Requests for such support have been denied for several reasons, including costs, fear of adverse reactions from subjects, and questions about reliability. When complex studies are done without funding there are serious impediments to data collection, data analysis, and presentation of the results.

Besides opportunity and cost, there are several major methodological problems in doing clinical assessments of terrorist victims:

1. Time Frame—If assessment is not performed within a short time after the experience, there are problems in evaluating the relative effects of such contingencies as starvation syndrome, imprisonment and overcrowding, and the effects of readjustment. Most of the prisoners examined in Portugal and Chile were examined after they had been released and relocated.[13, 14] Many of the Norwegian victims studied by Eitinger and Strøm had been returned to their original homes.[8, 15] Differences in recorded consequences may be related to the complexities of refugee status.

2. Techniques of Assessment—To evaluate the condition properly, the clinician should have access to such equipment as the Halstead-Reitan Battery and other psychoneurological procedures. The Halstead-Reitan Battery, a series of neuropsychological tests designed to detect the

presence of organic brain dysfunction and to evaluate the nature and extent of disability, has been widely used in Norway and Sweden.

In the past, examinations of prisoners have often had to take place in secret or in the prison itself, thus requiring instruments that were portable, concealable, and quick. The same tests should be given to all available victims, whenever possible, to build up a bank of comparable data.

3. Base Line Data—The clinician dealing with the effects of terrorist victimization ordinarily will not have recourse to any information on the original condition of the victim. While Eitinger and Strøm were able to consult hospital and clinic records on the Norwegian victims, Eitinger was unable to acquire baseline data on his Israeli sample, nor was it possible to do so on the Northern Irish, Chilean, or Portuguese cases. Therefore, these studies must proceed as longitudinal studies and include fairly large samples if the findings are to have any significance.

In spite of these barriers, research into the effects of terrorism continues in a limited way.[16, 17, 18] My own work has focused mostly on child victims, particularly those in Israel and Northern Ireland.[19, 20] In the remainder of this chapter I will briefly discuss some of the background and research findings on children in Northern Ireland.

After a decade of examining torture victims and hostages from several different countries and as many wars, after after eight years of testing children age 6 through 15 growing up in conditions of constant violence, I have been led to conclude that "little victims into big terrorists grow." It has become evident to me that some societies ameliorate and others exacerbate the effects of ongoing stress consequent to violence. I have been particularly interested in the means of this amelioration or exacerbation, such as the legal system and other instruments of social control. Therefore, let us briefly examine the various background conditions affecting these children. The following section illustrates how necessary it is for the investigator to become acquainted with the background of terror before attempting to understand the sequelae.

Growing Up Into Terror

An examination of recent history suggests that terrorism appears in waves about once every two decades, i.e., about once every generation. This might be explained by considering the childhood experiences of the terrorists-to-be in terms of national and social turmoil characterizing their early lives. Not all children growing up in turmoil and violence become terrorists. We have only to look at the post-war young adults of continental Europe to see that in the 1950s young French, German, Dutch, Italian, and Scandinavian adults whose childhood fare had been a nightmare of bombings, strafings, and fixed battles did not become a terrorist generation. On the other hand, there is much evidence to suggest that the youthful Irish and Palestinians are more likely to be involved in terrorist actions than were their parents and that persons living in these places are more likely to become terrorist victims.

The ameliorating and exacerbating conditions for a social group are a product of the components of the social system in which they exist. They affect the children of the society through socialization and as social control processes. In this way, the relationship of a subgroup to the established institutions can provide an ameliorating condition or effect in otherwise stressful circumstances. The subgroups we are exploring have very different kinds of relationships with their larger societies and hence different problems in the socialization and social control processes.

The Northern Ireland groups are significant in that the institutions and thus the social control agents of that society are not indigenous to either group, although the Northern Ireland Protestants at one time considered them advantageous to their own survival needs and became "Loyalists" in politics. During the past five years, the social control agents of that society through their parent institutions have been ambivalent about Protestant privilege and position. This uncertainty has, in turn, compelled a change in the conditions of life for individuals and groups in the Protestant community and has led to significant changes in the position, and even geographic residence, of the urban Protestant working class community in Belfast and environs.

Irish society has historically survived genocidal experiences, some of which are still within memory of the oldest members of these groups and, at times, even some of the younger ones. The round of violence unleashed in Northern Ireland through the 1971 internment when the Special Powers Acts were applied has produced a child population growing up under conditions of ongoing and repeated stressful trauma.

Since 1971 in Northern Ireland over 2,000 civilians and 1,245 members of the security forces have been killed in various shooting and bombing incidents. Between 1965–75 live births declined by 20 percent and birth defects reached a peak for the twentieth century in that place, rising to 2.9 and 3.2 percent between 1970 and the end of 1972, when the major utilization of CS gas against the Catholic population amounted to 25,767 CS gas projectiles. Since 1971 there has been an 81 percent increase in alcoholic admissions to mental hospitals and during one six-month period in 1977 3,000 persons were interrogated in depth at one police barracks outside of Belfast (depth interrogation at that place, according to Amnesty International, amounting to torture). Between July 1972 and the end of December 1976 there were 3,340 explosions in Northern Ireland and a ratio of 1 death for each explosion, 6 in-depth interrogations per explosion, and 3 incarcerations per explosion.[21]

The effects of these continuing scenarios of violence and suffering have been very marked among children of all ages. Generally, children experience stress through their "meaningful adults." However, in the case of trauma-induced stress such as this there is an objective element—a destructive imbalance in the ecological system that imposes a tremendous burden on the cognitive, the affective, and sometimes also on the physical system of the child. In contrast to the stress of introducing a new member into a family or accustoming oneself to a new environment, events that are stressful but may be viewed as positive, negative, neutral, or confusing, trauma-induced stress is the introduction of a destructive force into the system. Ofra Ayalon has reported that child witnesses to violence and/or children who are physically violated suffer a systematic shock that transcends subjective valuation and incorporates distress.[17]

Over the past decade I have intensively studied the moral and social development of children ages 6 to 15 growing up in Northern Ireland. My research indicates that moral judgment in these children halts at a primitive level, so that it is no surprise to find that the bombers and gunmen of Belfast are often adolescent boys and girls of working-class families.

In their early years, ages 4, 5, and 6, these were the children whose houses were burned down around them by mobs augmented by uniformed "security forces"; whose fathers and sometimes mothers were dragged off to interrogation centers and tortured; whose older brothers and sisters were interned or assassinated by terror squads; and who, in telling their stories to the TAT card stimuli I presented in my field research, saw no one as having control over his own fate. The TAT (Thematic Apperception Test) is a projective test in which the subject is asked to tell stories in response to a set of pictures. The responses reveal basic attitudes toward significant figures and situations in the subject's environment. As part of the research, a number of projective tests, including the TAT, were administered semiannually to Belfast working class children over a period of seven years. There have been several highly significant changes, including consistently downward scores on the Story Sequence Analysis of the TAT that measures motivation.[22] These children, not surprisingly for children who see the future as beyond their control, began with below-average scores. These scores decreased from 1971 to 1974 and have since remained low but stable.

I also asked the Tapp-Kohlberg questions, which are a test of moral development in which the subject is asked to make choices for action in hypothetical situations involving complex ethics. The final score reveals the level of moral development that the subject has reached.[23] Here, the responses did not show the expected progression from level one to level two at ages 8–12. A few children did reach level two by age 12, but no more than 10 of the entire 350 studied were at level three. Again, in their responses to these questions there was a decrease in the number of children reaching level two at the appropriate age, which is commensurate with each succeeding year of violence and leveling out at its present curve since 1974.

The first analysis of the 1971 samples indicated a greater difference in both measurements between the children of Belfast and the children of Dublin (a comparably urban Irish city utilized for sampling a control population) than between the Protestant and Catholic children of either city. Differences were particularly striking when story imports were analyzed for themes of death and destruction. In 1971, Belfast children ages 6–8 were obsessed with such themes and saw themselves and their parents as helpless against these adversities. By 1977, the entire Belfast sample through age 15 was characteristically telling stories around death and destruction themes and unable to fantasize alternatives to violence. There was also a notable decline in fantasy content and fluency after age eight during 1971–72 and a general decline in fantasy productions among all age groups in the succeeding years.

As a group the people in the stories told by the Belfast children had little or no control over their own fate. There were some slight differences between Protestant and Catholic children on this dimension. Protestant children saw adversity as the product of malevolent "others" whereas Catholic children saw adversity as the effect of a malevolent "fate." This appears to reflect something of the theological metaphysics of their respective religious affiliations. In responding to "troubles," the Belfast children might choose to run away from their troubles but are pursued by them. Their story characters have incomprehensible drives for destruction, and both the children and (since 1973) the adults in their stories were quite helpless to combat them.

In 1971 and 1972 the Protestant children ages 8–14 who felt themselves helpless to deal with adversity referred to their elders, according to the TAT stories. However, even during that period they seemed aware that their elders could not successfully overcome the adversity either. Their stories in the years since then indicate that few if any problems can be taken to authority figures for successful solution. By 1973 they, along with their Catholic age peers, became obsessed with a passion for personally attempting to right the wrongs they had experienced; to do so meant injuring, killing, or destroying other people and places. This pattern may be a product of the fact that the 8-year-olds who in 1971 were obsessed with death and destruction and were feeling helpless and afraid by 1975 were among the older segment of the sample and had grown into adolescence with the conviction that death and destruction were constraints and that being afraid is commonplace. This pattern was undoubtedly exacerbated when they were lifted and beaten by soldiers—supposedly the representatives of authority and justice; attacked by older members of the paramilitary groups for minor infractions of discipline; or experienced first-hand the death or crippling of a close relative or friend. In addition, both groups of children see themselves as members of minority groups that are targets of strong prejudice, and both groups—the entire population of Northern Ireland—must be examined through the perspective of disadvantaged minority groups.

Since the historical events predisposing a violent recourse are usually well under way before a child is of an age to comprehend them, we may suppose that these events are acting on the child long before there is any possibility of his or her acting on them. Thus a generation or several generations are processed into a scheme of reacting and coping in certain psychological, social, and political ways. Clinical studies of children growing up in extreme stress strongly indicate that these young victims of a traumatic, violent event develop a kind of psycho-numbing that permeates their lifetimes. Furthermore, as my test results indicate, children growing up under conditions such as these may not achieve the level of moral development requisite to resolving legal and political conflicts nonviolently. Not surprisingly, moral development is further interrupted when the legal system is one imposed on an indigenous population by either a foreign nation or a governing system that has goals and objectives inconsistent with those of the nationals.

This research substantiates what common sense and experience tell us: that people who are badly treated or unjustly punished will seek revenge. In fact, even some whose punishment is appropriate will struggle to wreak vengeance on those who imposed that punishment. It should not be surprising then that young adolescents who have themselves been terrorized may later become terrorists and that, in a situation in which they are afforded a kind of sanction by their compatriots because of the actions of an unjust government, the resort to terror tactics becomes a way of life. A few highly publicized examples in the United States illustrate this point very vividly. Khalis, the Hanafi Muslim leader whose actions resulted in the 39-hour captivity of over 100 persons and the death and crippling of several others in Washington, D.C., during March 1977 was, a few years earlier, terrorized himself when members of his family were brutally murdered in their home. In that instance he extended his religious vendetta to scapegoat another beleaguered minority group— Jews. Donald De Freeze, later known as Cinque, of the Symbionese Liberation Army, had been a subject in aversive conditioning "experiments" in the Vacaville Medical Facility of the California Penal System. Not surprisingly, he and his band subjected the kidnapped heiress Patty Hearst to some makeshift variations of the same techniques. Just past adolescence herself, Patty Hearst was unable to withstand the ego assault; she was terrorized and converted to terrorism. Her experience epitomizes the dynamic relationship between terrorization and the terrorist particularly because of its combination of crucial factors: i.e., psychological and psychotechnological forces operating in a social context that exacerbates stress through denial of institutional supports and prolonged threat to life, bodily integrity, and identity presented in a circumstance of powerlessness, helplessness, and unpredictability to victims with varying levels of strength. These factors have even more significance when the victims or witnesses are children or adolescents whose ego capacity is not yet developed enough to withstand such a series of shocks. Further research in this area should not only attempt to add to the slowly growing fund of data but should also identify and examine the amelioration factors in the various settings. If the same evaluative instruments can be used as soon after trauma as possible and then again at appropriate intervals, data will be comparable and hence more useful. The usefulness of this research is inadequately appreciated, in view of the researcher's ultimate goal: to increase our understanding of how to intervene in the sequence that too often dooms innocent victims to become victimizers themselves.

Notes

1. Lazarus, R.: "The concepts of stress and disease." In Levi, L. (ed.): *Society, stress and disease*. New York, London: Oxford University Press, 1971.

2. Milgram, S.: "Some conditions of obedience and disobedience to authority." *International Journal of Psychiatry*. 6:259–276, 1968.

3. Haney, C.; Banks, C.; and Zimbardo, P.: "A study of prisoners and guards in a simulated prison." *Naval Research Reviews*. Washington, D.C.: Office of Naval Research, Department of the Navy, pp. 1–17, September 1973.

4. Hinkle, L. E., Jr., and Wolff, H. G.: "Communist interrogation and indoctrination of the enemies of the state." *Archives of Neurological Psychiatry*. 76:115–174, 1956.

5. Schein, E. H.: "Man against man: brainwashing." *Corrective Psychiatry and Journal of Social Therapy*. 8:90–97, 1962.

6. Strassman, H. D.; Thaler, M.; and Schein, E. H.: "A prisoner of war syn-

drome: Apathy as a reaction to severe stress." *American Journal of Psychiatry.* 112:908–1003, 1956.

7. Lifton, R. J.: *Thought reform and the psychology of totalism: A study of "brainwashing" in China.* New York: W. W. Norton Co., 1963.

8. Eitinger, L.: *Concentration camp survivors in Norway and Israel.* Oslo, Norway: Universities Press, 1964.

9. Chodoff, P.: "Effects of extreme coercive and oppressive forces: Brainwashing and concentration camps." *American Handbook of Psychiatry III.* New York: Basic Books, 1956.

10. Nathan, T. S.; Eitinger, L.; and Winsik, H. L.: "A psychiatric study of survivors of the Nazi Holocaust." *Israel Annals of Psychiatry and Related Disciplines,* 2, 1964.

11. David, J.: "Pathology of the captivity of the prisoners of World War II." Works of the International Medical Conference, Brussels, 1962, published as *Ex-prisoners of War,* Paris, 1962.

12. Trautman, E. C.: "Fear and panic in Nazi concentration camps." *International Journal of Social Psychiatry.* 10:134–141, 1954.

13. Vasquez, A., and Ryczynzki, K.: "Ethical questions submitted to psychologists on torture techniques used in Chile." Presentation at American Psychiatric Association, Miami Beach, Florida, 1976.

14. Albuquerque, A., and Fields, R.: "Portuguese torture victims." Unpublished paper, 1974.

15. Eitinger, L., and Strøm, A.: *Mortality and morbidity after excessive stress.* New York: Humanities Press, 1973.

16. Jacobson, S.: "Leadership patterns and stress adaptations among hostages in three terrorist captured places." Presented at the International Conference on Psychological Stress and Adjustment in Time of War and Peace, Tel Aviv, Israel, 1975.

17. Ayalon, O.: "Coping with terrorism: The Israeli case." In Meichenbaum, D. and M. Jahmko (eds.): *Stress prevention and management: A cognitive-behavioral approach.* New York: Plenum Press, 1980.

18. Belz, M.; Parker, E. Z.; Sank, L. I.; et al.: "Is there a treatment for terror?" *Psychology Today.* 11(5):54–56 and 108–112, October 1977.

19. Fields, R. M.: *A society on the run: A psychology of Northern Ireland.* Hammondsworth, England: Penguin Ltd., 1973.

20. Fields, R. M.: *Society under siege.* Philadelphia: Temple University Press, 1976.

21. Official U.K. Statistics, obtained through Institute for Peace and Conflict Research, University of Lancaster, U.K.

22. Arnold, M. B.: *Story sequence analysis.* New York: Columbia University Press, 1961.

23. Tapp, J. L., and Kohlberg, L.: "Developing senses of law and legal justice." *The Journal of Social Issues.* 27(2)65–91, 1971.

8

The Stockholm Syndrome: Law Enforcement Policy and Hostage Behavior

Thomas Strentz

The Bank Robbery

At 10:15 A.M. on Thursday, August 23, 1973, the quiet morning routine of the Sveriges Kreditbank in Stockholm, Sweden, was destroyed by the clatter of a submachine gun. As clouds of plaster and heaps of shattered glass settled around the 60 stunned occupants, a heavily armed lone gunman called out in English, "the party has just begun."[1]

The "party" was to continue for 131 hours, permanently affecting the lives of four young hostages and giving birth, in name at least, to a psychological phenomenon subsequently called the "Stockholm Syndrome." During the 131 hours from 10:15 A.M. on August 23 until 9:00 P.M. on August 28, four employees of the Sveriges Kreditbank were held hostage. They were Elizabeth Oldgren, age 21, then an employee of fourteen months working as a cashier in foreign exchange, now a nurse; Kristin Ehnmark, age 23, then a bank stenographer in the loan department, today a social worker; Brigitta Lundblad, age 31, an employee of the bank; and Sven Safstrom, age 25, a new employee who today works for the National Government of Sweden.[2] They were held by a 32 year-old thief, burglar, and prison escapee named Jan-Erik Olsson. Their jail was an 11- by 47-foot carpeted bank vault that they came to share with another criminal and former cellmate of Olsson—Clark Olofsson, age 26. Olofsson joined the group only after Olsson demanded his release from the Norrkoping Penitentiary.[3]

This particular hostage situation gained long-lasting notoriety primarily because the broadcast media exploited the fears of the victims as well as the sequence of events. Contrary to what had been expected, it was found that the victims feared the *police* more than they feared the robbers. In a telephone call to Prime Minister Olaf Palme, one of the hostages expressed these typical feelings of the group when she said, "The robbers are protecting us from the police." Upon release other hostages puzzled over their feelings: "Why don't we hate the robbers?"[4]

For weeks after this incident, under the care of psychiatrists, some of the hostages experienced the paradox of nightmares over the possible escape of the jailed subjects and yet felt no hatred for their captors. In fact, they described feeling that the subjects had given them their lives back and that they were emotionally indebted to their captors for this generosity.

The Phenomenon

The Stockholm Syndrome seems to be an automatic, often unconscious, emotional response to the trauma of becoming a victim. Although some victims may think it through, this is not a rational choice by a victim who decides consciously that the most advantageous behavior in this predicament is to befriend his captor. The syndrome has been observed around the world and includes a high level of stress, as participants are cast together in a life-threatening environment where each must achieve new levels of adaptation to stay alive. This phenomenon affects both the hostages and the hostage-taker. The positive emotional bond, born in, or perhaps because of, the stress of the siege serves to unite its victims against all outsiders. A philosophy of "it's us against them" seems to develop. To date there is no evidence to indicate how long the syndrome lasts. Like the automatic reflex action of the knee, the bond seems to be beyond the control of the victim or the subject. The Stockholm Syndrome generally consists of three phases: positive feelings of the hostages toward their captors, negative feelings of the hostages toward the police or other government authorities, and reciprocation of the positive feelings by the captors. Although this relationship is new in the experience of law enforcement officers, the psychological community has long been aware of the use of an emotional bond as a coping mechanism by people under stress.

In the structural theory of Sigmund Freud, the ego, governed by the reality principle, assumes an "executive" function. In doing so the ego mediates between the demands of reality, the instinctual demands of the id, and the moralistic dictates of the superego. The ego in a healthy personality is dynamic and resourceful; it utilizes, as needed, a host of psychological defense mechanisms that Anna Freud summarized and described in *The Ego and the Mechanisms of Defense*.[5] The number of defense mechanisms varies depending upon the author. However, all serve the same basic purpose—to protect the self from hurt and disorganization.[6] When the self is threatened, the ego must adapt under a great deal of stress. The ego enables the personality to continue to function even during the most painful experiences—such as being taken hostage by an armed, anxious stranger. The hostage wants to survive, and the healthy ego is seeking a means to achieve survival.[7] The defense mechanisms utilized most frequently by the hostages I have interviewed have been regressive, involving a return to a less mature and often unrealistic level of experience and behavior.

Several theories have been advanced in an attempt to explain the observable symptoms that law enforcement professionals and members of the psychiatric community have come to call the Stockholm Syndrome. One of the earliest concepts formulated to explain it involved the phenomenon of "identification with the aggressor" that Anna Freud described. This type of identification is summoned by the ego to protect itself against authority figures who have generated anxiety.[8] The purpose of this type of identification is to enable the ego to avoid the wrath and potential punishment of the enemy. The hostage identifies out of fear rather than out of love.[9] It would appear that the healthy ego evaluates the situation and selects from its arsenal of defenses a mechanism that had served it best in the past during similar trauma.

Related to identification is the defense mechanism known as "introjection." Like identification, this mechanism is often associated with imitative learning in which young people take on the admired or wanted characteristics of parents or other models. A person may also introject the values and norms of others as their own even when they are contrary to their previous assumptions. This occurs when people adopt the values and beliefs of a new government to avoid social retaliation and punishment, following the principle, "If you can't beat 'em, join 'em."[10] Identification with the aggressor and the introjection of alien values have been used to explain the behavior of some people in Nazi concentration camps who radically altered their norms under those terrible circumstances.[11]

Though identification with the aggressor is an attractive explanation for the Stockholm Syndrome, and may indeed be a factor in some hostage situations, it does not totally explain the phenomenon. Identification with the aggressor is commonly associated with the period at around age 5 when children begin the resolution of the Oedipal complex, give up the dream of being an adult, and begin to work on the reality of growing up. This is often accompanied by identification with the parent of the same sex, which is generally healthy. When this parent is abusive, however, we see the identification serving multiple purposes, including protection, and some of the circumstances of the Stockholm Syndrome are reproduced.

I view the Stockholm Syndrome as a regression to a more elementary level of development than is seen in the 5-year-old who identifies with a same-sex parent. The 5-year-old is able to feed himself, speak for himself, and has locomotion. The hostage is more like the infant who must cry for food, cannot speak, and may be bound and immobile. Like the infant, the hostage is in a state of extreme dependency and fright. In addition, like the infant or extremely young child, the hostage is terrified of the outside world and of the prospect of separation from the "parent."

A normal infant is blessed with a mother figure who sees to his needs. As these needs are satisfactorily met by the mother figure, the child begins to love this person who is protecting him from the outside world. The adult is capable of caring and leading the infant out of dependency and fear. So it is with the hostage—his every breath a gift from the subject. He is now as dependent as he was as an infant; the controlling, all-powerful adult is again present; the outside world is threatening once again. The weapons that the police have deployed against the subject are also, in the mind of the hostage, deployed against him. Once again he is dependent, perhaps on the brink of death. Once again there is a powerful authority figure who can help. So the behavior that worked for the dependent infant surfaces again as a means to survival.

Domestic Hostage Situations

Since 1973 local law enforcement agencies have been faced with many hostage situations. The subject-hostage bond is not always formed, yet case studies show that it frequently is a significant factor. As such, the Stockholm Syndrome should be kept in mind by police when they face such a situation, plan an attack, debrief former hostages, and certainly when the subjects are prosecuted.

Hostage situations seem to be on the increase. Today, more than ever, police can respond to armed robberies in progress in a fraction of the time it took a few years ago. Unfortunately, this increased skill in incident response promotes a perpetrator's need to take hostages. In the past, the armed robber was frequently gone before the employees felt safe enough to sound the alarm; today, silent alarms are triggered automatically. Computerized patrol practices place police units in areas where they are more likely, statistically, to encounter an armed robbery. An analysis of past armed robberies dictates placement of patrol units to counter future attempts. Progress in one phase of law enforcement thus has created new demands in another.

The vast majority of these domestic hostage incidents are accidental. In cases such as these, it is likely that the robber did not plan to take hostages. However, if the police arrive sooner than anticipated, as a new form of flight—a method of escape—the suddenly trapped armed robber takes a hostage so he can bargain his way out.

In his desperation the armed robber compounds his crime with kidnapping and assault charges. These considerations are initially minimal to him. His emotions are running high; he wants to buy time; and in this he succeeds. The armed robber or other criminal hostage-taker often has a prior history of felony arrests. Therefore, although desperate, he is not ignorant or inexperienced in the ways of the criminal justice system, and eventually realizes the consequences of his new role.

The trapped subject is outgunned and outnumbered, and with each fleeting moment his situation becomes less tenable. Perhaps he takes hostages as a desperate offensive act, one of the few offensive acts available to him in his increasingly defensive position. Whatever his motivation, the subject is now linked with other individuals, usually strangers, who will come to sympathize and in some cases empathize with him in a manner now recognized and understood. The stranger— the victim—the law-abiding citizen—is forced into a life-and-death situation and is unprepared for this turn of events. Suddenly his routine world is turned around. The police, who should help, seem equally helpless. The hostage may feel that the police have let him down by allowing this to happen. It all seems so unreal.

Stages of Hostage Reaction

In the early development of a hostage incident certain stages of hostage reactions occur with regularity, in my experience. The vast majority of hostages share this sequence of emotional events: denial; delusion of reprieve; busy work; and taking stock. The alliance that forms between the hostages and the subject comes later. Anna Freud distinguished denial, which is a reaction to external danger, from repression, in which the ego is struggling with basically internal instinctual stimuli.[12] Denial is a primitive but effective psychological defense mechanism. There are times when the mind is so overloaded with trauma it cannot handle the situation. To survive, the mind reacts as if the traumatic incident is not happening. Former hostages have reported responding: "Oh no"; "No, not me"; "This must be a dream"; or "This is not happening."[13]

Denial is but one stage of coping with the impossible turn of events. Each victim who copes effectively has a strong will to survive. One may deal with the stress by believing he is dreaming, that he will soon wake up and it will be over. Some deal with this stress by withdrawing through sleep; I have interviewed hostages who have slept for over forty-eight hours while captive. Some have fainted, although this is rare.

Some of the denial and repression of fear of the hostage-takers and the transfer of these feelings of fear to the police has a realistic basis. Research has shown that most hostages die or are injured during the police or military assault phase,[14] although this is not to say that the police killed them.

Frequently hostages gradually accept their situation, but find a safety valve in the thought that their fate is not fixed. They view their situation as temporary, and are sure that the police will come to their rescue. This gradual change from denial to delusions of reprieve reflects a growing acceptance of the facts. Although the victim accepts that he is a hostage, he believes that freedom will come soon.[15]

If freedom does not immediately relieve the stress, many hostages begin to engage in "busy work," work they feel comfortable doing. Some knit, some methodically count and recount windows or other hostages, and some reflect upon their past lives. I have never interviewed a former hostage who has not taken stock of his life and vowed to change for the better, thus attempting to take advantage of a second chance at life.

Time

Time is a factor in the development of the Stockholm Syndrome, and its passage can produce a positive or negative bond, depending on the interaction of the subjects and hostages. If the hostage-takers do not abuse their victims, hours spent together will most likely produce "positive" results. Time alone will not do so, but it may be the catalyst in nonabusive situations. In September 1976 when five Croatian hijackers took a Boeing 727 carrying ninety-five people on a transatlantic flight from New York to Paris, another case of the Stockholm Syndrome occurred. Attitudes toward the hijackers and their crime reflected the varying exposures of those involved. The hostages were released at intervals—the first group was released after a few hours of captivity; the second group after a day. The debriefing of the victims in this situation clearly indicated that the Stockholm Syndrome is not a magical phenomenon, but a logical outgrowth of positive human interaction.

TWA Flight 355, originally scheduled to fly from New York to Tucson, Arizona, via Chicago, on the evening of September 10, 1976, was diverted somewhere over western New York to Montreal, Canada, where additional fuel was added. The hijackers then travelled to Gander, Newfoundland, where thirty-four passengers deplaned to lighten the aircraft for its flight to Europe, via Keflavik, Iceland, with the remaining fifty-four passengers and a crew of seven. The subjects, primarily Julianna Eden Busic, selected passengers to deplane. She based her decision on age and family responsibilities. The remaining passengers, plus the crew of seven, were those who were single, married with no children, or who had volunteered to remain on board, like Bishop O'Rourke. After flying over London, the aircraft landed in Paris, where it was surrounded by the police and not allowed to depart. After thirteen hours the subjects surrendered to the French police. The episode lasted a total of twenty-five hours for most of the passengers and about three hours for those who had deplaned at Gander.[16]

During the months of September and October 1976, all but two of the hostages and all of the crew were interviewed. The initial hypothesis—before the interviews—was that those victims released after only a few hours would not express sympathy for the subjects while those released later would react positively towards them. In other words, time was viewed as the key factor.

This hypothesis was not proven. Instead, it seemed that the victims' attitudes toward the subjects varied from subject to subject and from victim to victim regardless of the amount of time they had spent as captives. Although this may seem illogical, interviews with the victims revealed understandable reasons. It was learned that those victims who had negative contact with the subjects did not evidence concern for them, regardless of time of release. Some of these victims had been physically abused by the subjects; they obviously did not like their abusers and advocated the maximum penalty be imposed.

Other victims slept on and off for two days. This could have been a form of denial, a desperate ego-defensive means of coping with an intolerable event.[17] These victims had minimal contact with the subjects and also advocated a maximum penalty. They may not have had distinctly negative contact, but they experienced no positive association. Their only contact with the subjects was on three occasions, when hostage-taker Mark Vlasic awakened them in Paris as he ordered all of the passengers into the center of the aircraft where he threatened to detonate the explosives unless the French government allowed them to depart.

The other extreme was evidenced by victims, regardless of time of release, who felt great sympathy for their abductors. They had positive contact with the subjects, which included discussing the hijackers' cause and understanding their motivation and suffering. Some of these victims told the press that they were going to take vacation time to attend the trial. Others began a defense fund for their former captors.

Some recommended defense counsel to the subjects and others refused to be interviewed by the law enforcement officers who took the subjects into custody.

Perhaps one of the most self-revealing descriptions of the Stockholm Syndrome was offered by one of these hijack victims: "After it was over and we were safe I recognized that they (the subjects) had put me through hell, and had caused my parents and fiancé a great deal of trauma. Yet, I was alive. I was alive because they had let me live. You know only a few people, if any, who hold your life in their hands and then give it back to you. After it was over, and we were safe and they were in handcuffs, I walked over to them and kissed each one of them and said, 'Thank you for giving me my life back.' I know how foolish it sounds, but that is how I felt."[16] Another hostage in this incident expressed the same feelings: "They didn't have anything (the bombs were fake), but they were really great guys, I really want to go to their trial."[18]

Despite all these positive expressions, the feeling of affection seems to be a mask for great inner turmoil. Most victims in the Croatian skyjacking, including those who felt considerable affection for the subjects, reported nightmares after the incident. These dreams expressed the fear that the subjects would escape from custody and recapture them. Similar findings have been reported by Ochberg[19] and by police officers involved in the original Stockholm incident.[20] The negative aspects of the hostage-takers are, of course, fully expressed in the reactions of others involved in the incident. In describing the same action of the Croatians, New York City Police Commissioner Michael Codd said in an interview, "What we have here is the work of madmen—murderers." The interview of the Commissioner followed an attempt to defuse a bomb left by the hijackers; the bomb killed one officer and seriously injured three others.[21]

The situation in 1973 in Stockholm was not unique. These same feelings were generated in the Croatian hijacking and more recently by the Japanese Red Army hijacking of JAL Flight 472 in September–October 1977,[22] as well as the hostage situation that took place at the German Consulate in Chicago in August 1978.[23]

Isolation

The Stockholm Syndrome relationship does not always develop, however. Sir Geoffrey Jackson, the British Ambassador to Uruguay, was abducted and held by the Tupamaro terrorists for 244 days. He remained in thought and in action the Ambassador, the Queen's representative, and so impressed his captors with his dignity that they were forced to regularly change his guards and isolate him for fear he might convince them that his cause was just and theirs foolish.[24] Others, such as the American agronomist, Dr. Claude Fly, held by the Tupamaros for 208 days in 1970, have also avoided identification with the abductor or his cause. Dr. Fly accomplished this by writing a 600-page autobiography and by developing a 50-page "Christian Checklist," in which he analyzed the New Testament. Like Sir Geoffrey Jackson, he was able to create his own world and insulate himself against the hostile pressures around him.[25] Persons of the stature of Dr. Fly and Sir Geoffrey Jackson have been able to influence their captors to the extent that the terrorist organizations found it necessary to remove the guards who were falling under their influence.[26] In these, and in most situations, the Stockholm Syndrome is a two-way street.

Most victims of terrorist or criminal abductors, however, are not individuals of the stature of Dr. Fly or Ambassador Jackson, and as such do not retain an aura of aloofness during their captivity. As yet, there is no identified single personality type more inclined to the Stockholm Syndrome. The victims do share some common experiences, though.

Positive Contact

The primary experience that the victims of the Stockholm Syndrome share is positive contact with the subject. The positive contact is determined by *lack* of negative experiences such as beatings, rapes, or physical abuse, rather than by actual, specific, positive acts on the part of the abductors. The few injured hostages who have evidenced the syndrome have been able to rationalize their abuse. They have convinced themselves that the abductor's show of force was necessary to take control of the situation, that perhaps their resistance precipitated the abductor's force. Self-blame on the part of the victim is very evident in these situations.

Stockholm Syndrome victims share a second common experience. They sense and identify with the human quality of their captors. At times this quality is more imagined than real, as the victims of Fred Carrasco learned in Texas in August 1974. On the afternoon of July 24, 1974, at the Texas Penitentiary in Huntsville, Fred Carrasco and two associates took approximately seventy hostages in the prison library. In the course of the eleven-day siege most of the hostages were released. However, the drama was played out on the steps of the library between 9:30 and 10:00 on the night of August 3, 1974. It was during this time that Carrasco executed the remaining hostages.[27] This execution took place in spite of his letters of affection to hostages who had been released earlier due to medical problems.[28]

Some hostages expressed sympathy for Carrasco.[29] A Texas Ranger who was at the scene and subsequently spoke to victims told me that there was evidence of the Stockholm Syndrome.[30] Although the hostages' emotions did not reflect the depth of those in Sweden a year before, the hostages admitted some affectionate feelings toward a person they thought they should hate. They saw their captor as a human being with problems similar to their own. Law enforcement has long recognized that the trapped armed robber believes he is a victim of the police. We now realize that the hostage tends to share his opinion.

When a robber is caught in a bank by quick police response, his dilemma is clear. He wants out with the money and his life. The police are preventing his escape by their presence and are demanding his surrender. The hostage, an innocent customer or employee of the bank, is also inside. His dilemma is similar to that of the robber—he wants to get out and cannot. He has seen the arrogant robber slowly become "a person" with a problem just like his own. The police on the outside correctly perceive the freedom of the hostages as the prerogative of the robber. However, the hostages perceive that the police weapons are pointed at them; the threat of tear gas makes them uncomfortable. The police insistence on the surrender of the subject is also keeping them hostage. Hostages begin to develop the idea that "if the police would go away, I could go home. If they would let him go, I would be free,"[23] and so the bond begins.

Reactions of the Hostage-Taker

As time passes and positive contact between the hostage and hostage-taker begins, the Stockholm Syndrome also begins to take its effects upon the subjects. This was evident at Entebbe in July 1976. During this incident there were major variations in the quality of interaction between the hostage-takers and the hostages. These ranged from relatively friendly conversations to sadistic taunting. During the final assault, one of the male terrorists, who had engaged in conversations with the hostages from Air France Flight 139, elected at the moment of attack to shoot at the Israeli commandos rather than to execute the hostages.[31] The same process was probably at work in the decision of the South Moluccan terrorists not to execute Gerard Vaders. After Vaders had told his fellow hostage, Prins, about the problems he was currently having in his marital relationship and with his daughter, the Moluccans could no longer see him as a faceless symbol to be executed. He was now a human being who might be spared. Tragically, the Moluccans selected another passenger, Bierling, and led him away to be executed before they had the opportunity to know him.

Most people cannot inflict pain on another unless their victim remains dehumanized. When the subject and his hostages are locked together in a vault, a building, a train, or an airplane, a process of humanization apparently does take place. When a person, a hostage, can build empathy while maintaining dignity, he or she can lessen the aggression of a captor.[32] The exception to this is the subject who can be characterized as having an antisocial personality. As Fred Carrasco demonstrated in August 1974, such hostage-takers experience little guilt and have an ability to abuse and even kill their captives if they feel this will be in their own interests. Fortunately, extreme cases of this type are in a minority, and in most situations the Stockholm Syndrome is a two-way street. With the passage of time and the occurrence of positive experiences, the victims' chances of survival increase. However, isolation of the victim precludes the formation of this positive bond.

In some hostage situations the victims either have been locked in another room or have been in the same room, hooded or tied, gagged, and forced to face the wall and away from the subject. This type of interaction occurred frequently during the Hanafi Muslim siege in Washington, D.C., in March 1977.[33] Consciously or unconsciously, the subject has dehumanized his hostage, thereby making it easier to kill him. As long as the hostage is isolated, time is not a factor. The Stockholm Syndrome will not be a force that may save the victim's life.

Hostage-Captor Interaction

In interviewing victims of the Hanafi Muslim siege, I observed that even though some of the hostages responded positively toward their captors, they did not necessarily evidence Stockholm Syndrome reactions toward all of the subjects. It was learned, as might be expected, that most of the victims reacted positively toward those subjects who had treated them, in the words of the victims, "fairly." Those hostages who gave glowing accounts of the gentlemanly conduct of some subjects did not generalize to all subjects. They evidenced dislike, even hatred, toward one hostage-taker whom they called "an animal."

A hypothetical question was posed to determine the depth of these victims' feelings toward their captors. Each former hostage was asked what he would do in the following situation: A person immediately recognizable as a law enforcement officer, armed with a shoulder weapon, orders him to lie down. At that same instant one of his former captors orders him to stand up. When asked what he would do, the response varied according to the identity of the captor giving the "order." If a captor who had treated him fairly were yelling "stand up," he would stand up. Conversely, if he thought it was the command of the subject who had verbally abused him, he would obey the law enforcement officer. This would indicate that the strength of the syndrome is considerable. Even in the face of an armed officer of the law, the former hostage would offer himself as a human shield for his captor. As absurd or illogical as this may seem to those who are not familiar with the Stockholm Syndrome, such behavior has been observed by law enforcement officers throughout the world and on many different occasions.[34]

Whether the incident is a bank robbery in Stockholm, Sweden, a hijacking of an American aircraft over western New York, a kidnapping in South America, or an attempted prison break in Texas, there are behavioral similarities despite geographic and motivational differences. In each situation a relationship, a healthy relationship (healthy because those involved were alive to talk about it), seems to develop within and between people caught in circumstances beyond their control and not of their making, a relationship that reflects the use of ego defense mechanisms by the hostage. This relationship seems to help victims cope with excessive stress and at the same time enables them to survive—a little worse for wear, but alive. The Stockholm Syndrome is not a magical relationship of blanket affection for the subject. This bond, although strong, does have its limits. It has logical limits. If a person is nice to another, a positive feeling toward him develops even if he is an armed robber, the hijacker of an aircraft, a kidnapper, or a prisoner attempting to escape.

The victim's need to survive is stronger than his impulse to hate the person who has created his dilemma. It is his ability to survive and to cope that has enabled man to advance to the top of the evolutionary ladder. His ego is functioning and has functioned well, performing its primary task of enabling the self to remain alive. At an unconscious level the ego has activated the proper defense mechanisms in the correct sequence—denial, regression, identification, or introjection to achieve survival. The Stockholm Syndrome is merely another example of the ability of the healthy ego to cope and adjust to difficult stress brought about by a traumatic situation.

The application for law enforcement is clear, although it does involve a tradeoff. The priority in dealing with hostage situations is the survival of all participants. This means the survival of the hostage, the crowd that has gathered, the police officers, and the subject. To accomplish this end, various police procedures have been instituted. Inner and outer perimeters are well-recognized procedures designed to keep crowds at a safe distance. Police training, discipline, and proper equipment save officers' lives. The development of the Stockholm Syndrome may save the life of the captor as well as the hostage. The life of the captor is usually preserved, because it is highly unlikely that police will use deadly force unless the subject makes a precipitous move. The life of the hostage may also be saved by the Stockholm Syndrome: the experience of positive contact, thus setting the stage for regression, identification, or introjection on the part of all those involved in the siege. The subject is less likely to injure a hostage he has come to know and, on occasion, to love.[35]

It is suggested that the Stockholm Syndrome can be fostered while negotiating with the subject by asking him to allow the hostage to talk on the telephone, by asking him to check on the health of a hostage, or by discussing with him the family responsibilities of the hostages. Any action the negotiator can take to emphasize the hostages' human qualities to the subject should be considered by the negotiator.

The police negotiator must pay a personal price for this induced relationship. Hostages will curse him as they did in Stockholm in August 1973. They will call the police cowards and actively side with the subject in trying to achieve a solution to their plight, a solution not necessarily in their own best interests or in the best interests of the community.

Unfortunately, it may not end there. Victims of the Stockholm Syndrome may remain hostile toward the police after the siege has ended. The "original" victims in Stockholm still visit their abductors, and one former hostage has been engaged to Olofsson.[36] Some American victims visit their former captors in jail.[37] Others, such as some of the hostages in the Croatian skyjacking of TWA Flight 355 in 1976, have begun legal defense funds for some of their jailed captors.[16] A hostile hostage is the price that law enforcement must pay for a living hostage. Anti–law enforcement feelings are not new to the police. But this may be the first time it has been suggested that law enforcement seek to encourage hostility, hostility from people whose lives law enforcement has mustered its resources to save. However, a human life is an irreplaceable treasure and worth some hostility. A poor or hostile witness for the prosecution is a small price to pay for this life.

Notes

1. Lang, D.: "A Reporter at Large." *The New Yorker*, November 1974, p. 56.
2. Interviews by author with Stockholm, Sweden, police officers, Quantico, Virginia, 22 March 1978.
3. Interviews by author with Stockholm, Sweden, police officers, Quantico, Virginia, 8 November 1978.
4. Lang, D.: *op. cit.*, p. 118.

5. Freud, A.: *The Ego and the Mechanisms of Defense*. New York: International University Press, 1974, p. 42.

6. Coleman, J. C.: *Abnormal Psychology and Modern Life*. 5th ed. Glenview, Illinois: Scott Foresman Company, 1972, p. 122.

7. Bellak, L.; Hurvich, M.; and Gediman, H. K.: *Ego Functions in Schizophrenics, Neurotics and Normals*. New York: John Wiley and Sons, 1973, p. 51.

8. Freud, A.: *op. cit.*, p. 120.

9. Hall, C. S.: *A Primer of Freudian Psychology*. New York: The World Publishing Company, 1954, p. 78.

10. Coleman, J. C.: *op. cit.*, p. 129.

11. Bluhm, H. O.: "How did they survive? Mechanisms of defense in Nazi concentration camps." *American Journal of Psychotherapy* 2:205, 1948.

12. Freud, A.: *op. cit.*, p. 109.

13. Jenkins, B. M.; Johnson, J.; and Ronfeldt, D.: *Numbered Lives: Some Statistical Observations From Seventy-Seven International Hostage Episodes*. Santa Monica: The Rand Corporation, 1977, p. 18.

14. Jenkins, B. M.; Johnson, J.; and Ronfeldt, D.: *op. cit.*, p. 25.

15. U. S. Congress, Senate Committee on the Judiciary: *Terrorist Activity: Hostage Defense Measures*. Hearings Before a Subcommittee To Investigate the Administration of the Internal Security Act and Other Internal Security Laws, Part 5. 94th Congress, First Session, 1975, p. 265.

16. Interview by author with victims of the hijacking of TWA Flight #355 in New York City, Chicago, Illinois, and Tucson, Arizona, 1976.

17. Laughlin, H. P.: *The Ego and Its Defenses*. New York: Appleton-Century-Crofts, 1970, p. 57.

18. Alpern, D. M.: "A Skyjacking For Croatia." *Newsweek*, 20 September 1976, p. 25.

19. Ochberg, F. M.: "The victim of terrorism: Psychiatric considerations." *Terrorism, An International Journal* 1(2):151, 1978.

20. Interviews by author with police officers in Stockholm, Sweden, 22 March 1978.

21. "Skyjackers Are Charged With Murder." *The New York Times*, 12 September 1976, p. 3.

22. Interviews by author with American victims of hijacking of JAL Flight #472 in Los Angeles, San Francisco, and Tokyo, 1977.

23. Interviews by author with victims of hostage situation, German Consulate, Chicago, Illinois, 19 August 1978.

24. Jackson, Sir Geoffrey: *Surviving the Long Night*. New York: Vanguard, 1973, p. 49.

25. Fly, C. L.: *No Hope But God*. New York: Hawthorn, 1973, pp. 151–220. This book by Dr. Fly provides a more detailed discussion of how he achieved his particular psychological adjustment.

26. U.S. Congress, Senate Committee on the Judiciary: *op. cit.* Testimony by Brooks McClure, p. 267.

27. "Murder-Suicide Found In Huntsville Case." *Houston Post*, 4 September 1974, pp. 1–2.

28. House, A.: *The Carrasco Tragedy*. Waco, Tex.: Texian Press, 1975, pp. 104–107.

29. Cooper, L.: "Hostage Freed by Carrasco Aided Prison Officials in Assault Plan." *Houston Chronicle*, 5 August 1974, p. 4.

30. Interview by author with Texas Ranger Captain G. W. Burks, Austin, Texas, December 1975.

31. Stevenson, W.: *90 Minutes at Entebbe*. New York: Bantam Books, 1976, p. 116.

32. Aronson, E.: *Social Animal*. San Francisco: W. H. Freeman, 1972, pp. 168–169.

33. Interview by author with victims of Hanafi Muslim siege, Washington, D.C., March 1977.

34. This was observed as well in the hijacking of a Philippine Airlines Flight on 9/17/78; during a hostage situation in Oceanside, California, 2/3/75; during an aborted bank robbery in Toronto, Canada, in November 1977; and during a hostage situation that grew out of an aborted bank robbery in New York City in August 1976, that was later made into a movie entitled "Dog Day Afternoon."

35. Aronson, E.: *op. cit.*, p. 168.

36. "Swedish Robin Hood." *The Washington Post, Parade Magazine* supplement, 14 November 1976.

37. This was evident during the hostage situations in Cleveland, Ohio, on 29 October 1975, and in Chicago, Illinois, 18 August 1978.

9
Interactions of
Law Enforcement and
Behavioral Science Personnel

Conrad V. Hassel

The police service has always reflected the most entrenched American middle-class values and has, therefore, faced criticism and attack from those who represent other values. This phenomenon was particularly noticeable during the campus demonstrations of the 1960s when police were often the main targets of student demonstrators and radical groups. During the resulting confrontations, however, particularly those before the television camera, some commentators accused the police of over-reacting to either newsmen or demonstrators. As a result, it became fashionable in many circles to describe the police as brutal and op-pressive.

Some of those engaged in critical comment on the police happened to be behaviorists, sociologists, or others in the academic world, but many had no knowledge of the sometimes tremendous stresses and even the basic problems that law enforcement officers were facing. During the 1960s and early 1970s, governmental studies and professorial treatises were highly critical of police action and the police community generally. Feelings between police and behaviorists, never very positive, became in-creasingly hostile and intense. Any mutual animosity, however, cannot be placed solely at the door of the behaviorist, because some persons in law enforcement have always been suspicious of behavioral scientists.

Attempts since the mid-nineteenth century to explain crime and criminals in medical, behavioral, and social terms have met with little in-terest from law enforcement personnel. Efforts to explain and understand criminal behavior found no sympathy among officers exposed to the un-fortunate victims of crimes and the suffering brought about by appar-ently senseless acts of violence. Some officers felt that behavioral scien-tists were basically on the side of the criminal element and were willing to forgive almost any crime if it could be shown that the criminal was in some way deprived in childhood. Many police officers were brought up in the same conditions of poverty and deprivation as those they dealt with on the street. They were, and largely still are, quite resistant to some of the sociological and behavioral views expressed by a small segment of the behavioral science community. The task of overcoming the gulf between the two types of professions is currently proceeding with encouraging speed, but much remains to be done. This chapter describes briefly how recent attempts at collaboration in the area of police stress have led to a readiness and an ability to work together fruitfully and harmoniously on the problem of hostage negotiations.

The Recognition and Treatment of Police Stress

Police were struggling with the concept of stress long before there was any thought of developing domestic programs to deal with potential hostage situations. Several departments were paying close attention to the particular stresses under which a police officer works. Like an aircraft controller, he may undergo hours of boredom and moments of panic. He may also suffer a kind of culture shock when the reality of his work experience matches neither his expectations nor his ideals. Particularly vulnerable to this culture shock is the young, idealistic policeman who, immediately after training, is placed in a high crime area where his full set of rather stringent middle-class values does not seem to apply. He sees almost complete contempt for the rules by which he lives and works. At first the officer looks at this new environment optimistically and attempts to bring some understanding and friendliness to his contacts with people on the beat. Later he sees his efforts are regarded as naive by the community, and he may be ridiculed or held up to contempt not only by the community, but by some fellow officers for being a "social worker" rather than a police officer. His entire attitude may change to an extremely hard-line view of the community, full of suspicion and mistrust.

Normally this phenomenon lasts for two or three years until the policeman regains his equilibrium. The best resolution occurs when the officer starts to take a more balanced view of the community in which he is placed. The stresses from this culture shock, as well as the shift work and various peer pressures, put a severe strain on the officer's family life that can lead to divorce, heavy drinking, or other family and social maladjustments.

To deal with this stress, police departments have hired psychologists to counsel those with stress-related problems and, whenever possible, to eliminate some of the causes of this stress. It is a particularly difficult role; there is a conflict between the therapist-patient relationship and the screening function within the police department. It may be damaging to the psychological health of a police officer to recommend to the Chief of Police that he be relieved of street duty for a time, even though it may be necessary to keep the officer from overreacting in a street situation, causing death or injury to himself and someone else. As a result of this double bind, police are often reluctant to consult with the department psychologist, feeling that their careers might be damaged or that their fellow officers will think they are unfit to continue their role as "street cops." Use of a departmental psychologist is a highly delicate and sophisticated management problem. Police management, the police psychologist, and the officer himself must understand that the psychologist is a resource person for the troubled officer.

Some departments prefer to use staff counselors who are sworn police officers with advanced degrees in psychology and, usually, considerable police experience. This method tends to diminish the barriers often faced by the police psychologist who has had no experience in police work. Many officers feel that anyone who has not experienced the actual stress of police work on the street is really not in a position to understand the problems of the job.

Very few departments, however, are fortunate enough to have former police officers who have gone on to become psychologists or psychiatrists. Even then, suspicion is not completely overcome. The psychologist, whether a police officer or not, still has a duty to the department and to the community; he is still in the position to relieve an officer of his present assignment or suggest transfer to other duties.

The stigma of consulting a psychiatrist or psychologist still exists within the larger community and the same reluctance is reflected within the police community. Even so, efforts to use staff psychologists more effectively are continuing and improving. As more and more police officers begin duty with higher degrees of education, the real necessity for this type of service is being accepted and recognized. The responsibility for its success still rests heavily with police management. When mental health professionals have had the opportunity to demonstrate their value, however, they have become an inseparable part of the law enforcement system.

Use of Behavioral Scientists in Hostage Negotiation

The growing appreciation of the dangers of police stress and the grudging acceptance of some police administrators that psychiatrists and psychologists could be helpful allies has dispelled much of the suspicion between the two groups. Working together on outside problems, however, used to be an unlikely prospect. The idea of real collaboration has come about only in an atmosphere of shock and apprehension.

The televising of the Munich Olympics tragedy, when several Israeli athletes were abducted and killed, brought the problem of terrorism before the eyes of the entire world. It was only then that police began to think seriously of the possibility of similar incidents occurring here in the United States. The New York City Police Department (NYCPD) immediately began to plan for such events. They used the considerable talents of one of their policemen, Harvey Schlossberg, who also holds a Ph.D. in psychology, to set up a hostage negotiation program for the NYCPD, and from his seminal work in this area police departments around the country developed similar techniques. The success of such techniques is reflected in the record of NYCPD Captain Frank Bolz, who is currently in command of the Hostage Negotiation Squad in that city. He has successfully negotiated hundreds of hostage situations without loss of life using the basic techniques developed by the NYCPD.

In view of their recognized contributions to the study and amelioration of police stress, behavioral scientists have been welcomed into this new area of police work and have already had a considerable impact on new programs. Psychological and sociological thinking that would have been soundly rejected before has become invaluable in this new endeavor. Using basic psychological theory and an understanding of the sociological factors within a particular community that might affect a hostage situation, the police community, especially in the United States, has been eminently successful in defusing potentially disastrous situations.

Although to date the United States has not had to deal with the problem of terrorism at the same level as the Western European nations, the basic groundwork in the area of hostage negotiatons has been laid should terrorism escalate in this country. So far, the most serious terrorist incident to occur in the United States has been the Hanafi Muslim takeover of three buildings in downtown Washington, D.C., in 1977. In that case, the cool-headedness and psychological awareness of the Washington, D.C., Metropolitan Police Department, especially former Chief of Police Maurice Cullinane and Assistant Chief Robert Rabe, were major factors in the resolution of the incident. The police showed an ability to wait out the hostage-takers even under strong provocation. They used sophisticated tactics of delay and negotiation and, with the help of three Middle East Ambassadors, defused the situation with the loss of only one life. It was psychological sophistication, effective use of time, and emphasis on negotiation rather than force that brought this episode to a relatively successful conclusion.

Although it was perhaps the most spectacular incident in recent memory, this kind of hostage incident has by no means been an isolated one. Police officers have been dealing for years with trapped armed robbers who have used hostage-taking as a method of escape. The officers' expertise is increasing because of the education and training currently available in this area. Through the help of behavioral specialists, such training is becoming more and more sophisticated and the concept of hostage negotiation is being recognized and accepted by the police community. There is a growing readiness among police as well as federal agencies to learn techniques of hostage negotiation. Groups of local and state police and federal employees now take courses at the FBI Academy in Quantico, where they study with psychiatrists, sociologists, and other experts in the behavioral sciences. Similar courses are available in various parts of the country, such as excellent seminars sponsored by state police units.

There are now two recognized major themes in embarking on negotiations in a hostage situation. First, the psychological theory applied when negotiating with the trapped criminal or the mentally ill person is extremely similar to the theory used with a sophisticated terrorist group. Consequently the courses in hostage negotiation just described teach techniques that are constantly in use. Second, the stages of a hostage siege situation appear to coincide with the normal physical reaction to situations eliciting stress or panic. Time, then, is the most important factor in the beginning. The aim of the initial negotiation is to reduce the stress on the hostage-takers. Their rational faculties must be given a chance to gain preeminence over the first panic reaction. The most dangerous period of time during any hostage negotiation situation is usually the first ten minutes; this is when the hostage-takers appear to be most dangerous and their stress level is the highest. If the first phase can be traversed and communications established, chances of a successful outcome, in which all persons held hostage and the hostage-taker himself are recovered unharmed, are extremely good.

As time passes, the human body, as well as the human psyche, tends eventually to wear down. This wearing down affects the firm resolve of even the most dedicated terrorist. Admittedly, the fanatical terrorist group presents a situation that is much more difficult to defuse; experienced police know it will take much longer to bring about their surrender than that of the ordinary criminal hostage-taker. Even so, techniques taught by behavioral scientists to police negotiators have been of critical importance in bringing about eventual surrender. These behavioral concepts applied by trained hostage-negotiators have saved many lives. Seeing these visible successes, the police officer and administrator is able to appreciate the value of behavioral techniques and, therefore, the value of the behavioral scientist.

In some foreign countries, most notably the Netherlands, behaviorists have been used as actual negotiators in terrorist hostage situations. Dr. Dick Mulder (a psychiatrist), for instance, played a central negotiating role during the Moluccan train sieges. However, it is generally believed in the United States and in the United Kingdom that the behavioral scientist should not be the negotiator. There is a particular kind of expertise needed to deal with criminals; this expertise exists to a much greater degree within the police community than it does within the realm of the psychiatrist or psychologist. Part of this expertise consists of a familiarity with dangerous persons and situations, although not an enjoyment of them. In this perspective, a case can be made for using seasoned police officers as negotiators.

As part of the negotiating team, however, a psychiatrist, psychologist, or other behavioral scientist can provide critical assistance to the negotiator and to the overall command structure. The behavioral scientist can point out not only the nuances in mood—the emotional highs and lows of the hostage-taker—but also the psychological implications of such changes. If the behaviorist has access to psychiatric records on the hostage-taker and some of the hostages, he can interpret them for the police negotiator and the command. These records have a potentially important role in the decision-making procedure in any siege situation. In addition, the psychiatrist-psychologist, knowing something about the hostages, might be able to predict and interpret some of their reactions, both during and after the incident. He can also serve as an extremely effective support and resource person for the negotiator. His presence, advice, and encouragement may also help the negotiator deal with his own stress during a time when human lives hang in the balance.

Although the rise in terrorism and the increasing willingness to take hostages are deplorable trends, they have had the effect of bringing the disciplines of law enforcement and behavioral science much closer. Cooperation has educated both communities to the problems of the other and created an appreciation and respect for each other's capabilities.

Research and collaboration between the two fields is by now well established. The FBI has established within its Training Division a Special Operations and Research Unit that is observing terrorist and hostage incidents internationally and gathering information about both behavioral and tactical methodology. This unit performs writing and research functions in the area of terrorism and presents symposia and classroom instruction to local police, federal police, and military personnel on this topic. It has leaned heavily on behavioral science expertise, not only the knowledge of its own Special Agent staff members who hold advanced degrees in the behavioral sciences, but also on the knowledge and training of experts outside the police community. It is increasingly likely that law enforcement units such as the Special Operations and Research Unit will have a salutary effect in blending behavioral with law enforcement expertise.

10
Planning for the Future: Means and Ends

Frank M. Ochberg
David A. Soskis

Introduction

After all has been said, it remains for us to determine what should be done about the victims of terrorism. In the realm of terrorism a fairly stable, although not static, dynamic equilibrium has begun to form during the last few years. The initial wave of terrorist incidents in the early 1970s that left democratic countries stunned and found them unprepared has passed. As democratic states prepare counter-responses of their own via negotiation, Entebbe-type assaults, and co-opting the major grievances of the terrorist groups, the sense of a living counterpressure exerted by target states in the interest of their own survival begins to emerge. However, it is clear that terrorism is not going to go away, and in the case of those like the Palestinians or the Northern Irish, evidently this mode of conflict will be with us for a very long time. The debilitating effects of this activity can easily be seen by those who knew the Beirut or Belfast of ten years ago. Although no major government has yet fallen in the West, several have been significantly disrupted and the United States, with the Iranian incident, has joined the group of government victims. There are certainly no longer any illusions that terrorism is a phenomenon that can have a serious impact only in faraway places.

If we must plan for a future of which terrorism will be a part we should at least do so both rationally and realistically. The previous chapters of this volume have explored both concepts and past experiences that may form the basis for this planning as it relates to the victims of terrorism. A useful framework for discussing these efforts is the one that Gerald Caplan provided with the terms primary, secondary, and tertiary prevention. Primary prevention reduces the incidence of disorder in a community; secondary prevention reduces the duration of a significant number of those disorders that do occur; tertiary prevention reduces the impairment that may result from those disorders that do occur.[1] We shall discuss each of these in turn as it relates to programs for victims. For all three types of prevention it is especially important to keep in mind the relationship of means to ends, even more so when terrorism is involved. The relationship of means and ends is far from unidirectional and linear; means determine ends quite actively. Recent history has clearly shown that terrorist groups are decreasing their focus on political ideology and that a "terror for its own sake" subgroup is rising. Thus the means of the older generations of terrorists have been transformed into ends. In planning helping programs, the translation of "means" into "costs" (financial and human) clarifies that means are indeed used to evaluate and often to modify what were originally seen as ends. There is no planning strategy that avoids this interrelationship. The only safety that we can find is in jointly determining means and ends, and in being very specific in defining the values we are   for   and under what conditions they apply.

Primary Prevention

On the broadest level the primary prevention of terrorism consists of withdrawing its rewards and punishing its perpetrators promptly. Rewards may be withdrawn by refusing to pay or to publicize, by co-opting the demands of terrorist groups, and by attempting to explore and undermine the emotional wellsprings that feed movements based on revenge. Punishment, in the behavioral sense, works best when it is applied quickly and when it is not relied upon too heavily. One of the stated aims of many terrorist groups is to provoke a wave of repression and police-state tactics that will undermine people's trust in their government. We must not give in to this temptation and lose our values in their defense. Yet we must also be as clear as possible about the point at which we say, "No! Beyond this point we cannot go!" In the end this may come down to choosing which side we are on, and which we oppose; our choice of enemies, after all, says a great deal about who we are. We will not change human nature, which changes slowly, if at all. We can, however, change human behavior, choose the way we shall behave and articulate the limits of acceptable anti-terrorist tactics. The translation of these concepts into programs is beyond the scope of this volume but the specific tactics chosen will form a background of common knowledge shared by both hostages and hostage-takers in any terrorist incident.

All primary prevention programs for potential victims of terrorism start with the assumption that incidents will occur. If such programs are to be cost-effective they should probably be applied initially to those whose geographical or occupational situation puts them at high risk for becoming hostages. Some techniques that have already proved their usefulness can be given more general publicity and this list should grow as our experience increases. Government and private groups have made several significant efforts in this direction already. Recently, the State Department's eight-hour "counter-terrorism" seminar has been expanded to two days and now includes segments on psychological techniques for coping with hostage-taking incidents that have been drawn from analyses of contemporary experiences.

Dr. Jared Tinklenberg's chapter in this volume on "Coping with Terrorist Victimization" reviews some of the strategies that such programs should seek to enhance. To prepare someone for possible captivity by *Solution* political terrorists it is important to formulate cognitive strategies that bear on the experiences of unjustified suffering, willingness to suffer injury and death, and transcendental purpose that can match the dedication and fervor of religious or political extremists. Dr. Tinklenberg suggests that military training may help in this area. Although this training usually does force people to face issues of sacrifice, obedience, and violence, in its current form it seems to inadequately prepare the average soldier for terrorist captivity. Therefore, the concept of courage needs to be broadened to include the physical and mental endurance that helps people successfully handle prolonged captivity as well as the concentrated discipline that is so valuable in a brief military attack. In short, there must be articulated ways to be strong through and while waiting.

Traditionally, religious systems have provided the sustaining cognitive framework for such crises. Our long-standing commitment to the separation of church and state should not blind us to the resources that these traditional systems may offer to potential victims of terrorism. Recent hostages, including several of the American captives returning from Iran, have testified to the usefulness of these resources. We feel that any person who thinks he might possibly become a victim or hostage would do well to examine his personal and family religious beliefs and find out what his religion says in explanation and support of victim experiences. An obvious and valuable source for this kind of examination is the Book of Job, both in itself and through the efforts that scholars and literary figures throughout the ages have made to understand and interpret its message. Some people will be able to see hostage experiences as a time of testing, others will see them as a time of punishment for past misdeeds, and others will more or less successfully accept God's will or their own personal destinies.

These types of explanations are inherently very personal, and what works for one victim may be totally useless for another. The structure of many hostage incidents makes this kind of personal preparation even more important, since it is clear that potential hostages must be prepared for isolation or for confinement in small groups of strangers. Isolation far short of sensory deprivation can have major negative physical and psychological consequences to those accustomed to a more gregarious existence. This possibility of isolation makes it more important for potential victims to set their religious and ethical houses in order. In dealing with political or other ideologically motivated terrorists it is especially important to have a clear view of those sustaining principles that the victim himself feels are truly moral and thus related to intrinsic consequences. This is in contrast to actions and values that may be expressions of prudence, and thus related to extrinsic outcomes. One of the major weapons of captors, especially in prolonged captivity situations, is to extort or bribe captives to compromise their moral values and thus their self-esteem in the name of being "prudent" or "reasonable." When captivity is prolonged, maintaining self-esteem may be decisive in terms of psychological and physical survival. As Gerald Caplan has noted, "A clear and positive concept of his own enduring identity [is] a major fulcrum for the leverage efforts of an individual in pressing forward with problem-solving efforts in a situation of stress."[2]

Efforts for personal preparation should also include an understanding that highly stressful events will have different meanings for different individuals depending on their own past experiences. These experiences give a meaning to an event such as terrorist captivity that may interact with areas of vulnerability, conflict, or psychological "unfinished business" in the particular victim; the total reaction of the victim is thus a function of his own individuality. A good example of this process is what being a survivor meant to Gerard Vaders, which was clearly linked to two intense past experiences. The first was when he was arrested by the Nazis at age 17, placed briefly in a concentration camp, and released after he lied about his age. The second was during the war when a grenade landed at his feet but failed to explode. These events had a major impact on Vaders, both in terms of how he behaved during the Moluccan incident itself and how he felt about it later. These particular experiences, and therefore the specific context of personal meaning that grew out of them, were not shared with other hostages.

Preparation of the potential victim's inner environment should be accompanied by a thorough familiarization with the physical and cultural environment in which he or she will work, and with what is known about potential terrorist captors. This kind of specific, detailed cognitive preparation may go a long way toward helping a hostage make realistic and rational decisions about chances for escape, areas of personal vulnerability, and strengths of commitment in various dimensions. In addition, this kind of acquaintance can help diminish the sense of bewilderment and of dealing with the unknown that seems to have aggravated stress in hostage experiences.

In our view, former hostages should have a major role in the planning and execution of primary prevention programs relating to the minimization of hostage-related disorders. It is especially from those who have coped well with experiences as hostages and captives that we can learn the range of positive coping techniques that work best in these situations. Victims of analogous situations, such as POWs and victims of conventional violent crime, can also provide valuable insights into how people make the best of the worst. We feel that former hostages should be cast in the role of valuable advisors to experts, rather than being set up as experts themselves. This distinction is an important one, since the task of overall evaluation and planning requires that the experiences of individuals be integrated and the relevant aspects of each selected and blended into a coherent policy. Since former hostages are, correctly, highly invested in their own individual adaptations to their experiences, it is unfair to ask them to be too objective about what happened to them and how they dealt with it.

Despite these limitations, the experience of contemporary hostages provides important help to planners; it is even more valuable because of its specificity. An example was the crucial role that reading played for several of the American hostages held recently in Tehran. Dr. Robert I. Hauben, one of the psychiatrists who debriefed the hostages, commented that "one of the most important things that pulled them through was the library. The Iranians allowed the hostages to read and this alone sustained many of them. Richard Queen, who was released early . . . was allowed by the captors to be librarian for the group, and he told us there was a great run on books. And games. By keeping their minds alive, these people kept themselves alive."[3]

Other coping techniques, such as humor, that have gotten many people through extremely difficult situations are poorly taught by abstract principles and only come alive when concrete examples are given. Former CIA Agent John Downey, who spent twenty years in a Chinese prison after being shot down in 1962, explained his captivity by the comment that "I had a rather long run of bad luck."[4] Perspectives like these work for some better than others, and should ideally be "tried out" before an incident occurs.

One helpful technique for mastering coping skills and evaluating individual vulnerabilities during captivity is the use of simulations or "gaming" exercises. These have been used quite successfully to train hostage negotiators and may play a major role in reducing the shock of an actual terrorist incident. It is important to have these exercises as realistic as possible so that potential hostages can experience at least some of the emotions they will have to deal with during an actual incident. Techniques such as the evaluation of escape possibilities, the collection of data concerning captors, the "humanization" of the hostage to captors, and the use of special communication devices or codes are mastered most effectively in a training program that combines study with practice. Some coping techniques that have proved extremely useful to hostages may be difficult to teach even in a relatively realistic simulation, but examples should still be given to potential hostages. A good one is the use of fantasy, which has been extremely useful in facilitating adjustment to prolonged captivity, including that experienced by the American hostages in Iran. Potential hostages may be reassured by being prepared for the potential vividness and importance of dreams and fantasies so that they do not mistakenly identify their use as psychopathological.

The dissemination to the general public of some of these positive coping techiques can be and has been partially accomplished through the media. Several television programs portraying prisoners of war have focused on successful coping by prisoners, reactions of their families, and problems of readjustment. In addition to giving viewers a chance to wonder "what would I do?" these programs promote a needed shift of public attention from the harm-doers to the persons who have been injured. We discussed the importance of this shift in our previous chapter in this volume, "Concepts of Terrorist Victimization," in relation to Melvin Lerner's work on the "just world theory." Lerner found that people are less likely to unrealistically condemn the victim if they can identify with him in *any* way and more likely to condemn him if they identify with the harm-doer. Thus this type of public presentation may function directly in the primary prevention of post-hostage disorders. On a broader level of primary prevention, the portrayal of positive coping responses that do not involve violence or revenge may have some role in shaping future events.

Any realistic program of primary prevention should involve the preparation of family members along with that of the potential captive. Families of captives should think through for themselves what it would be like to have one of their members as a hostage and experience and work through some of the predictable feelings associated with this. Families should also identify in advance who will be called upon both within and without the family to perform various support roles and, significantly, who will need special support in such situations. Although it may seem morbid, it is worthwhile for families to put wills and trust funds in order when one or more members are entering a situation of potential terrorist captivity. Hostages have to process enough information that is relevant to their survival without also having to worry or feel guilty about financial arrangements for their families. In planning these and other programs of primary prevention, the goal is to balance the need to provide potential victims with useful information and experiences against the cost and emotional strain of such educational experiences. In general, we believe that the natural human tendency to avoid thinking about or preparing for unpleasant future events will help ensure that these kinds of preparatory activities will be adequately controlled.

Secondary Prevention

Once a terrorist incident has occurred, helping efforts must concentrate on reducing the harm that it causes. The first phase of these efforts includes the attempt to resolve the situation itself as quickly as possible with a minimum loss of life. While concern for victims plays a major role in the planning of these interventions, many other political and situational factors influence decision makers. Options in this phase include assault, refusal to submit to demands, negotiation by governments, and the more traditional forms of hostage negotiation. These procedures, which attempt to resolve the incident as a whole, have been discussed elsewhere.[5, 6, 7] In this chapter we will focus on secondary prevention measures directed specifically toward victims after the incident has been concluded. First, we will discuss broad issues of program design; specific techniques that may be helpful to clinicians involved in the care of hostages will be presented later in this chapter.

There are special reasons for separating issues of care for specific victims from those of program design. The empathic clinician engaged in a therapeutic relationship should be sensitive to feedback from those whom he or she is trying to help. In the field of program design, however, the concrete needs of victims are sometimes played down or even forgotten in view of the competing demands of publicity, political expediency, career advancement, or grantsmanship. The perception of these competing demands has already made some hostages and hostage families suspicious of organized helping efforts. To us, it seems particularly important to limit program planning to those techniques that either have demonstrably worked in the past or to those that seem sensible to the former hostages or hostage families who are acting as consultants. We feel that any program that incorporates techniques that work will eventually be accepted by the group it is supposed to serve. Our caution in this area is meant to prevent a double victimization that might turn victims of terrorism into socially stigmatized psychiatric patients and intrude on their privacy with no real benefit to them. Dr. Martin Symonds has described the "second injury" to victims that may result from poorly planned helping programs.[8]

The importance of using former hostages in this planning process cannot be overemphasized. Their involvement in official efforts to plan secondary prevention programs will benefit not only the programs but also the former hostages themselves, as was clearly demonstrated in the case of Gerard Vaders discussed elsewhere in this volume. The case of Dutch efforts to help hostages from the two Moluccan train incidents can be particularly instructive from several points of view. Not the least of these efforts was the role that former hostages' families played in helping the families of hostages in the second incident—both during the incident and after it was concluded.

The experiences both of prisoners of war and of former hostages have made it clear that major therapeutic and preventive efforts must be directed toward the families of victims. Mrs. Vaders, for instance, experienced depression and guilt over her hostility toward the Moluccans who had held her husband captive. When captivity has been prolonged, hostages may have to readjust to family members who have undergone significant changes that have altered the nature of important relationships. One of the American hostages returning from Iran found that his wife had become "very self-reliant and independent." "I am dealing with a new and stronger person," he commented, "and that's difficult for me to adjust to."[9] Knowing that these changes are normal under such circumstances and discussing them with helping professionals who are familiar with family dynamics may make it easier for both the victim and his family to adjust and capitalize on the positive aspects.

The structuring and delivery of secondary prevention services is still a matter of much discussion and debate. One major point of contention is whether these services should be provided by specialized professionals or "official" therapists working for the government agencies or private corporations for which the hostages worked, or through educational efforts directed toward the general community of clinicians or made available to those who may be treating hostages. Good arguments can be made for both of these options, but right now it seems likely that neither will prevail. It is clear that officially sponsored helping services must be available but also that some hostages and hostage families will feel realistically or unrealistically embittered and seek help "outside the system" or even from clinicians conspicuous for their oppositional stance. In our efforts to help victims of terrorism we should not be averse to providing educational assistance to anyone who is willing to help and professionally competent to provide the needed services.

The analogies between victims of terrorism and victims of rape have been explored in a previous chapter in this volume, "Concepts of Terrorist Victimization." The organization of specialized helping services for rape victims may serve as a model for one approach to the same issue in terrorist incidents. In general, these services do not attempt to replace traditional medical or legal systems but rather to provide referral, advocacy, and often companionship to victims as they encounter the "helping" system. This particular structure can provide the kinds of specialized referral and counseling that would be difficult to impart to the average practitioner, especially when issues such as the collection of evidence for later prosecution are involved. In addition, staff members or volunteers in these services are frequently psychologically desensitized to the first phases of curiosity and fear with which many average people greet the victims of rape or of terrorism. Involving former victims adds another helpful element of peer support. Clearly the availability of such specialized services either to victims or to helping clinicians must be made known to their target groups. This raises the issue of how far outreach should go, an issue that is of particular concern to a group that has been used and publicized as part of their actual victimization. Our own position is that helping services for victims should advertise, but not "knock on doors." We believe that the right to privacy and to say "no" to helping services is especially important for former hostages and other victims of terrorism, and justifies a less aggressive helping stance on both moral and clinical grounds.

Events surrounding the return of the American captives from Iran have highlighted an aspect of secondary prevention related to negative consequences of a warm welcome and a well-organized readjustment program. These negative consequences are suffered not by the current hostages themselves, but by other victims of past captivity or similar trauma. Currently, Vietnam veterans and former prisoners of war feel neglected, undervalued, and underserved compared with the hostages who returned from Iran. There are realistic bases for some of these feelings and they should be addressed as ongoing services are planned for these other groups. Resentment can also be lessened by secondary prevention programs that keep this aspect of the hostages' symbolic function in mind. Official statements and welcoming programs should include reference to and recognition of other groups of victim-survivors.

Tertiary Prevention

Our knowledge of effective techniques in the tertiary prevention of disability due to terrorist victimization is still in an embryonic stage. What we do know from studying analogous victimization situations —especially prisoners of war and Nazi concentration camp victims —is that late effects and residual disability do occur in a significant proportion of such victims.

Intelligent planning for services involving tertiary prevention must, more than for any of the other types of prevention, be based on an accurate and objective knowledge of the victim's premorbid state and present level of functioning. It is only within this context that an evaluator/clinician can assess how much damage has been done and whether the pre-incident baseline has been reached or surpassed. A particularly useful perspective for this process of longitudinal evaluation has been provided by the study on precaptivity personality and the development of psychiatric illness that was conducted by psychiatrist Robert J. Ursano. Dr. Ursano studied six former Vietnam Air Force prisoners of war who had undergone psychiatric evaluations at the School of Aerospace Medicine before being shot down. These men had also been evaluated regularly following their release from captivity. Keeping in mind the small number of subjects, Dr. Ursano felt justified in drawing the following conclusions based on his data: "First, the presence of antecedent psychiatric disturbances or symptoms usually thought to represent a predisposition to illness is not necessary to the development of psychiatric illness after long-term trauma. . . . Second, the presence of antecedent psychiatric disturbance is not sufficient for the development of post-traumatic illness. . . . These cases support the view that neurotic illness can develop under unusually stressful conditions in individuals with no predisposition to psychiatric illness."[10]

The experience to date of clinicians caring for the American hostages released from Iran has confirmed this cautionary perspective. Extensive study of the histories of American prisoners of war, victims of past hostage incidents, and concentration camp survivors formed a background for the helping efforts of these clinicians. In general, clinicians have agreed that the amount of psychopathology observed so far has been much less than expected. This has led to some concern over the possible negative effects that could have occurred due to the highly publicized speculations about possible post-captivity disorders that were made as the hostages were being released. A research study done in a medical context has provided an objective basis for this concern. Apparently, communicating the presence of hypertension to previously asymptomatic individuals in a work setting leads to higher rates of absenteeism and increased illness reports that are unrelated to the actual control of blood pressure.[11]

The tertiary helping efforts with the least likelihood of producing negative results may be those in support of internal, subjective resolution of the event and its aftermath. Morton Bard and Dawn Sangrey have explored the process of attribution in victims of conventional crimes and the various pathways that this process can take both in the victim and her or his family.[12] Politics (including clinical politics) being as fickle as it is, it may be safer and more prudent for a former victim to make his or her peace and reach closure and a sense of purpose about the event on an internal, cognitive basis.

Despite the wisdom of concentrating on internal psychological resolution, the issue of compensation inevitably arises, and correctly so when victims of terrorism are discussed. The victim of terrorism holds a special position among victims of premeditated human violence. He or she often literally represents the government that the terrorist is challenging when he takes the victim hostage. One of government's core functions is to provide basic security. When this function fails, as it does in a successful terrorist assault, a strong argument can be made that government itself should take up a central responsibility for restitutive care. Over one-half of our states currently have crime victim compensation laws, usually involving payments for lost work time and medical expenses. The programs function imperfectly, but they do function; they may provide some models for planning services to victims of terrorism.

Guidelines for the Clinical Care of Ex-Hostages

It is unlikely that many therapists will encounter ex-hostages as patients at all, let alone be involved in treatment programs in the immediate aftermath of group captivity. However, we feel that some general observations regarding treatment theory and practice in the re-entry period and later stages of re-equilibration are worth mentioning for those who may be called upon.

A group of persons, just liberated and received by government authorities, will be propelled in individual directions and anxious to return to familiar surroundings. Predictably, their desires for quiet or for ventilation will vary. Few groups have, when given the choice, opted to stay together for more than a day in order to graduate the reentry process. In June 1977 the staff of Groningen Psychiatric Hospital, under the direction of Dr. Willem Van Dijk, arranged an optional twenty-four hour decompression program for the hostages held on the second hijacked train. Gerard Vaders assisted with the preparation, and suggested, as many ex-hostages have, that time spent in group debriefing and in anticipation of adjustment problems at work and at home is desirable between liberation and homecoming. However, Van Dijk's and Vaders's plans did not come to fruition, as the liberated hostages chose to leave for home as quickly as they could. Therapists at the scene were prepared to help individuals and groups look backward and forward. Therefore, tension may have possibly developed among the hostages immediately after they were released. Within the suddenly contrived extended family, antagonisms or at the very least ambivalences may have arisen. Since these feelings are colored by the primitive affects that have been released in the infantilizing hostage experience, they are potentially intense, enduring, and linked to similarly intense interpersonal feelings from past relationships. There would hardly be time, energy, or interest in working these feelings through on the spot. However, a minimal amount of reflection and revealing in a sympathetic environment, moderated by a skillful group therapist, might be quite beneficial in the long run.

The clinician skilled in group work has a definite therapeutic opportunity to facilitate optimum exposure, undoing, resolution, and mature leave-taking under these circumstances. This process could help individuals avoid later self-recrimination and unconscious longing to maintain or restore transference relationships. Furthermore, group work could help prevent victims from transferring ambivalent feelings to their genuine family members. Occasionally, ex-hostage groups have formed an ongoing support system for themselves and for future victims. Hours of decompression can give newly released hostages time to build such a network. The experience of clinicians who had worked with the Dutch hostages and with victims of other incidents was used in planning for the release of the American hostages from Iran. Partly because initial proximity to family members often leads victims to understandably reject therapeutic debriefing and working through, Wiesbaden, Germany, was chosen as the location for the initial helping program.

Prior to any group interaction, individual exploration in a therapeutic setting would be useful for diagnostic purposes and for gathering a sense of the potential for group cohesion and for the sensitive points of group conflict and individual vulnerability. The clinician should be particularly vigilant in looking for denied or consciously suppressed psychological wounds. Hints may come from fellow hostages about victims who were singled out for physical or psychological abuse and individuals who showed signs of stress or depression during captivity. Supportive comments and a secure atmosphere might help such individuals use ventilation, insight, and support systems to advantage rather than to follow a stoical instinct or retreat behind a veneer of bravado or lingering isolation.

On the other hand, it may not be advisable to press every personality relentlessly for a psychiatric encounter. It was noted in the Dutch incidents and in many others that a group of psychologically unscathed individuals emerged. These were frequently rural, religious, conservative persons whose faith and firmly held values cushioned the shock and provided a nonpsychological framework for reentry. Although such persons might abhor psychological intervention, they could be in the vanguard supporting victimized individuals and family members whose world view is similar to their own. The reluctance to share or to delve into psychological issues may be a personal as well as a cultural trait. As Dr. Walton Roth discussed previously in this volume, the tendency to acquaint psychological health with "letting it all hang out" may be more of a fashion than a fact. An intermediate level for some victims may be the need and desire to share their inner experiences only with trusted friends or family members. The wise clinician will respect such wishes and maintain his or her distance.

Medical clinicians helping in the immediate aftermath should also anticipate future difficulties. These would include physical problems such as constipation or diarrhea; insomnia; impotence; and exacerbation of any previous psychophysiological problems such as asthma or essential hypertension. Dr. Roth has explored the relationship of concepts of stress to an understanding of such disorders. There are, as we have mentioned, several schools of thought with respect to predicting possible symptoms. Some suggest that former hostages will develop predicted symptoms: the "self-fulfilling prophecy." Others suggest that a symptom that is predicted but explained will have a less disturbing effect. We believe in the latter theory, and would counsel clinicians to explore possible physical symptoms. We would consider semiannual medical examinations over a two-year period as the minimal level of monitoring necessary to provide care that is consonant with our knowledge of previous instances of terrorist victimization. Psychological support should ideally be provided on a more frequent ongoing basis. Along these lines, current plans for the follow-up of returned American hostages from Iran include weekly phone checks.

Potential interpersonal problems should also be explored. Family reunions could be difficult for the ex-hostage who does not realize that his loved ones have also, in a sense, been captured. They too will need support, ventilation, and a chance to share the sudden, short-lived limelight. Several marriages have been strained because hostages were not prepared to accept the role of comforter along with the role of comforted, or the changes in social role that a spouse had assumed in his or her absence. The clinician might well review previous separations and reunions for points of weakness and strength within the couple.

It would not be unusual for a clinician to receive the question, "Doctor, when will I be ready to return to work?" Military psychiatry proved during and after World War II that a brief rest and a rapid return to full responsibility prevented prolonged psychiatric illness when the diagnosis was "battle fatigue." "Hostage fatigue," without other complications, could be treated the same way. However, a hostage may have lost his or her place of employment. For instance, the State Department employees at the Iranian embassy could hardly be expected to return there. In such cases, a review of options and support for a preferred option might prove essential. Clinician and hostage together could force a more rapid return to work than would otherwise be the case with a business or public employer who is slow to realize the medical necessity for rapid reemployment. This approach of relatively rapid reentry has generally been followed in the cases of the returning American captives from Iran.

A clinical encounter with a former hostage may begin from several days to several months after the hostage incident and may be initiated through self-referral, family referral, or referral from an employer or friend. In such circumstances, the involved clinician should use standard procedure: take a thorough history; search for signs of organic impairment or personality disorganization that would require emergency measures; formulate a presenting problem; make a differential diagnosis; attempt to gain a longitudinal sense of pre-traumatic levels of adjustment in various areas; catalogue strengths and weaknesses, particularly coping skills and sustaining relationships with significant others that are relevant to the current situation; and finally, agree upon a collaborative approach. There is no singular "hostage syndrome," but there are unique issues that should be anticipated and explored. First, there is the Stockholm Syndrome, which has been described and discussed in detail in this volume. An ex-hostage may have a continuing attachment to one or more of the hostage-takers. This is best conceptualized as a pathological transference, forged in the infantilization that is an essential part of such incidents. There is little psychological or ideological reason to prolong an infantile love for a gun-wielding terrorist whose only act of decency was to refrain from pulling the trigger. However, the sudden, unanticipated loss of the Stockholm Syndrome may be accompanied by depression and humiliation. Not only is the object of transference love removed, but in its place stands a naked self-image of one who has been cruelly mistreated and deceived. Anticipating this, and removing obstacles to confronting such awareness, is a reasonable therapeutic course. For the clinician embarking on this type of resistance analysis, a prior knowledge of the complexes within the individual victim that underlie his resistance may be extremely helpful in designing strategies to aid in its resolution.

The Stockholm Syndrome includes negative feelings toward government and other authority figures. Gradual exposure of the former hostage to possible constructive roles for government officials, allowing empathy to develop and promoting appreciation for the limited available options, will help promote a realistic assessment of the situation. Once they overcame the Stockholm Syndrome, several ex-hostages have joined negotiator training classes and other activities that reunite victims with their government.

Celebrity status is another unique issue that the consultant may confront. Particularly after notorious incidents, the ex-hostage will have access to the mass media and be treated as a hero. However, this soon fades. Hero becomes curiosity; curiosity becomes nonentity; nonentity may even become pariah. The sudden fall from grace is a reenactment of hostage victimization, and loss of celebrity status could precipitate depressive illnesses in the same way as other meaningful losses in patients' lives. Family members may resent the sudden lionization of the ex-hostage, but may deny or suppress these feelings. A sensitive, supportive family may help restrain the ex-hostage who becomes hypomanic or grandiose in reaching for and accepting celebrity status. Similarly, a family-oriented therapist may call upon family resources to maintain a realistic outlook in the face of temptation to move beyond one's realm of comfort. We would certainly not suggest that all ex-hostages avoid media exposure. We would note that the ex-hostage's major psychological task is to readjust to a lifestyle compatible with his or her values and talents.

Publicity and celebrity status may also become a significant issue for the clinician. It is important for clinicians who contemplate involvement with former hostages or their families to evaluate their own needs for publicity in advance and to consider at whose expense these needs are to be filled. Such temptations may be far more seductive than financial ones to practicing therapists. It would also be worthwhile for the clinician to determine in advance how he will respond to requests from the press or from the patient for media exposure. This can become an even more complicated consideration when issues of support for or opposition to "official" government efforts are superimposed.

Compensation for physical, psychological, and vocational damages may enter into the therapeutic equation. Some physicians have specialized in compensation claims; it would be beyond the scope of this volume to explore the ethical and practical ramifications of such a topic. However, it would be prudent for the involved clinician to determine quickly whether the patient's ultimate quest is for help in a compensation claim or for help in readjustment. Certainly, one could legitimately seek both. The psychiatrist who becomes an expert witness in an ex-hostage compensation case would do well to review the limited documentation on the subject, much of which is likely to be recent.[13]

The ex-hostage patient is a victim and is therefore at risk for "pathological victimization." Just as Lindemann formulated concepts of grief and pathological grief,[14] we suggest the useful paradigms of victimization and pathological victimization. In pathological victimization one has been lowered in dominance and responds not only with rage or resignation, but with seriously lowered self-esteem and an extended period of rumination, preoccupation, or fantasies of revenge. This may have more to do with the victim's prior life events than with the details of the recent episode. If so, therapists should try to expose and resolve past intrapsychic conflicts.

The psychotherapeutic goal should be to enrich the life that follows a traumatic event by exploring the life that preceded it. In judging the intensity of a victim's response, however, the clinician should be careful to relate his or her comparisons to the extent of victimization injury. For example, one of the former American hostages from Iran commented: "I don't postpone things that I want to do any longer. If I want a new stereo for my pick-up I buy it. If I want to shoot skeet, I do it, because I don't know where I'll be next week."[15] A statement like this may be realistic and not unhealthy in the early phases of return from captivity, but would alert a clinician to monitor and foster the redevelopment of appropriate security feelings. It is important for the clinician to realize that brutal and prolonged mistreatment may be sufficient to cause prolonged rage and severe difficulty with readjustment. In these cases, thorough ventilation has often proved quite helpful. Clinicians should realize that this could, however, place an almost intolerable burden upon the therapeutic listener.

The nature and potential extent of this burden for therapists who deal with victims of terrorism and other forms of violent human victimization has been explored by several clinicians working in this area. Sarah Haley has poignantly described the problem of listening to graphic accounts of torture and atrocity (in her case, told by the torturer).[16] Dori Laub has described similar difficulties for clinicians working with victims of the Holocaust and pointed out the pervasive tendency to avoid listening to a full, frank account of the trauma through often unconscious devices such as frequently interrupting with questions.[17] The clinician should be prepared to encounter these particular stresses during therapy with such victims and should certainly not avoid this form of treatment because of his or her own limitation in withstanding the shock of morbid detail. The Task Force on Psychiatric Aspects of Terrorism and Its Victims of the American Psychiatric Association has formulated as one of its functions the provision of peer support for clinicians working with victims of terrorism. This will encompass both cognitive structure in terms of specific therapeutic techniques and, just as important, the opportunity to share some of these private burdens.[18]

Conclusion

In this chapter we have discussed broad strategies and specific techniques that can help prevent the harm done by terrorism to the men, women, and children who have been and will be its victims. As a nation we have clearly not been as compassionate toward victims in general as our wealth and publicly-stated moral code should allow us to be. To combat terrorism at home and abroad we must extend our commitment to the value of human life from simply withholding attack to providing concern and adequate care to victims.

While this book was being written, America suffered, raged, waited, and was finally rewarded and relieved by the return of our hostages from Iran. Contributors to this volume participated directly and indirectly in the planning for this return and in the helping efforts that have ensued. To give a specific example, State Department physicians debriefing the hostages in Wiesbaden were careful to prevent the "second injury" described by Dr. Martin Symonds. In interviewing, they asked the returnees' permission before coming in and sitting down, thus giving the hostages back some measure of control over their lives. In April 1981, Dr. Symonds himself addressed the former hostages at their "reunion" in the Greenbrier Hotel in West Virginia, sharing with them his experience and wisdom concerning the stages of resolution of victimization experiences.

The national outpouring of sympathy and affection that greeted the hostages was an important event in our history. Like astronauts, they had gone to a very strange and dangerous place and come back alive. This heartfelt welcome may mean that we are now mature enough to lavish our positive feelings on people who have suffered rather than on people who have inflicted harm. It represents a needed return to a more traditional form of hero—the man or woman who stands up against great odds, survives, and prevails.

Notes

1. Caplan, G.: *Principles of Preventive Psychiatry.* London: Tavistock Publications, 1964, pp. 16–17.

2. Caplan, G.: "Mastery of stress: Psychosocial aspects." *American Journal of Psychiatry* 138:413–420, 1981, p. 415.

3. Robert I. Hauben, M.D., quoted in *American Medical News*, February 13, 1981, p. 16.

4. *Newsweek*, April 13, 1981, p. 18.

5. Kupperman, R. H.: "Treating the symptoms of terrorism: Some principles of good hygiene." *Terrorism: An International Journal* 1:35–49, 1977.

6. Miller, A. H.: "Negotiations for hostages: Implications from the police experience." *Terrorism: An International Journal* 1:125–146, 1978.

7. Bolz, F., and Hershey, E.: *Hostage Cop.* New York: Rawson, Wade, Inc., 1979.

8. Symonds, M.: "The second injury to victims." *Evaluation and Change.* Special Issue, Spring 1980, pp. 36–38.

9. *Newsweek*, April 27, 1981, p. 42.

10 Ursano, R. J.: "The Viet Nam era prisoner of war: Precaptivity personality and the development of psychiatric illness." *American Journal of Psychiatry* 138:315–318, 1981.

11. Haynes, R. B.; Sackett, D. L.; Taylor, D. W.; et al.: "Increased absenteeism from work after detection and labeling of hypertensive patients." *New England Journal of Medicine* 299:741–744, 1978.

12. Bard, M., and Sangrey, D.: *The Crime Victim's Book.* New York: Basic Books, Inc., 1979, pp. 52–75.

13. A relevant case in this area is that of *James Pulley* v. *District of Columbia Workmen's Compensation Board.* Mr. Pulley won his claim based on psychological damage suffered during and after his ordeal as a hostage in the B'nai B'rith incident. Frank Ochberg provided a portion of the expert witness testimony, which is available upon request from the U.S. Department of Labor, Office of Workers Compensation Programs.

14. Lindemann, E.: "Symptomatology and management of acute grief." *American Journal of Psychiatry* 101:141–148, 1944.

15. *Newsweek*, April 27, 1981, p. 42.

16. Haley, S.: "When the patient reports atrocities." *Archives of General Psychiatry* 30:192–196, 1974.

17. Laub, D.: "The traumatic neurosis revisited: Traumas experienced during the Yom Kippur War by children of concentration camp survivors." Paper presented to the Association for Mental Health Affiliation with Israel, Eastern Pennsylvania Chapter, Elkins Park, Pennsylvania, May 20, 1979.

18. David Soskis is currently chairperson of this Task Force. The chapters in this volume by Drs. Martin Symonds and Leo Eitinger also provide some guidelines on this issue. The goal should be the desensitization of the clinician to the more psychologically disruptive aspects of terrorist victimization without the loss of therapeutically effective empathy and sensitivity.

About the Contributors

Leo Eitinger, M.D., is professor of psychiatry and head of the Department of Psychiatry at the University of Oslo in Norway. He is the author of *Concentration Camp Survivors in Norway and Israel, Mortality and Morbidity After Excessive Stress,* and *Psychological and Medical Effects of Concentration Camps* (a research bibliography).

Rona M. Fields, Ph.D., is a psychologist and sociologist who serves as senior partner with Associates in Counseling Psychology in Alexandria, Virginia. She is also adjunct professor of psychology at George Mason University and has written *Society Under Siege* and *The Armed Forces Movement And The Portuguese Revolution.*

Conrad V. Hassel, J.D., M.S., is a special agent of the Federal Bureau of Investigation and chief of the Special Operations and Research Unit of the FBI Academy in Quantico, Virginia. This unit is responsible for training in hostage negotiation, special weapons and tactics, and crisis management conducted by the FBI.

Frank M. Ochberg, M.D., practices psychiatry in Michigan and has served as director of the Michigan Department of Mental Health. He has served as a psychiatric advisor to the Federal Bureau of Investigation and participated in the National Security Council Special Coordinating Committee on Terrorism.

Walton T. Roth, M.D., is associate professor of psychiatry and behavioral sciences at the Stanford University School of Medicine and he is chief of the Psychiatric Consultation Service of the Veterans Administration Medical Center in Palo Alto, California. He is also coeditor (with Paul M. Insel) of *Core Concepts in Health.*

David A. Soskis, M.D., is clinical associate professor of psychiatry at Temple University School of Medicine, where he has served as director of residency training in psychiatry. He is chairperson of the Task Force on Psychiatric Aspects of Terrorism and Its Victims of the American

Psychiatric Association and serves as a psychiatric consultant to the Federal Bureau of Investigation.

Thomas Strentz, M.S.W., is a special agent of the Federal Bureau of Investigation working in the Special Operations and Research Unit at the FBI Academy in Quantico, Virginia. He has conducted extensive interviews with victims of terrorist incidents in the United States and abroad.

Martin Symonds, M.D., is director of psychological services for the New York City Police Department and associate clinical professor of psychiatry at the New York University School of Medicine. He has served as director of the Victim Treatment Center at the Karen Horney Clinic in New York City and is assistant dean of the American Institute For Psychoanalysis.

Jared Tinklenberg, M.D., is associate professor of psychiatry and behavioral sciences at the Stanford University School of Medicine. He is also assistant chief of the Psychiatry Service and director of the Clinical Diagnostic and Rehabilitation Unit of the Palo Alto Veterans Administration Medical Center.

Index

1-65, 78-80,
100-101, 123-126, 150-161
186-187